IRAN OIL

IRAN OIL

The New Middle East Challenge to America

Roger Howard

I.B. TAURIS

LONDON · NEW YORK

Published in 2007 by I.B.Tauris & Co. Ltd
6 Salem Road, London W2 4BU
175 Fifth Avenue, New York, NY 10010
www.ibtauris.com

In the United States of America and Canada distributed by Palgrave Macmillan, a
division of St Martin's Press, 175 Fifth Avenue, New York, NY 10010

ISBN: 978 1 84511 249 3

A full CIP record for this book is available from the British Library
A full CIP record for this book is available from the Library of Congress

Library of Congress catalog card: available

Typeset in Goudy Old Style by A. & D. Worthington, Newmarket, Suffolk
Printed and bound in Great Britain by CPI Bath

Contents

Acknowledgements		vii
Introduction		ix
1.	Why Iran's Natural Resources Matter	1
2.	Breaking US Alliances	45
3.	US Rivals and Non-Aligned States	87
4.	Supporting the Iranian Regime	125
	Conclusion	157
	Notes	167
	Index	175

Acknowledgements

Although I am indebted to numerous individuals for their assistance in the research and compilation of this book, I would like to express my particular gratitude to Lavinia Brandon for granting me access to the outstanding library at the Oxford Institute for Energy Studies, and to Reza Bayegan, Professor Sohrab Behdad, Fereidun Fesharaki, Dr Parviz Mina, Rosarie Nolan, Simon Shercliff, Professor Jonathan Stern and Mehdi Varzi for their comments and information. I am also particularly indebted to Abigail Fielding-Smith at I.B.Tauris, who has been a first-rate editor, to David Worthington, who has been such a good copy-editor, and to the Authors' Foundation for a generous grant.

Roger Howard
Oxford, August 2006

To Elaine C.

Introduction

L ike an individual who suffers sudden and unexpected misfortune, great powers can decline and fall with a rapid, even dramatic speed. Although the influence and prestige of many great empires has seeped away gradually and imperceptibly over many decades, or even centuries, in the way that was true of the British Empire or what Edward Gibbon called the 'slow decay' [1] of the Roman, the sudden demise of others can sometimes elicit as much surprise among contemporaries as the historian. Such a startling transformation eventuates most obviously after military defeat, of the sort that befell ancient Persia, or as a result of political turmoil and revolution, similar in scale to the upheavals that brought a tumultuous end to tsarist Russia.

At the present moment it seems possible that the United States could suffer a serious loss of global influence with a comparable rapidity. The same country that on the eve of the invasion of Iraq in March 2003 appeared to be an untrammelled colossus, confident of its ability to stride with ease through the Middle East and elsewhere, prompting admiration among its friends and allies in equal proportion to the hostility and contempt it provoked among its rivals and enemies, could in the next few years conceivably look defensive and vulnerable, with the loyalties of its long-standing allies increasingly uncertain, its former allies even more distant and its enemies ever more emboldened. At the same time, the predictions of those who had heralded 'the next American century', and looked forward with joyous anticipation to the peace, democracy and progress it would supposedly bring, might equally look hollow and premature.

Should it come about, the single most important factor in engineering this change of fortune will not be America's experiences in Iraq, where its name, reputation and resources have been undermined by insurgency, civilian casualty and atrocity. The USA, after all, survived defeat in Vietnam and maintained its global pre-eminence despite the war's serious damage on every party. Nor will it be simply because of the fiery rise of the Chinese dragon, whose raw economic power is currently on course to make it the world's biggest marketplace and knock the United States into second place. Even if this happens, America can still remain a global superpower, if not a superpower quite as pre-eminent as before. Instead, much more important is the world's economic dependence on oil and natural gas, and the degree to which political power has suddenly begun to move into the hands of those who do possess the resources to feed that dependency at the expense of those who do not.

Of course this presents a clear irony. Throughout the twentieth century, the governments of the developed nations were frequently accused of exploit-ing the resources of the less developed, and alleged to be using their over-whelming military superiority to plunder and take advantage. Nationalist leaders such as Mohammed Mossadeq in Iran and Gamal Abdul Nasser in Egypt played this card to great effect before seizing with resolute hand the Western-owned oil enterprises, the Anglo-Iranian and Suez Canal compa-nies, that had long enjoyed lucrative local concessions. Similar accusations were ventured by those who argued that the US invasion of Iraq in March 2003 was essentially motivated by an interest in its vast deposits of high-quality oil. But in the course of the present century, a clear change of empha-sis has quickly come about, as the leaders of Europe and America openly accuse their counterparts in energy-rich states of exploiting their oil and gas deposits to devastating political effect. As US Vice-President Dick Cheney claimed in a telling phrase in May 2006, the Russians are using their energy resources as 'tools of intimidation or blackmail'.[2]

A glance at the wider geopolitical picture in 2006 illustrates the degree to which political power is in the process of rapidly migrating into the hands of those countries that do possess deposits of oil and gas. In January, Moscow had briefly cut off supplies of gas to the Ukraine amid a price dispute, and four months later, as its giant energy supplier Gazprom considered making a bid for Centrica, the Western European utility company, Russian premier Vladimir Putin warned that his country would simply switch its energy supplies to Asia if Western governments blocked the expansion plans of Gazprom and any other Russian energy groups. With an overwhelming dependency on imported oil, one that has for some time caused deep conster-nation within the highest offices,[3] the United States can only listen to such demands with a mixture of envy and alarm.

On the other side of the world, in Venezuela, President Hugo Chavez has been voicing a stridently anti-American rhetoric and has pursued poli-cies deliberately antagonistic to Washington with a vehemence that has been fuelled by the rise in the price of oil. When first elected as president in 1998, at a time when a barrel fetched a mere $12 on the world's market, Chavez had neither the spare cash nor the political influence to antagonize Washington. But ever since the price subsequently began to spiral, the Venezuelan leader has been a moving force of regional anti-Americanism, furnishing Castro's cash-strapped Cuba with some 90,000 barrels of oil a day and funding left-wing political parties throughout Latin America.[4] While many of those who listen may be lukewarm towards, or disagree strongly with, his anti-Washington line, the threat of retaliation by such a key regional oil exporter does not always give them much room for choice. And although Chavez continues to export more than half of his oil to the USA while speaking in such vituperative terms about his best customer, both he and the Americans know that, in the event of any clash, Venezuelan oil would find new markets much more readily than Washington would ever find new suppliers.

Besides allowing governments that produce petroleum to openly defy Washington, the world scarcity of oil also undermines American global power in another way. For given a choice between respecting American interests and wishes on the one hand, and securing a source of energy supplies on the other, foreign governments are being increasingly tempted to prioritize their energy concerns. One stark illustration of this prioritization came in September 2004, when Beijing abstained from a US-sponsored UN resolution condemning the genocide in Sudan, and instead promised to block moves to enforce an oil embargo on a country that was a major oil exporter to China. This was no easy option for the Chinese government, which was anxious not to tarnish its international image by being seen to pass easy excuse for a Sudanese regime that was complicit in mass-scale atrocities against innocent civilians.

Lying at the heart of the new petropolitics lies an imbalance between the supply of and demand for refined oil. Although there have been numerous occasions when a similar imbalance has wreaked serious economic havoc – during the OPEC oil embargo on 1973, for example, or in the early days of the Iran–Iraq War in 1980 – the present situation is differentiated by the dramatic, prolonged and seemingly inexhaustible economic growth of China and, to a lesser extent, India. Since 1993, when it was last self-sufficient in oil, China's GDP has trebled and its demand for oil has almost doubled, thereby creating a 'demand shock' with far-reaching political and economic tremors. While China's overall share of the world's oil market is a relatively meagre 8 per cent, its economic expansion has accounted for nearly a third of global growth in demand since 2000.

Of course it is impossible to tell if the price of oil will continue to remain so high in the years ahead, before alternative forms of energy become available: predicting the energy market is notoriously difficult. But the International Energy Agency, the oil sector monitoring body, expects global demand to more than double by 2030, with many of the world's current producers, notably Saudi Arabia, facing real hurdles if they are to maintain, let alone increase, current levels of supply.[5] And even a semblance of such a market imbalance cannot fail to have major political repercussions, putting more power and influence into the hands of those countries that possess natural resources of oil and natural gas at the expense of the rest.

It is in this big picture of the new petropolitics of the twenty-first century that Iran's challenge to the United States forms part. The rise in the price of oil has been profoundly important, for example, in creating the newly found nuclear defiance of Iran, one of the world's leading oil exporters. In October 2003 Iranian negotiators had suddenly and unexpectedly caved in to international pressure by granting extra powers to the inspectors of the International Atomic Energy Agency and by immediately halting uranium enrichment. But just two years later the same regime was willing to openly defy the threat of referral to the United Nations, its subsequent deadlines and the passage of condemnatory resolutions. The key difference was not the election as premier of the hot-headed Mahmoud Ahmadinejad, who came to power in the summer of 2005, but the rise in the price of oil from a relatively meagre $33 per barrel in early 2004 to a peak of $70 in August the following year. Not only did this make the passage of meaningful sanctions impossible but it also gave Tehran scope to threaten retaliation against its critics while rewarding those countries, notably China, that took its side. Hence the brazen defiance of the president, who in a typical statement openly declared, the day before a UN deadline to stop sensitive nuclear work expired at the end of April 2006, that his country would 'not bow to injustice and pressure'.

Iran's vast resources of oil and natural gas have not only emboldened the Tehran regime but also put increasing strains on America's international influence. Washington's attempts to isolate Iran from foreign investment and build a united front with which to confront its nuclear ambitions are made considerably more difficult by the lure of these resources. Confronted by a growing domestic demand for oil and gas that they cannot readily ignore, numerous countries throughout the world have greater reason than ever before to sidestep or even openly defy Washington's wishes and instead prioritize their links with Tehran. The result is a growing tension between the US and its international allies and rivals, and with non-aligned countries, a tension that is posing a clear challenge to American political power.

As the conclusion of this book argues, however, these tensions do not render inevitable any negative impact on the global influence of America. Far from it, in international affairs, just as in an individual's everyday life, there is very rarely such a thing as inevitability. There are only a series of choices,

which can be taken with varying degrees of ease and difficulty. In this particular case, the question of how far Washington can adapt its political position
in order to meet the petropolitical challenge from Iran is ultimately reduc-
ible to one of the American mindset, for the choices that confront those
who pull the strings of political power are made difficult essentially because
they are obstructed by certain psychological barriers, such as the difficulty
of doing business with a 'terrorist regime'. It is this psychological barrier, not
Iranian oil, that ultimately presents the challenge to America.

CHAPTER ONE

Why Iran's Natural Resources Matter

From the dramatic moment in the early hours of 26 May 1908 when a British geologist, George Reynolds, was suddenly woken in his tent by earth tremors and the sound of something violently bursting through the ground outside, Iran's oil has always been an intensely political commodity. For in the years that followed their discovery at this remote wilderness spot known as Masjid-i-Suleiman, these enormous oil reserves were a prize of immense value over which numerous participants played desperate political games and fought often vicious military battles, typically sparing no expense in their determination to take possession or to keep rivals at bay. Great explorers of the British Empire, cunning Bolshevik agents, ruthless Nazi spies, theatrical Iranian nationalist martyrs and bitter Cold War rivals – all of these different types, some of them dark and sinister, others romantic and charming, have their place in the rich and fascinating story of Persian oil.[1]

Today, almost exactly a century after their discovery, Iran's superb natural resources of oil and gas are also standing firmly on the stage of world politics. But this is not so much because the outside world is fighting tooth and nail to win control over them, in the way that it once was, but because the possession of such supreme natural wealth is now allowing the Tehran regime to pose a subtle challenge to the global political influence exerted by the United States. This challenge may not as yet stand centre-stage – on the contrary it has hitherto played its part largely unnoticed by its audience – but it is one that is nonetheless growing fast in stature and, unless there is some dramatic and unexpected political transformation in either Tehran or Washington, seems destined to soon assume a starring role.

This is of course a very different type of 'threat' from the one that the Tehran regime is usually supposed to present both to America and the wider outside world, for in an age in which visions of nuclear catastrophe and terrorist violence loom large, contemporary Iran cannot fail to conjure up some very disturbing images. In American eyes, above all, Iran has long been viewed as 'the world's primary sponsor of terror', while its nuclear programme, ostensibly for the production only of civilian energy, is invariably regarded as disguising a secret bid for a warhead that could target not just the densely populated cities of southern Europe and Israel but also the Saudi oil fields and their Gulf transit routes on which the American and the wider global economy so strongly depend.

Yet Iran's challenge to the United States is not born of any military threat. Nor can it in any way be labelled as 'terrorist', whatever that elusive term really means. Iran instead poses a challenge to American interests that is less readily measured and, to those accustomed to viewing 'threats' only in more traditional terms, one that is more easily overlooked than any military menace of the sort that the United States faced in the Cold War and continues to face from the Al Qaeda terrorist network.

This contemporary challenge to the United States is instead a consequence of a political leverage that essentially hinges on the world's increasing need for the very resources that Iran possesses in such abundance. Their ownership inevitably bestows a degree of power and influence that exists in equal proportion to the need that others have for them, and this means that one country's possession of oil inevitably has powerful political repercussions in the same way that the possession of any highly valued commodity, like brains or beauty, also confers power and influence on its beholder.

Of course no oil or gas-rich country poses a political threat to another simply because it possesses such an enormity of natural resources: Saudi Arabia, to take one obvious example, has had a very strong diplomatic relationship with Washington since 1943, when President Roosevelt, declaring that 'the defence of Saudi Arabia is vital to the defence of the United States', extended a helping hand of large American aid to Riyadh.[2] Instead Iran's contemporary political challenge to the United States represents a convergence of two influences, one born of its possession of immense natural wealth, the other a result of nearly three decades of enmity, mistrust and outright hostility to the world's greatest superpower. And it is from the interrelationship between these political conditions and material resources that this challenge to the United States arises.

There are three distinct ways in which this convergence is undermining US power. On the one hand, it is putting increasing strain on America's relationship with many of its allies across the world, notably the European Union, Japan and Pakistan. For while all of these countries share America's great and growing need for Iran's oil and gas, no ally of Washington – with the exception of Israel – harbours any comparable strength of hostility towards the Iranians, and all therefore feel much more at liberty to trade with a regime that the Americans refuse to deal with. The result is that these countries are being increasingly tempted to build and cement ties with Iran that Washington does not share and which it has also desperately wanted to stop others from having.

While undermining Washington's ties with its allies, Iran is also creating stronger political links with American rivals such as China and Russia, and with a country, India, that is formally 'non-aligned'.[3] In the case of China and India, these links reflect the particularly important role that Iranian oil and gas is playing in feeding their rapid economic growth: Beijing's relatively new commercial and political relationship with Tehran, for example, one that is still only in its relative infancy, has been created and sustained by an insatiable Chinese thirst for oil that its domestic production has failed to quench since the early to mid-1990s. In the case of Russia, which is a net exporter of oil and gas, Iran's natural resources are important in another, more indirect, way because they create highly lucrative business opportunities that Russian enterprise is extremely keen to exploit, opportunities that are born both of Iran's need to develop its outdated energy infrastructure as well as the demand that has sometimes been created by the vast earnings generated by the international sale of oil and gas.

In each case, Iranian natural resources are undermining not just American power and influence over this 'international community' but also over the Tehran regime itself. For without the wider support of other countries, America speaks with a lone voice that is much less easily heard and listened to than a louder chorus. What is more, there are also a number of other ways in which the status and power of the Tehran regime – America's chief rival and enemy in the Middle East since the deposition of Saddam Hussein in 2003 – has been bolstered by the export of vast quantities of oil and gas. For the sale of these commodities has secured huge earnings that have allowed the regime to purchase political support with a series of populist measures, to expand the size and strength of its security apparatus and to pursue a vastly expensive nuclear programme that would be quite unsustainable, or even unthinkable, without them. So in these wider terms Iran's oil and gas are also presenting Washington with a clear challenge.

Of course the process by which Iran's energy resources are undermining American global power is far from linear but is instead highly sensitive to fluctuations in the temperature of the world's wider political climate. In the latter months of 2005 and in early 2006, for example, the global political pendulum was pushed subtly and inadvertently away from Tehran by the aggressive rhetoric of Iran's new hardline president, Mahmoud Ahmadinejad, whose highly charged speech before the United Nations General Assembly in September 2005 and fiery talk about 'wiping Israel off the map' confirmed all the worst fears of those who claimed that his election, three months before, spelt unmistakable trouble for the outside world. As a senior US official in Washington put it, such radical posturing meant that, for the moment at least, countries that had previously been prepared to side with Iran were now 'running for the doors' because 'nobody wants to be associated with someone that outlandish'.[4] As some international investors took fright and the Tehran Stock Exchange collapsed, these words looked far from exaggerated. Yet although an abrupt and sometimes broken course it may be, it is a process that is nonetheless unmistakably unfolding.

The Iranians are fully aware of the political fissures that they can use their natural resources to exploit, and adequate testimony to this awareness is their tactic of linking the rewards and penalties yielded by their energy resources with the outside world's cooperation on the hot political issues of the day. So it is probably no coincidence that the Iranian authorities have suddenly and unexpectedly announced the discovery – or supposed discovery – of new oil and gas fields, and the availability of new contracts to develop them, just as international negotiations on the nuclear issue have reached important junctures. So on 26 August 2002, just days after the world had been shocked by the exposure of a covert uranium enrichment programme, the Iranian Oil Minister, Bijan Namdar Zanganeh, held a press conference and announced that at least 50 billion barrels of new oil reserves had been found in Iran in the course of the preceding four and a half years. And when in the following year controversy over the issue flared up again, as Iranian officials denied weapons inspectors access to one of their suspected nuclear facilities, the director of Iran's Oil Development and Engineering Company (ODEC) on 14 July suddenly announced, without citing evidence, the discovery of another new reserve, not far from the Iranian Persian Gulf port of Bushehr, whose estimated 38 billion barrel deposits promised to make it the world's second biggest oil field after Saudi Arabia's Ghawar development. More was to come, for in March 2005, as the Iranians tried to extract as many concessions as they could from European negotiators in return for surrendering their nuclear ambitions, Zanganeh announced that new oil and gas fields had been discovered in the southern province of Khuzestan and south of the South Pars gas field in Bushehr province, with an estimated capacity of 5,700 million barrels of oil.

It is with these 'petropolitics', the politics of Iran's energy, that this book is concerned. But before looking at each of the different ways in which American power and influence is being undermined, this opening chapter now seeks to look in more detail at the background to the Iranian challenge that represents a convergence between two exceptional, if not unique, factors. One of these, it has been mentioned above, is its possession of outstanding natural resources that are of increasing value to the outside world. The other is the existence of a very considerable degree of animosity between the Tehran regime and the country that currently wields more political influence and power than any other – the United States. It is the interaction of these two exceptional influences that has given birth to a unique challenge to American hegemony, one that is already in its early stages of infancy and growing up fast.

Iran's natural resources

One of the two roots from which Iran's challenge to American global hegemony stems is its possession of outstanding natural resources. Its proven[5] oil reserves are undoubtedly vast and widely estimated to hold at least 95 billion barrels, meaning that they are outsized only by those of Saudi Arabia, whose deposits are estimated to contain 260 billion barrels, by Canada's 170 billion barrels, and perhaps by Iraq's, which are thought to contain around 115 billion. Moreover the size of Iran's underlying reserves, or 'oil-in-place', like those of many other countries, may well be considerably greater, since most experts feel sure that there are many more undiscovered deposits, particularly in Caspian waters. Its massive new oil field at Azadegan in the southwestern province of Khuzestan, for example, one which alone has the potential to provide a very large consumer like Japan with more than 6 per cent of its annual oil imports, was discovered only in 1999, while two important onshore oil fields near Gavaneh, which are thought to have combined reserves of over 100 million barrels, were also located in the same year. This means that Iran's hopes of increasing its production capacity to as much as 7 million barrels each day (b/d) by the year 2024 may also be assisted by the discovery of even more deposits, just as the announcement in July 2003 of the discovery near Bushehr also prompted a sharp upward revision of estimates of its reserves.

Of course no one knows exactly how big Iran's resources really are, or how much of those reserves are recoverable: 'oil data is [always] like paint thrown across a canvas – you get the broad outline of the situation, but even then the paint later moves of its own accord', as one analyst has put it.[6] In the autumn of 2003, some independent analysts were highly sceptical of Iranian claims about the size of the Bushehr field, which pushed the size of Iran's national reserves up from 95 to 130.8 billion barrels, putting it ahead of Iraq. So although this figure has been accepted by some highly respected sources,[7] a leading Honolulu-based consultancy claimed that the Iranians had double-counted existing reserves and assumed a recovery rate that was well above the average figure for the Middle East. Instead Iran's self-assessment, the analysts concluded, was really just a bid to convince OPEC that Iran should continue with a high export quota that Iraq's newly founded freedoms might imperil.[8] Put bluntly, they were cheating in the same way that they have sometimes made announcements about their oil industry at curiously convenient times, almost as if to provide international governments with carrots that can win them support just when Tehran most needs it.[9]

Yet no one disputes that Iran has huge potential as a major player in the future oil industry, and while in recent years Iranian wells have certainly been producing oil at a sharp rate – between 3.5 and 4.2 million barrels every day, which amounts to around 4 per cent of global production – most analysts reckon that, with sufficient investment, they have the potential to increase such capacity considerably. Even if, in the years ahead, the Iranians fail to inject the investment necessary to recover a higher proportion of their underlying reserves – Iran's recovery rate, which stands at around 24 per cent of their overall national reserves, is much lower than the Middle Eastern average of 32 per cent – then their oil is still important for another very simple reason: there would be an overall global shortfall if its supply was ever seriously disrupted, a shortfall that would cause the price of oil to increase dramatically and affect every country in the world, whether directly importing Iranian oil or not.

Besides oil, Iran also holds vast deposits of another commodity that has immense and rapidly increasing value to the outside world – natural gas. Because Iran's natural gas reserves are reckoned to total something around 940 trillion cubic feet (cf), second in size only to those in Russia, it clearly has huge potential as a key exporter of natural gas. Its current production, of only around 2.7 trillion cf each year, will also be considerably boosted if yet more important reserves are discovered, as most independent experts expect: Tabnak, a super-giant gas field containing 15.7 trillion cf of gas and 240 million barrels of condensate, was found only in April 2000, and as recently as June 2004 the Iranian news agency announced that two new natural gas fields had been discovered at Balal and Lavan Island in the Persian Gulf.

One of the great jewels in Iran's energy crown is the massive gas field at South Pars in the Persian Gulf whose reserves, which are really just an extension of Qatar's North Field, amount to somewhere between 280 and 500 trillion cf. Such is the size of this single field that the Iranians are having to develop it in a series of distinct phases, which are in the course of being offered to national and international bidders. Nor are there just a handful of these individual 'phases', for although the Iranian parliament has given the Oil Ministry authorization to go ahead with 18 phases in the development of this giant gas field, the Oil Minister has previously said that 28 different phases, maybe more, could eventually be required. Whatever its capacity may ultimately prove to be, the Iranians undoubtedly have immense ambitions for the field and have declared that they want the Pars Special Econo-Energy Zone, established in 1998, to become 'one of the most important industrial energy centres of the Middle East'.

Once again though, these figures, like those of the country's oil reserves, have to be viewed with a highly sceptical eye because it is likely that they have sometimes reflected ulterior motives, such as an effort to lure outside investment or the interest of the outside world when Tehran has needed it. In 2005, for example, another report by the FACTS independent consultancy[10] argued that South Pars might really be considerably overrated: 'most foreign companies with hands-on experience in South Pars believe the capability to be 13–15 billion cubic feet per day (cfd). [But] Iranian field engineers esti-mate the field to be more productive, based on the results of the first three phases and believe the upper limit is 20 billion cfd.' The enormous differ-ence between these two estimates could conceivably be explained by delib-erate Iranian distortion, although it will remain a distortion of academic importance until the field's production has reached a lot more than it has at present.

Of course the importance of Iran's superb natural resources cannot be assessed just in terms of either their raw size or the relative ease with which they can be extracted. Just as important is their accessibility to foreign markets, and on this count Iran certainly scores very high marks. Some of its most important potential customers include the states of the Middle East, notably Dubai, which has in recent years experienced a particularly urgent need to import gas, as well as Kuwait, Abu Dhabi, Oman and Bahrain, whose own needs are growing rapidly. Iran has already made some prelimi-nary agreements to supply some of these Middle Eastern countries: on 12 January 2003 initial deals were signed in Tehran by the Kuwaiti Foreign Minister, Sheikh al-Ahmad, for the eventual implementation of a plan to import around 300 million cf of Iranian lean gas into Kuwait every day along a 200km underwater pipeline, while on 15 March 2005 the Iranian Oil Minister, Zanganeh, and the Omani Energy Minister, Mohammed al-Rumhy, signed an agreement to supply the kingdom with 350 billion cf of Iranian gas every year, a quantity to be eventually increased to 800 billion cf each year by 2012.

Of course Iran is not alone in eyeing this Middle Eastern market, and Qatar in particular is a major rival. But Iran is geographically much better positioned than Qatar to serve some other potential markets, notably Turkey and the former Soviet Union, through which pipelines can move Iranian oil and gas to much wider European and Asiatic destinations. Moreover Iran also has two sophisticated deep-water ports and refinery facilities, at Asaluyeh and Kish Island, from which tankers can channel its oil or lique-fied natural gas (LNG) to even remoter destinations, such as South Korea and coastal China.

So far some important steps have been made towards linking Iran with these wider markets. In September 2004 Alikhan Malikov, the head of the Azeri Gas Company, announced that Iran would soon start supplying up to 12 billion cf of gas every year to the autonomous republic of Nakhichevan in Azerbaijan, while six months before the National Iran Gas Exporting Company (NIGEC) agreed to annually deliver 12.6 billion cf of natural gas over the next 20 years along a proposed $220 million pipeline to Armenia in return for receiving supplies of electric power from a state-run plant in Yerevan. One of the main customers, however, is Turkey, which in 1996 agreed to purchase Iranian natural gas over a 22-year period, starting in 1999. In practice, of course, things have not turned out to be as easy as everyone originally hoped, and a series of technical and political problems brought years of delay until 2002, when Iran and Turkey officially inaugurated a natural gas pipeline running between Tabriz and Ankara, along which 106 billion cf of Iranian gas is eventually expected to move each year. Although there have subsequently been persistent disagreements between the two countries on the price and quality of Iranian gas, the opening of this pipeline has put a much wider European market within Iran's grasp: on 13 March 2002 the Greek state gas company Depa signed a $300 million deal with NIOC to extend the Tabriz–Ankara link into northern Greece, from where it could be fed into the rest of Europe, while in January 2004 a joint Austrian–Iranian venture was initiated to extend the new pipeline, whenever it was completed, into southern Austria. If the Iranians decide to make a commitment to feed it, then this 'Nabucco' pipeline could move between 720 and 900 billion cf to Austria each year.

At the same time plans to feed the vast and rapidly growing markets of India and Pakistan have also been slowly fomenting. In February 2002 Tehran and Islamabad initiated a feasibility study to assess the prospects for a 1,600-mile, $4 billion pipeline that would cross southern Pakistan to supply India with Iranian natural gas, providing Islamabad with lucrative transit fees as well as its own gas supply in the process. For many months political tensions between India and Pakistan over the status of the disputed region of Kashmir seemed to make this project a mere chimera, particularly when, in the summer of 2002, the two countries appeared to be on the verge of full-scale nuclear war. Yet by mid-2005, as a thaw in relations between the two countries seemed to have melted a considerable amount of the 58-year ice that had hitherto made such a plan unthinkable, the Iran–New Delhi pipeline looked to be a very real prospect. And it certainly seemed to be much more realistic than another proposed solution to the region's energy needs – a pipeline that would move Turkmen gas across remote and lawless regions of Afghanistan, which would not only be very difficult to build but would be highly vulnerable to military attacks and acts of sabotage. By the spring of 2006, as the outside world closed ranks before Iran's unexpected nuclear confrontationalism, the Iranian–Pakistan section of the pipeline looked ready to proceed, even if the final leg, between Pakistan and New Delhi, looked far from certain.

Of course there are numerous other factors besides the size and accessibility of such resources, which one way or another may influence Iran's future as an oil and gas exporter. Above all its potential as a leading player in the regional gas market may eventually prove to be more limited than that of other countries, notably Qatar, because there is at present much stronger domestic opposition to the export of natural gas. Led by Dr Saeidi, the former head of the NIOC Reservoir Engineering Department, this body of opinion argues that Iran's own reserves are needed to meet growing domestic demand and should be injected back into the country's oil fields to boost their production. This uncertainty is compounded by the fact that no one is sure how much gas will in future be required for this re-injection to boost oil supply: the government estimates that 5 billion cfd will be needed for this purpose during the 2005–9 Five-Year Plan, a much lower figure than the 20 billion cfd cited by those who oppose gas exports. 'The Iranians,' as one leading authority, Professor Jonathan Stern, emphasizes, 'have not realized the export potential of their gas resources over the past 30 years. Whether they will choose to do so and succeed in doing so over the next 30 years, remains to be seen.'[11]

Whatever its growth potential may eventually prove to be, it is clear that such an exceptional natural wealth does not in itself create any political challenge to the hegemony of the United States, which has of course often had very strong and successful relations with numerous regimes that are just as wealthy as Iran and, in many cases, have human rights records that are at least as dubious. For example, other oil- and gas-rich countries like Russia and Venezuela have in recent years also grown in political confidence but have not provoked a comparable American reaction, just as Washington's relations with Riyadh have remained strong. What lies behind Iran's challenge to American global hegemony is rather an interplay between Tehran's massive natural wealth and the intense hostility and mistrust that have characterized US–Iranian relations since the Islamic revolution of 1979.

Viewed in these terms, it is obvious where a tension might lie. Such wealth in the hands of one's enemy inevitably provides economic muscle, financial earnings and a political bargaining power that can hold some sway over one's own allies, feed your rivals and buttress the enemy regime. Iran's contemporary challenge to the United States, in short, represents an explosive tension between politics and resources.

The US–Iranian political framework

For the United States, the immensity of Iran's natural resources is of no
benefit, or rather of no direct, immediate benefit because since 1995 there
have been no economic ties of significance between the two countries and
since 1980 no formal diplomatic relations either. In the eyes of many ordinary Americans and certainly for a very considerable number of highly influential US policymakers, the Iranian regime is simply a terrorist-supporting,
human-rights oppressing, nuclear-arming and even evil-embodying political
order with which Washington should not and cannot deal, unless a massive
change of policy, rhetoric and attitude comes about in Tehran.

   The background to such antagonism is well known. Until the attacks on
the World Trade Center 22 years later, there have in the post-war era been
few images more traumatic for the American public than those that emerged
from Iran during and in the immediate aftermath of the Islamic revolution
of February 1979, when Shah Mohammed Reza Pahlavi's monarchical order
was swept away by the violent demonstrations of millions of street protestors.
Having strongly supported the royalist regime for years, and having offered
the dying shah a place of temporary refuge after he fled his homeland, the
United States soon became a target for the revolutionary hotheads, and on 4
November, nine months after the revolution began, several hundred young
Iranian students overran the US embassy in Tehran. The pictures of what
followed shocked and horrified the American public, which watched foot-
age of some of the blindfolded diplomats and soldiers, 66 of whom were
held as hostage, being led around the embassy compound by their mocking
captors.

   If these images were not bad enough, worse was to follow when in April
1980 President Carter's bid to rescue the hostages by force, Operation *Eagle
Claw*, backfired badly. The mission, designed to fly special forces personnel
into Iran, attack the embassy, rescue the hostages and fly them out of the
country, got off to a disastrous start when three of the helicopters encountered severe and unexpected weather conditions in the Iranian desert which
forced the commander on the spot to cancel the operation. But as the Americans pulled away from their base, 200 miles south of Tehran, one of the
helicopters collided with a transport plane, killing eight American service-
men in a giant fireball that lit up the night sky and which, in its enormity,
was visible from hundreds of miles distant. America's sense of humiliation,
not long after the end of the Vietnam War, was of course overwhelming and
compounded by even more shocking images that emerged from Iran, this
time of revolutionary zealots gleefully pointing to the charred remains of the
unfortunate Americans killed in the aborted operation.

Over the decade that followed, Iran's image in the eyes of most Americans, and indeed most Europeans, as a brutal, fanatical and violent regime was reinforced by quite a few other incidents. During the eight-year Iran–Iraq War, which began in September 1980, stories emerged of very young Iranian soldiers, perhaps no older than 12 or 13, voluntarily undertaking suicide missions against the Iraqi army, although to most members of the general public much better-known cases were the American allegations, never conclusively proven, that Tehran had instigated the 1982 car-bombing of a US compound in Beirut in which 241 marines died. But the Iranians undoubtedly did have links of some kind with the Beirut kidnappers who seized high-profile figures such as Terry Waite and John McCarthy, and who in 1984 tortured and killed the local CIA chief, William Buckley. Nor did the regime appear to have lost much of its fervour and fanaticism when, a decade after the revolution, a death sentence was pronounced against the British writer Salman Rushdie for the publication of his allegedly blasphemous work *The Satanic Verses*, or, for that matter, when Iranian Kurdish leaders were gunned down in a Berlin restaurant by regime assassins in 1992.

Yet this background does not in itself explain either the divide between Iran and the United States or the depth of animosity and mistrust that we see today. Although the 444-day US embassy siege had prompted both the immediate rupture of diplomatic relations between the two countries, which were formally broken off on 7 April 1980, as well as the cessation of trade with Iran, this economic impasse had began to break down significantly by the early 1990s. So while Ronald Reagan's Executive Order 12613, signed on 29 October 1987, had imposed a new import embargo on goods that originated from Iran, it did not technically prevent the overseas subsidiaries of American companies from importing them into the United States or stop US-based companies from exporting these Iranian goods to other foreign markets elsewhere in the world. Such loopholes meant that by the mid-1990s US companies were buying and exporting very large quantities of Iranian oil: throughout 1994, for example, Iran exported a daily output of 2.6 million barrels, 23 per cent of which was moved by American companies such as Exxon, which was contracted to buy 250,000–300,000 barrels each day, Coastal (130,000), Bay Oil (70,000) and Caltex (60,000). By 1995, two years into the Clinton presidency, this trade had grown substantially as American businesses continued to find and exploit legal loopholes that had by now allowed the United States to become Iran's third largest trading partner and its sixth largest export market.

It was also at this time, in March 1995, that Washington had a major opportunity to patch up relations with Tehran, or at least to establish some kind of relations. The opportunity came when Iranian premier Hashemi

Rafsanjani offered an American company, Conoco, a lucrative $1.6 billion contract to develop two of its offshore oil fields that did not require prior US government approval because the deal involved only its Dutch affiliate, Conoco Iran NV. This was a dramatic gesture by Tehran, one that stunned Washington because it would have opened a gateway to a much wider economic relationship and, by extension, a window of opportunity through which political and diplomatic dialogue could be started.

US sanctions against Iran

Although business leaders proclaimed the Rafsanjani offer as a golden opportunity for both countries, the deal was soon scuppered in Washington, but not because anyone of influence harboured traumatic memories of the days of revolution, or because they remembered the fate of Buckley or the threats against Rushdie. Though these perhaps influenced the image of Iran in the public mind, it was the 'high politics' on Capitol Hill, where so much foreign policy was determined, that now mattered. Claiming that Iran was directly implicated in many of the violent attacks on Israeli targets in the Middle East by groups such as Hamas and Islamic Jihad, Senator Alfonse D'Amato (Rep-NY) had already introduced draft legislation into Congress that sought to impose a blanket ban on all American trade, including deals struck by the overseas subsidiaries of US companies. Two months later, as Rafsanjani made his offer to Conoco, D'Amato found strong support from the Israeli government, which pressed Clinton to impose the trade ban on the grounds that, unless such pressure was exerted on Tehran, premier Yitzhak Rabin could not 'take risks for peace' in the ongoing negotiations to find a lasting Middle East settlement.

The Rafsanjani offer had brought matters to a head and led to Washington decisively turning a cold shoulder. Echoing D'Amato's claim that 'all trade with Iran must stop so we don't provide terrorists with hard currency', President Clinton argued that 'there are times when important economic interests must give way to even more important security interests, and this is one of those times'. On 15 March, barely a week after the offer was made to Conoco, Clinton signed a new Executive Order, number 12957, prohibiting all oil development deals with Iran, and on 6 May, as he declared a state of emergency with Iran, issued Order 12959 [12] which effectively imposed a blanket ban on all commercial and financial transactions with Iran. This more-or-less outright prohibition on Iranian imports was complemented by similarly sweeping restrictions on exporting US goods to Iran.

There are at present some minor exceptions to this outright prohibition, exceptions that allow particular items of value and interest such as carpets and caviar to be imported,[13] and the export of humanitarian goods and services, which found their way into the country in the aftermath of the massive earthquake that devastated the Bam region of southern Iran in December 2003. Although on 17 March 2000 President Clinton's Secretary of State, Madeleine Albright, did announce a slight easing of sanctions, these regulations have nonetheless remained substantially unchanged since they were introduced, having been renewed by President George W. Bush in March 2006, who argued that 'because the actions and policies of the government of Iran continue to pose an unusual and extraordinary threat to the national security, foreign policy, and economy of the United States, the national emergency declared on March 15, 1995, must continue in effect beyond March 15, 2006'.

The US authorities vigorously enforce these sanctions and the various other laws that supplement them. In 2002, for example, the Houston-based oil-field services company BS & B Process Systems was fined almost $1 million by the US Department of Commerce for illegally exporting oil-field equipment to Iran, after a lengthy investigation by the Department's Bureau of Export Administration (BXA) revealed that the company had made the sales to Iran in April 1996 for a sum that was far less than the fines imposed. The BXA brought its case not under the 1995 sanctions legislation but under a more general foreign export policy that calls for the prevention of exports of any equipment to any listed country which 'could make a significant contribution to that country's military potential or could enhance its ability to support acts of international terrorism'. Other companies have also fallen foul of similar prosecutions, such as Pars Company Inc of North Carolina which was fined $10,000 in September 2001 for exporting gas monitors to Iran without a Department of Commerce licence.[14]

Secondary sanctions

But what makes the scope of US sanctions highly unusual is their applicability to foreign nationals wanting to do business with Iran. Washington has at times passed and enforced comparable legislation against other countries but does so only very rarely in order to avoid the fierce political battles that are likely to ensue. In the 1980s, for example, attempts by the Reagan administration to prevent international companies from supplying Russia's trans-Siberian pipeline project proved to be immensely controversial, while from 1996 the introduction of the Helms–Burton bill for secondary sanctions against Cuba had led to litigation in international courts – a complaint was lodged before the World Trade Organization in 1997 against a US law that blocked investments in Cuba – and had eventually forced Washington to strike a compromise with the European Union.

Yet such obstacles did not prevent a determined number of Congressmen from pushing their case forward and in the summer of 1996, only a year after first proposing new sanctions against Iran, Senator D'Amato put forward a new bill that called for secondary sanctions on any 'extra-territorial' investment in Iran's oil and gas sectors that exceeded $40 (later $20) million. Under this legislation, the US president has the discretion to impose up to two of six possible sanctions on any company that falls foul of its terms. These include a ban on its imports of goods and services into the United States, a federal government ban on the purchase of its goods and services, the imposition of a loan ceiling of $10 million by all US financial institutions, a prohibition on the sanctioned business from acting as a primary dealer of US treasury bonds, a ban on US export–import assistance, and a denial of licences that approve the export of controlled technology to that business. After Senator Kennedy added Libya to its remit, the legislation became the Iran–Libya Sanctions Act (ILSA) as it passed through Congress in July 1996.

To date ILSA has not been enforced, although its spectre has occasionally been raised, most notably in the six months after an international consortium – led by the French oil giant Total SA but also including Malaysia's Petronas and Russia's Gazprom – signed a $2 billion contract with the Tehran authorities in October 1997 to develop part of the massive South Pars field. After seven months of perusal, President Clinton eventually gave in to strong international pressure and used the discretionary powers under Section 9(c) of the legislation to waive the enforcement of the sanctions on the grounds that doing so is 'important to the US national interest'. Since then the State Department has conducted official investigations into a number of other deals, notably those struck by Shell, Eni and Sheer Energy, the Canadian company that in 2002 was awarded an $88 million contract to redevelop the Masjid-i-Suleiman field.

The reluctance to enforce ILSA against Total encouraged other international oil companies to consider making new arrangements with Tehran. 'Dozens of foreign companies are watching our reaction to the Total deal,' D'Amato and Rep. Ben Gilman, the House International Relations Committee chairman, had argued in 1997; 'if we do not sanction Total as an ILSA violator, it is likely that foreign investment will pour into Iran's oil and gas fields'. They were proved right, and within months there was a flurry of international interest in the Iranian market. On 1 March 1999 the Iranian government signed a deal with the French Company Elf Aquitaine and Italy's ENI to develop the Dorood oil field near Kharg Island in the Persian Gulf, while the following month Elf made its second deal with Iran, this time siding with Bow Valley Energy of Canada to strike a $300 million contract to develop the Balal offshore oil field, another vast deposit with recoverable reserves of around 100 million barrels. In both Iranian and American eyes, each and every one of these deals undermined the credibility of the Iran–Libya Sanction Act by driving, as one Iranian official has put it, a 'nail into the coffin' of the US embargo.[15]

This is not to say that the threat of US sanctions does not continue to loom large for many would-be international companies, particularly those that feel highly vulnerable to retaliation because they happen to have a large number of American investors or because they hold a large stake in the American economy. Even after Clinton backed down from penalizing Total's 1997 deal to develop South Pars, the threat of ILSA, though receding, probably still played some part in subsequently deterring an Indonesian company, Bakrie, from making a bid to develop the Balal oil field and has subsequently continued to significantly restrain international development in the Iranian petroleum industry. Perhaps the main example of the dark shadow that ILSA continues to cast is provided by the proposed pipeline to move Caspian oil across Iran to the Persian Gulf: although on paper this proposal is easily the most attractive option, American pressure always made another much less viable option by far the most likely contender.

Yet the political obstacles that inhibit ILSA's enforcement have not led to any strident demands in US political circles to repeal the legislation and to rethink the economic or political relationship with Tehran. Nor, for that matter, has the huge cost to American industry of a trade embargo with a country that after 1995 immediately found other international purchasers of its oil and whose domestic market has yielded huge profits that American businesses have had to watch their rivals reap. Far from it. Iran continues to be castigated in American politics as a 'terrorist' and 'nuclear-arming' state, and in Congress a powerful call to restore economic and political ties with Tehran continues to be heard only rarely.

It is from the fusion of these two factors – Iran's natural resources and an American economic embargo on that country – that a very volatile political creation has been born. The tensions are obvious. If American businesses cannot trade with Iran, then of course a void is created that can be filled by other countries that Washington would ordinarily consider rivals or even enemies. Moreover American allies and 'non-aligned' countries are being pulled in one direction by the looming shadow of the Iran–Libya Sanctions Act and by the more general political and economic weight of the United States, which wants to stop them from supporting the Tehran regime. But they are also being pulled in the other direction by their need for Iran's natural resources and by the huge profit that the demands of its domestic market, created in large part by the oil and gas industry, increasingly offer.

Why, though, are such tensions particularly evident now rather than at any previous time? After all, as this chapter began by saying, Iran's natural resources have in some sense always been deeply 'political'.

The politics of energy

If Iran's possession of such outstanding natural resources has always had powerful political ramifications, then those that are in evidence today are no more or less potent than those that have preceded them.

Right from the onset, there was bitter international rivalry to gain control over Iranian reserves. This was initially a privilege that belonged exclusively to the British government, which took full advantage of a deal struck in 1901 between William Knox D'Arcy and Shah Muzzaffar al-Din that gave the British entrepreneur an exclusive right to search for oil in a vast area of Persian territory. After 1908 British ministers helped establish the Anglo-Persian (later Iranian) Oil Company (AIOC) to explore and develop the Persian oil that was particularly indispensable to the Royal Navy after Churchill's decision, as First Lord of the Admiralty, to convert the fuelling of ships' engines from coal to oil. But such a valuable asset inevitably raised the strong interest of foreign governments, and equally strong fears in London of their plots to seize the Persian jewel. In 1919 the British government effectively assumed control over Persia under the terms of a new Anglo-Persian agreement that was partly intended, as Foreign Secretary Lord Curzon announced, to prevent 'enemy intrigue' in a country that could be 'overrun by Bolshevik influence from the north'. And when, in the early stages of the Second World War, thousands of Nazi agents arrived in Tehran hoping to strike a deal with the shah in case the German armies in North Africa or Russia got close enough to the Iranian border, the British did not fail to act, launching a full-scale invasion of the country in August 1941 that, together with Russian actions further north, took just two weeks to overwhelm the shah's army.

Having been ruled by outsiders for so long, a nationalist reaction within Iran always seemed likely, and it emerged most unmistakably in April 1951, five years after a serious outbreak of rioting in the refinery port of Abadan had yielded clear proof that popular attitudes among Iranians to British involvement were hardening considerably. On 28 April, as a chorus of nationalist rhetoric at all levels of Iranian society grew louder, the Iranian parliament, the Majlis, voted in favour of the proposals made by Prime Minister Mohammed Mossadeq to nationalize the Anglo-Iranian Oil Company. Under the terms of the legislation, the Iranian government would now audit the AIOC's books and establish a new National Iranian Oil Company while giving British shareholders some unspecified amount of compensation for the loss they would incur.

So many years on, the strength of the feelings of devastation, panic and anger that such a move provoked in London is difficult to imagine. Keen to recapture some of its lost status in Iran, the British government initiated an operation to topple Mossadeq but was foiled when his security chiefs got wind of these efforts and closed down the embassy in Tehran where the operation was based. But London's efforts to implement regime change were then resumed by a US administration fearful that the Soviets might succeed in winning Mossadeq's sympathy and, by extension, get some degree of control over Iran's resources. As Secretary of State John Dulles was reported as saying: 'The communists might easily take over [Iran]. ... Not only would the free world be deprived of the enormous assets represented by Iranian oil production and reserves but the Russians would secure these assets and thus henceforth be free of any anxiety about their petroleum situation.'[16] In an operation of astonishing ingenuity, audacity and cleverness, the CIA operation, led by the highly resourceful and daring Kermit 'Kim' Roosevelt, succeeded in finding key opponents of the premier, mainly within the Iranian armed forces, while bribing others whose loyalty was wavering, and on 19 August 1953 succeeded in forcing Mossadeq to step down and hand over the premiership to his Washington-sponsored successor, Fazlollah Zahedi. Operation *Ajax*, against seemingly impossible odds, had worked.[17]

Over the next three decades, until the eve of the Islamic revolution in 1979, Washington was extremely concerned to keep Iran's resources, as well as those that moved along the Persian Gulf that straddled its southern borders, out of Soviet hands. Sharing a long and in places porous border with the Soviet Union, Iran seemed highly vulnerable not just to a military attack but to a campaign of infiltration and subversion of the sort that the Russians were often thought to excel at, and this prompted the Americans to nurture and sustain a very close relationship with Shah Mohammed Reza Pahlavi's regime. Successive Washington administrations now provided Iran with vast amounts of economic assistance – around $200 million in the three years that followed the 1953 coup – and very considerable military support, as vast numbers of American soldiers and advisers as well as huge quantities of equipment poured into the country. Not surprisingly, the shah was adept at playing the Soviet card in order to maximize concessions from Washington: just before the 1962 Cuban missile crisis, for example, he openly pledged not to allow the deployment of foreign – and, by deliberate implication, American – nuclear missiles on Iranian soil, even though this pronouncement was really just a clever tactic designed to increase his political leverage over the Kennedy administration.[18]

So from a glance at its history, it is clear that Iran's possession of such immense natural resources has always had very powerful repercussions, both within and outside its own borders, and this means that there is clearly no novelty in the assertion that there is, in its own right, a discernible 'politics of energy': it is self-evident that any country's possession of such resources of oil and gas has such strong political repercussions in the same way as the possession of any other valuable asset. But the novel impact of Iran's natural resources on the outside world lies not in their politicization but in the unique challenge to American power that they are now posing.

This, in turn, prompts another obvious question: why is this challenge of particular importance now rather than, for example, in 1995 and 1996, when the existing US economic sanctions were first introduced, or for that matter in the year that followed the 1979 revolution, as relations between Washington and Tehran crashed and reached a nadir? Put simply, the main reason is that Washington is now seeking to put more pressure on a country with which other governments and businesses have more reason than ever before to strike deals.

Why Iran's resources matter now

Greater American pressure

The basic reason why Iran is now posing a greater challenge to American interests than ever before is simply that Washington is currently more anxious than at any previous time to pressurize its allies into toeing its own line at the expense of doing business with Tehran.

This can be measured by drawing a contrast between the events of 1997, when the Clinton administration weighed up the arguments for and against invoking ILSA to penalize the Total-led consortium, and events in US Congress in the course of 2005. On the one hand, Clinton's 1998 decision not to invoke ILSA against Total provoked only relatively isolated cries of protest from lobby organizations such as the American–Israeli Public Affairs Committee (AIPAC) and from within Congress. Furthermore only a small number of senators had also actively sought to penalize the two other companies in the project, Petronas and Gazprom, even though both were particularly vulnerable to American retaliation: the giant Russian firm Gazprom, for example, signed the deal to develop South Pars at the same time that it was seeking to raise $1 billion in US capital markets for Russian projects and to purchase of $750 million in US goods and equipment.

But in the course of 2005, on the other hand, Congressional demands to tighten the economic noose on international trade with Iran were becoming louder and more insistent and, by the early summer, support for a revision of ILSA had grown considerably. In April 2006 the House of Representatives approved by an overwhelming majority of 397 to 21 the Iran Freedom and

Support bill,[19] which tightened and codified the 1996 legislation, widening its scope while also threatening to slash or even cut out any US foreign aid received by a government that fell foul of the bill's terms: one section of the new legislation, for example, proposed extending ILSA's reach to insurers and creditors, greatly multiplying the number of people who fell within its remit, while another removed the 'sunset provision' originally written into the legislation which ensured that it would be reviewed in Congress every five years. Finding equal support among Republicans and Democrats, the proposed legislation was also strongly supported by AIPAC, which at its annual meeting in Washington in May made its implementation a high priority, and by some other pressure groups. Although the bill still faced big hurdles before it became law, its passage was an unmistakable sign that, among many highly influential people on Capitol Hill, attitudes were hardening.

Other critics of Iran wanted to take things further still. On 7 February 2005 Senator Ron Wyden had also introduced the Investor in Iran Accountability bill, which was intended to shine a spotlight on those American companies that were still using independent foreign subsidiaries to defy the US trade embargo and do business with Iran in the energy sector. The new bill required the Treasury Secretary to publish a list of those American companies whose overseas subsidiaries continued to do energy deals with Iran and had more than $1 million invested in these concerns. The legislation also sought to frighten off these businesses by making their dealings with Iran more transparent to American investors: it proposed to do this by requiring the Treasury Department to publish a list of all public and private US financial interests that held more than $100,000 worth of investment in those companies. It was this increasing pressure from within Congress and from American investors that in February 2005 prompted Halliburton to stop its independent overseas subsidiaries from dealing in Iran. Threatened with an official investigation into any possible breach of existing sanctions, and under mounting pressure from a number of shareholders about its ties with Iran, the company initially responded to shareholder concern by listing its Iranian activities, which included an annual $30–40 million of oil-field service work plus a number of comparatively small engineering and design projects, before finally withdrawing its subsidiaries from the country altogether.[20]

Later on in the year new legislation was also introduced into the Senate to restrict American businesses from obtaining nuclear fuel assemblies from any other company that also sold them to Iran. Originally proposed in September by Senator Rick Santorum, just as the Iranian nuclear controversy appeared to be reaching a diplomatic climax in Vienna,[21] the Iranian

Nuclear Trade Prohibition Act of 2005 targeted fabricated nuclear items that contained enriched uranium and outlawed their purchase by any American business from another business, entity or government that also sold to Iran. 'Iran's support for terrorist organizations, its past record of nuclear enrichment deceit and its opposition to US foreign policy objectives in the Middle East make Iran one of the most pressing national security issues facing the US and the democratic countries of the world,' Santorum said, 'and the US must take this important step toward eliminating nuclear activity in Iran.' This proposal, as well as the other legislative proposals, prompted Nicholas Burns, the Under-Secretary of State for Policy, to write to Santorum on 13 October pointing out that the administration was worried that the new rules 'would impair our ability to continue working closely and successfully with our allies' on the Iranian issue.

These proposals formed part of a growing chorus for action against Iran that had been increasingly audible over the preceding two years. In the summer of 2003, for example, moves had been made to reduce the president's scope to waive and exempt foreign companies that fell foul of ILSA, notably Rep. Ileana Ros-Lehtinen's bill, introduced on 21 October 2003, to limit these exemptions. Known as the Iran–Libya Sanctions Act Enhancement and Compliance Act (ILSA-ECA), the bill sought 'to address the concerns, loopholes and changes in the world since the original bill's passage in 1996' not only by narrowing the conditions under which the White House could waive the law but also by extending the classification of the parties subjected to sanctions to include public and private financiers and lenders. The bill also made the removal of sanctions contingent on a presidential certification that Iran and Libya no longer pose a 'threat to the national security of the United States, its interests or allies'.

There are two main influences that have made the case for primary and secondary sanctions against Iran more pressing in the course of George W. Bush's successive presidencies. These are Iran's nuclear project, which had taken sudden and unexpected strides since ILSA was first introduced, and its association in many American eyes, stronger than ever before, with 'terrorism'.

The nuclear issue

Undoubtedly the single most important reason why Iran's natural resources are now undermining American global power is the increasing sophistication of the Tehran regime's nuclear programme. Although Iran is still reckoned to be some years away from developing a warhead, its nuclear programme is now known to be vastly more sophisticated than at the time when the existing range of US economic sanctions against Iran were drawn up and enforced.

Until the summer of 2002 most independent experts harboured little doubt that Iran had a covert nuclear weapons programme, which its supposedly peaceful programme to provide civilian energy was intended to disguise. But the Iranians painfully lacked the core ingredient of a bomb, notably the heavily enriched uranium or weapons-grade plutonium from which the fissile material is derived, and it was widely assumed that the prohibitive costs of developing such a facility would force the Iranians to import these ingredients from foreign sources, probably looking to the cash-starved former Soviet Union where such resources were likely to be available and where local authorities could perhaps be easily bribed.

The revelation in the summer of 2002 that Iran had secretly constructed much of its own infrastructure to enrich uranium therefore sent shockwaves of alarm and outrage throughout many international capitals. At a press briefing in August, spokesmen for a dissident organization made dramatic revelations, based on information said to have been supplied by Israeli intelligence, about the existence of two nuclear complexes of which the outside world was wholly unaware. One was a vast uranium enrichment facility at Natanz, approximately 200 miles south of Tehran, made up of six buildings that in total covered around 100,000 square metres, while the other was a site at Arak where the Iranians intended to build a heavy-water reactor from which the plutonium required for the fissile material of a warhead could easily be extracted.

By failing to declare the existence of these facilities to the International Atomic Energy Agency (IAEA), the Iranians had not strictly violated the terms of the 1968 Nuclear Non-Proliferation Treaty (NPT) or the subsequent Safeguards Agreement that gave substance to the earlier deal. Yet this hardly reassured either critics of Iran or enemies of proliferation. With a capacity to house as many as 50,000 of the centrifuge machines used in the enrichment process, the Natanz complex potentially could produce between 400 and 500 kilograms of weapons-grade uranium, enough to make perhaps as many as 20 nuclear warheads, while according to non-governmental estimates the Arak reactor, when completed, could also annually produce between 8 and 10 kilograms of plutonium. After an IAEA visit to these other sites the following February, the Iranian nuclear programme was judged to be 'extremely advanced',[22] far more so than even the most audacious independent assessments had ever expected.

In February 2003, a few months after the original revelations were made, Iran appeared even closer to attaining its own self-contained nuclear fuel cycle when President Khatami announced that deposits of uranium had been discovered in Iran for the first time and that these were already being

mined in the Savand area, 200km from the historic city of Yazd. Although
the process of converting this natural uranium into the highly refined product used by a warhead is very difficult and time-consuming, this was not
much reassurance to those for whom the prospect of an Iranian bomb has
always been an unacceptable proposition.

The further revelations certainly continued to electrify political circles in
Washington and elsewhere, and as preparations for the invasion of Iraq gathered pace, many people began to wonder if it was really Iran, not Saddam
Hussein, that the Bush administration should be focusing its sights on.
Administration spokesmen such as the State Department's Richard Boucher
announced their 'very grave concerns that Tehran is using its supposedly
peaceful nuclear programme, including the construction of a reactor in Bushehr, as a pretext for advancing a nuclear weapons programme'. In practice
Iran was probably still years away from completing such a programme, as the
National Intelligence Estimate and highly respected independent experts[23]
pointed out, but it was nonetheless much further along the road to doing so
than had previously been realized.

From this moment on, the task of preventing the prospect of an Iranian
bomb from becoming a much feared reality became a particularly pressing
concern for Washington, even if it was for the moment overshadowed by the
task of removing Saddam Hussein from power and subsequently keeping
the peace in the new Iraq. In order to obstruct the Iranian nuclear project,
the Bush administration echoed the Clinton line by seeking not just to pressurize Tehran into renouncing its nuclear ambitions but also to starve the
regime of the foreign exchange it needed to fund such a project, even if that
meant persuading the international community to minimize its trade with
Iran. But when the outside world has a dire and growing need for oil and
gas, this pressure can only be politically highly volatile.

The nuclear issue is one reason why the advocates of sanctions against
Iran have been able to withstand the strong opposition of American business. Organizations such as 'USA Engage', an association of more than 675
US companies, has reckoned that these sanctions cost American business a
total of $19 billion per annum in lost revenue, along with 250,000 jobs.[24]
But there is also one other reason why anti-Iranian feeling on Capitol Hill
has not only been able to withstand this pressure but has also been strengthening.

Terrorism

The other main reason, besides its nuclear programme, why Iran is an even
more contentious issue in contemporary American politics than when ILSA
was first drafted is its association with 'terrorism'. For although Iran has

been consistently labelled by the US State Department as 'the world's most active sponsor of terrorism' for more than a decade, several recent developments appear to have considerably strengthened this argument.

From an American perspective, the Bush administration's post-9/11 preoccupation with defeating 'terrorism' has played straight into the hands of Iran's enemies on Capitol Hill, who have emphasized to great effect Iran's qualifications as a terrorist state. In particular, Israel's strongest supporters point to Iran's association with an organization that many influential American politicians have always wanted to put in the firing line of the 'War on Terror' – the Lebanese movement Hezbollah. Within days of the attacks on the World Trade Center, Tehran had earned a prominent place on the target list produced by an influential pressure group, the Project for the New American Century, 41 of whose members had addressed an open letter to President Bush urging retaliation against Iran if it failed to bring an immediate end to its support for the Lebanese militia.

Iranian actions, or rather alleged Iranian actions, have also helped to reinforce this impression. In January 2002 the ship *Karine A* was intercepted by the Israelis as it moved through international waters 300 miles off Israel's Red Sea coast and was found to be carrying more than 50 tons of arms, including Katyusha rockets and anti-tank missiles, that had allegedly been loaded at the Iranian port of Kish before being sent on their way to areas of the Gaza Strip controlled by the Palestinian Authority. The cargo's seizure, said the Israelis, gave 'incontrovertible evidence' that Iran was supplying military equipment to the radical Palestinian cause. 'The connection between the Palestinian Authority and the smuggling operation is unequivocal, clear and undeniable,' stated Chief of Staff Shaul Mofaz at a press conference in Tel Aviv on 4 January 2002, as Prime Minister Sharon, inspecting the cargo at Eilat, argued that it proved the existence of a 'network of international terrorism spearheaded by Iran'. Although many large question marks continue to hang over the story of the *Karine A* – even if the Israeli claims are taken on trust, there is no indication of who in Iran had ordered and organized the operation or why – such an incident received massive publicity in Washington and certainly tarnished Iran's image more than ever before.

More important, however, has been the alleged involvement of Iran in the militant insurgency in post-Saddam Iraq. From the moment this campaign began in earnest, in the summer of 2003, American leaders have pointed an accusing finger at neighbouring Syria and Iran, claiming that their respective governments have not just turned a blind eye to the insurgents' cross-border movements but given them proactive assistance and training. Although such claims were initially treated with scepticism, they later appeared to be taken much more seriously by other countries. By September 2005, for example,

British military officials claimed that attacks on allied personnel in Basra were to some important degree being orchestrated by the Iranian government, probably in a bid to intimidate a British government that was strongly opposed to Tehran's nuclear programme and which was at that time lobbying hard for the Iranians to be referred to the UN Security Council.[25] Similar claims were made in more mysterious fashion on 5 October, when an anonymous senior British official addressed a group of correspondents in London and stated that the Iranians were strongly supporting Shiite insurgents in Iraq. Not all independent analysts were quite so convinced,[26] especially when Prime Minister Blair admitted on 6 October that 'we can't be sure' of such support, but once again the terrorist label had been firmly pinned on to Iran.

Events in Iraq and the *Karine A* incident have accentuated, rather than caused, Iran's identification in American political circles with 'terror', which had been forged well before the onset of the attacks on the World Trade Center. Several political moves against Iran's 'terror' were made shortly before the 9/11 attacks, for example, and in the summer of 2001 AIPAC organized demands for the renewal of sanctions against Iran on the grounds that the clerical regime posed a clear threat both to Israel and the prospects for Middle East peace. And on 23 May 2001 a bill for the renewal of ILSA, which had originally been introduced in 1996 only for a five-year term, was introduced into the House of Representatives with over 200 co-sponsors, and was followed shortly afterwards by a parallel bill in the Senate backed by a veto-proof majority of senators. This strong and well-organized campaign took advantage of the new administration's post-electoral uncertainty and confounded the hopes of many American businesses that Bush's election would herald a significant change of stance in favour of US economic interests.

Yet Iran's image has undoubtedly suffered even more since 9/11, and on Capitol Hill the sponsors of new legislation have certainly strongly emphasized Iran's credentials as a terrorist state. The 2003 ILSA-ECA Act, for example, was intended to find 'ways to restrict the increasing wave of foreign investment into Iran and Libya and must be an integral part of the same effort to suppress terrorist financing', claimed Ros-Lehtinen as her bill was debated in June 2003. She added that 'neither Iran nor Libya have shown signs of relenting in their support for international terrorism. Those companies who continue to pursue investment in the oil sectors of these rogue nations, thus enabling this aggression, must realize that they are bankrolling terrorism. ILSA must be amended to address its continued financing of terror.'

Taken together, Iran's nuclear programme and its alleged support for Middle Eastern 'terror groups' have reinforced the case for economic sanctions against Iran, and in 2003 both were cited by Secretary of State Colin Powell in support of George W. Bush's decision to renew the sanctions first imposed in 1995: 'We've raised this issue repeatedly. We've talked about the "axis of evil" and been criticized for it,' Powell argued, 'and lo and behold, we discover they had a far more robust nuclear infrastructure that could be used for weapons development than people had thought, or wanted us to believe. We were seen as suspicious, and we shouldn't be moving in this direction, but now we have a real concern. When you marry that up with their continued support for terrorist organizations that foment terror in Lebanon and other places throughout the Middle East, I believe that our concerns with respect to Iran were well founded.'[27]

The strength of US concerns about terrorism and the nuclear issue helps explain why Washington appeared to actively seek regime change in Tehran, or at least to pave the way for such a radical approach, rather than emphasizing any constructive role for economic inducements or any other 'carrots' designed to dissuade the Iranians from pursuing their nuclear course. Only in March 2005, four months after the negotiations, did Secretary of State Condoleezza Rice announce a policy shift by agreeing in principle not to block Iran's application to join the World Trade Organization, having blocked a similar move to join the WTO the previous December after labelling the EU–Iran negotiations as 'a toothless enterprise'. But even then the 'policy shift' in Washington fell far short of what EU negotiators had hoped for: the only sanctions lifted by the US government, Rice announced in March, was a virtually meaningless offer to sell spare parts to Iran's decrepit fleet of civilian airliners. Such reluctance probably reflected the strong scepticism towards EU3 diplomacy that was reputedly harboured by Under-Secretary of State Nicholas Burns, National Security Adviser Stephen Hadley and his deputy, Elliot Abrams, who were said to argue that the negotiations with Tehran would never succeed but who were prepared to offer some 'carrots' to back them, not because they felt such incentives would work but in order to secure the support of European powers for American moves to sanction Iran when the negotiations eventually failed.

But at the same time that Washington, for political reasons, is increasingly trying to pull the outside world in one direction, another force is also pushing it in another. This force is a growing need for Iran's energy resources, and the other main reason why Iran's natural resources are now beginning to create more political fissures than ever before is that the outside world is more dependent on its supply of oil and gas. This means that Iran is now better placed to do deals with America's rivals and sustain their energy requirements or to tempt Washington's allies into breaking any US-led embargo on Iranian trade.[28]

Increasing global demand for oil and gas

The world's growing need for Iran's oil and gas reflects both increasing global demand as well as the diminishing capacity of many existing sources of supply to satisfy those demands in the long term. This lack of confidence in the capacity of existing sources partly reflects the fact that the world's oil reserves, even if they are consumed at a steady rate, are becoming increasingly inaccessible. So although Saudi Arabia, like all the other Gulf states, still harbours vast deposits of oil, some of which are perhaps still undiscovered, billions of dollars would need to be invested in its infrastructure if these reserves are to be tapped. According to the International Energy Agency, the Persian Gulf producers would have to spend an estimated $523 billion on new equipment and technology in the three decades between 2001 and 2030 in order to increase output and meet global demand.[29] This represents not just a huge financial and technological hurdle but also a political one, since it would have to be backed by international loans that would offend the Saudis' proclaimed wish to retain complete control over their nationalized energy sector, which is dominated by the state oil company Saudi Aramco.[30] Other political and legal obstacles to foreign investment also obstruct the development of oil fields in Kuwait, the Emirates and Qatar.

This was the message from the International Energy Agency, the oil sector monitoring body, which struck a note of alarm in 2005. 'It is not a problem of availability of reserves or capital,' as Fatih Birol, the group's chief economist told a British newspaper; 'we need to be sure that the increase in production will be high enough and a sustained production capacity increase is in place. That will need sustained political will.' But although Saudi Arabia would need to almost double current output of 10 million b/d to meet the level of demand anticipated in 2030, Mr Birol said that the kingdom might muster the long-term political will to produce just over half the extra barrels deemed necessary.[31]

Outside the Gulf, oil production has been stagnating, sometimes declining, in areas that were once highly productive. The output from Mexico's major oil field, the Cantarell site in the Bay of Campeche, for example, has naturally depleted over a number of years and is not expected to recover,[32] while many of Venezuela's fields, some of which have been in operation for a century or so, are also unmistakably waning. In 2005 Britain also became a net importer of oil for the first time in more than three decades, as its North Sea reserves became depleted. In other parts of the world, some of the most plentiful oil reserves are also the most inaccessible: Kazakhstan's newly discovered fields, for example, are located in a section of the Caspian Sea that freezes over in winter, making drilling operations extremely difficult, while Angola's fields are situated in very deep ocean waters. International investment in developing these deposits is also deterred by high political obstacles, notably endemic corruption, political instability and complex legal and financial barriers.

But while international governments may feel less sure than before about securing long-term supplies, global demand is also growing, and US Department of Energy figures show that between 2001 and 2025 major Middle Eastern oil producers will have to double their total daily output to satisfy growing demand.[33] This is partly because there is much greater demand in the developing world, whose populations and economies are rapidly expanding and whose consumers have higher expectations of material comfort than ever before. A classic case in point is India, whose annual rate of population growth averages between 3 and 4 per cent – roughly the same as Pakistan – and whose fast-expanding economy has created a new 'middle class' with a sophisticated taste for Western comfort. Another example is China, whose consumption of oil alone in the next 25 years is expected to jump from 6.5 to 12.8 million barrels per day, while demand in Asia as a whole will rise from 15 million to 32 million. Yet this increase in demand is certainly not just specific to any particular country or region but is instead a global phenomenon: in the United States, for example, demand for petroleum is projected to increase to around 27 million barrels of oil per day by the year 2020, compared with its daily demand of 20 million barrels in 2000.[34] The United States has had the occasional glimpse of this pending oil crisis, when, for example, Hurricane Katrina crashed through New Orleans in 2005 or after the steep oil price increases of 1999–2000 prompted the Bush administration to dramatically assert that 'America in the year 2001 faces the most serious energy shortage since the oil embargoes of the 1970s'.[35]

Most experts also expect a dramatic increase in global demand for natural gas over the next quarter century or so, even though this is likely to be tempered by high prices. In 2005 the *International Energy Outlook* forecast an average annual increase of 2.3 per cent, well above the 1.9 per cent increase it predicted for oil consumption. This overall 70 per cent increase in global demand, from 92 trillion cf in 2002 to 156 trillion cf in 2025, partly reflects the robust growth of the developing world, which needs natural gas to power electricity, but also the increasing tendency to view gas as a more efficient, cost-competitive and cleaner fuel than oil. These considerations also explain why European demand is projected to grow at a high annual rate, estimated to be around 1.8 per cent, which will make its governments far more dependent than ever before on imports. On the assumption that the production of

European gas stays flat at 10.6 trillion cf this means that gas imports will have to increase to 17 trillion cf each year by 2020.

For those countries that are not hindered by geographical or political obstacles from doing business with Iran, the rest of the world's growing need for oil and natural gas has clear consequences. Most obviously it means that no such country would be able to join any US-led embargo on Iranian oil. In an ideal world, the US would of course always have liked to see its European allies follow its example and impose an oil embargo on Iran, in the same way that in the two years following Mossadeq's nationalization of the AIOC in 1951 the British navy successfully imposed a blockade of oil exports that crippled the Iranian economy. But many of America's allies import huge quantities of Iranian oil: in 2004 Japan imported 572,000 barrels a day, Korea 105,000 and Western Europe 620,000.

The key difference is simply that the British embargo was made possible by a glut of world oil, whereas today's relative shortage means that Washington cannot make any comparable such demands on its European and other allies whose economies are both very oil-dependent and highly susceptible to any increase in its price. Similarly the oil-importing countries were in a much stronger position in the early 1980s, when they successfully withstood the major oil supply disruption that followed the outbreak of war in September 1980 between two countries, Iraq and Iran, that were both leading members of the Organization of Petroleum Exporting Countries (OPEC). Although this conflict suddenly reduced world oil supplies by approximately 4 million barrels a day, most countries had very substantial oil reserves that had been built up after the shocks of the Iranian revolution had exposed the need for contingency measures. Weak oil demand and a prompt increase in Saudi production partially offset lost Iranian and Iraqi oil exports and allowed the importing nations to avoid the disastrous pressures that had done so much to cause the price explosion of 1979.

Rather than seeking to restrict their oil and gas imports, Washington could more realistically expect its allies to sacrifice some of their trade and investment with Iran in order to pressurize Tehran into renouncing or at least freezing its nuclear programme. But this, too, is ambitious because Iran's energy infrastructure – the exploration, development and production of oil and gas ('upstream' contracts) as well as work in refineries and the petrochemical sectors ('downstream') – offers huge profits. Not only this but Iran is also awash with the revenue earned from the rise in the price of oil, which has helped to generate both sufficient cash to fund a hugely expensive nuclear programme as well as a domestic market for imported goods. So Washington's European allies have in recent years had more reason to ignore any such calls made by successive US administrations to restrict their trade and investments in Iran: in particular there have for some years been very strong German–Iranian commercial ties, and although Iran comes only 35th on the list of Germany's trading partners, it is an up-and-coming market with a high growth potential. Such interests doubtless play an important, probably decisive role in explaining why Germany has often been at odds with Britain and France in the negotiations with Iran over the nuclear issue, prompting some of those involved in the talks to humorously talk of the 'E2' rather than the 'E3'.

Even if any country ever did impose such trading sanctions while continuing to import Iranian oil, then Iran could clearly retaliate. In the summer of 2005, as Tehran defied international pressure by resuming parts of its uranium enrichment programme, Iranian negotiators hinted that they would respond to any bid to impose UN sanctions on their country by withholding the export of oil. Interviewed by the *Khaleej Times* on 1 October 2005 about possible Iranian counter-measures if such sanctions were enforced, newly elected President Mahmoud Ahmadinejad replied tersely that 'if Iran's case is sent to the Security Council, we will respond in many ways – for example by holding back on oil sales or limiting inspections of our nuclear facilities'. And in a clear warning to the EU the previous month, he also informed Iran's parliament that 'economic ties are not irrelevant to political ties' especially with 'hostile' countries that 'fail to recognize Iran's legitimate rights'.

Any such retaliation would of course greatly injure an Iranian economy whose foreign exchange earnings are highly dependent on oil exports, and most analysts are divided on the question of whether Tehran would really be willing to carry out its threats. Yet there are many countries that are far too dependent on both the importation of Iranian oil or on the price of oil whatever its origin to be willing to take that risk. So when the cost of a barrel rose sharply in the aftermath of Hurricane Katrina in 2005 and briefly reached $70, EU ministers warned that economic growth throughout Europe would be seriously imperilled. With growth in Europe already slower than expected, warned British Chancellor of the Exchequer Gordon Brown at an EU conference in Manchester in September 2005, fuel prices had made a recovery 'more fragile'.[36] Of course many of those who heard this warning wondered if oil prices were really just a convenient excuse for his own failings, but no one disputed that they made things worse. Not just that, but higher fuel prices for ordinary consumers also exact a painful political cost for a government that gets the blame for not reducing the levies that constitute much of the price at the pumps. In September 2000, for example, the British government was rocked by a blockade of fuel refineries by protestors who blamed high petrol costs on exorbitant levels of government taxation, while prices at the pump were also expected to be a big issue in the US mid-term elections in November 2006, as polls showed that a large majority of Americans disapproved of how President Bush was handling gasoline prices.[37] Such adverse consequences, political and economic, would affect every country that imports oil, no matter where it comes from: because Iran is the second largest producer of oil in OPEC, any embargo of its oil would have an impact that extended far beyond just those countries that directly imported it.

Not surprisingly, Iranian negotiators have been quick to play on such fears. So on 5 March 2003 Iran's top nuclear official warned the United States and Europe of the danger of an oil crisis if Tehran was sent before the UN Security Council over its nuclear programme, before rejecting outright their demands to halt uranium enrichment. Taking the matter to the Security Council would be 'playing with fire', claimed Hassan Rowhani, emphasizing that 'the first to suffer will be Europe and the United States themselves', and that 'this would cause problems for the regional energy market, for the European economy and even more so for the United States'. And in November the following year, as the nuclear crisis reached one of its many climaxes, a top aide to Iran's supreme leader declared that Tehran was completely unafraid of being taken to the Security Council over its nuclear programme and warned that if the UN imposed an oil embargo, world prices would go above $100 a barrel. This prompted Ali Akbar Nateq-Nuri, one of Ayatollah Ali Khamenei's closest advisers, to dismiss as 'ridiculous' some suggestions from Europe aimed at persuading Tehran to end uranium enrichment to avoid being summoned by the Security Council.[38] After Iran's referral to the Council by the IAEA in February 2006, the Iranians continued to make similarly threatening noises. On 8 March an official statement threatened 'harm and pain' in the event of confrontation over the nuclear issue, while on 14 March the new Oil Minister, Kazem Vaziri-Hamaneh, said that Tehran could revise oil supply contracts with those countries that supported the passage of UN sanctions. The Economy Minister, Davoud Danesh-Jafari, had made similar threats a few weeks before by warning that 'any possible sanctions on Iran from the West could possibly, by disturbing Iran's political and economic situation, raise oil prices beyond levels the West expects'.

Iran and foreign investment

There is another, less important reason why Iranian natural resources present an increasingly important challenge to American power. For not only do international governments have better reason than ever before to import Iranian supplies of oil and gas but the Tehran regime is also making greater efforts to lure international investors into its exploration, production and development. The importance of these efforts should not be exaggerated, because the Iranians are currently still almost as far from making the most of their resources as they have ever been, but they have certainly not gone unnoticed by international business.

Iran's drive to attract foreign investment is not just confined to the oil sector but is part of a much wider economic drive that was spelt out in 2004 when Mohammed Khazai, the Deputy Minister of Economy and Finance, acknowledged that the Iranian economy as a whole would need a $20 billion sum of investment over the next five years if its economy was to expand quickly enough to absorb the demands of a rapidly growing population. But the country's oil infrastructure is in particular need of such investment and the National Iranian Oil Company (NIOC) has estimated that at least $70 billion is needed over the next ten years to modernize it. The Tehran government knows that such targets will never be reached without a massive flow of capital from abroad and hopes that foreign investment will eventually make up not less than 40 per cent of the overall total: as the Deputy Petroleum Minister, Akbar Torkan, told the National Seminar on the Attraction of Foreign Investment, held in Tehran on 5 December 2004, roughly $17 billion of this overall figure was expected to come from domestic sources, $25 billion through a programme of contracting foreign companies and a further $28 billion through the international financial markets. 'We should be thinking of drawing foreign investments and [of] preparing the ground for [an] inflow of foreign capital,' as Khazai has emphasized.

There are a number of reasons why Iran's oil sector needs such vast sums. During the eight years of war with Iraq, some of the most important fields were badly damaged by overproduction, neglect or military action: several platforms on the Soroush and Nowruz fields were badly damaged by the Iraqis, while others at the Resalat and Reshadat fields were attacked and hit by US warships in the latter stages of the conflict, prompting Iran to make a bid, ultimately unsuccessful, for compensation in the International Court of Justice. Furthermore over the past 20 years Iran has been a politically isolated country that painfully lacks the technical expertise needed to develop its resources, especially when many of its most skilled workers have emigrated. The Iranian authorities have also been reluctant to invest the proceeds of oil sales back into the industry because much of this exchange is needed for other purposes, such as subsidies in the manufacturing or agricultural sectors, which are considered to be politically more pressing.

Yet such difficulties have not deterred the Iranians from entertaining high hopes for their oil industry. Wanting to increase their oil production essentially in order to generate more foreign exchange, NIOC officials hope to steady daily output of oil at 4.5 million barrels by the end of 2005 and increase production capacity to 5.4 million by 2009 and to 7 million by

2024. Although Iran has previously come close to reaching such a staggering rate of output – in 1974 its maximum daily output was a colossal 6 million barrels – such targets look unrealistic to most independent analysts. These figures look even more daunting because of the rate at which Iranian output has in recent years been levelling off, with the rate of onshore production declining at a rate of around 8 per cent per annum and offshore around 13 per cent per annum: 'this means Iran is losing 350,000 b/d of capacity each year', one leading consultancy has claimed.[39]

Some significant steps in attracting the billions of dollars it needs have been taken, however. In November 1995 Iran made new and sudden efforts to woo international investors for help in developing 11 large oil and gas offshore projects, reviving pre-revolutionary ambitions to make maximum economic use of its reserves. To this end it held a major conference in Tehran at which NIOC officials gave technical details for these projects to representatives of foreign companies. And in late 1997, two years after declaring an ambition to fully develop the country's massive oil and gas reserves, the Majlis broke new ground by announcing that foreign companies would in principle be eligible to bid for forthcoming onshore exploration and development projects, even though foreign involvement in such schemes had previously been considered by many to be a violation of Iran's 'territorial integrity'.

In May 2002 a very limited step towards attracting foreign investment was also taken when Iran's Expediency Council approved a 'Law on the Promotion and Protection of Foreign Investment', streamlining the complex procedures that were thought to be restricting the flow of capital and to give foreign investors more guarantees that they would not lose their funds. This legislation, which came into effect five months later, retains many of the features of its predecessor, which had been unchanged since it was first introduced in 1956, but also extended its scope by bringing nearly every different type of foreign investment under its wing. Its importance should not be exaggerated, however, since many of its terms are just too nebulous to give would-be investors proper reassurance.[40]

The Iranian authorities have made particular efforts to attract foreign investment in the petrochemicals that are manufactured from the natural gas supply. The first Iran Petrochemical Forum was held in April 1999, at which more than 600 potential foreign investors heard Bijan Namdar Zanganeh outline plans to attract international interest. Special economic zones would be set up, it was announced, where joint venture operations would receive extended tax holidays of up to six years as well as exemptions from import–export regulations. Kish Island, on the Gulf Straits, is one such economic haven for investors, and an increasing number of foreign busi-

nesses are avoiding their tax liabilities by registering in Kish while setting
up representative offices in Tehran. In its bid 'to give assurance to potential international investors', the Iranians also hired the German investment
bank Dresdner Kleinwort Benson to conduct a detailed study of Iran's petrochemical expansion and prepare a comprehensive report that foreign investors could use as a guide.

Iran has also been reviewing and modifying some of the other rules to
which international investment has previously been subjected and by which
many investors feel themselves to have been unreasonably constrained.
From 2003, for example, it has taken some steps to alter the workings of the
'buyback' model of contracts, established under the 1987 Petroleum Law,
that were intended to circumvent a constitutional prohibition on the granting of petroleum rights to foreign concerns.

Buyback contracts

A buyback contract is a fixed-term agreement under which the relevant
company undertakes to finance, construct and commission all facilities not
in return for a direct equity stake in the venture but for a fixed share of oil
or gas production. Thus a company that contracts to spend $1 billion on
developing an oil field would recoup its expenditure, together with interest
and profit, from the field's output when it starts to produce oil, after the
contract has been completed. At the end of the contract term, the ownership of that fixed share reverts back to the National Iranian Oil Company,
which is obliged to recoup the contractors' agreed costs even if the output of
the particular project is insufficient to meet them. Such deals replaced the
granting of *emtiaz* (concessions) that allowed foreign companies not only to
unilaterally explore, develop and produce oil but also to subsequently retain
ownership in the concession area. These were outlawed at the time of the
1979 revolution, when they were strictly prohibited by Article 81 of the new
constitution, drafted as it was by a number of 'Islamic Marxists' and 'red
clerics'.

The buyback contract has been widely used since July 1995, when Total
and Malaysia's Petronas signed a deal to develop the Sirri A and Sirri E gas
fields and became the first foreign contractors since the Islamic revolution to
fix a stake in the heart of Iran's energy sector. By 2004, as its annual report
pointed out, Total had four main buyback deals in Iran that gave it 60 per cent
of the production share in the Sirri A and E fields, 40 per cent in South Pars,
46.8 per cent in Balal and 55 per cent in Doroud. Overall NIOC allocated
Total an average production of 26,000 barrels of oil a day to recoup its upfront
expenditure on these various projects, a figure that was much lower than the
2003 figure of 50,000 mainly because of the impact of higher crude prices.

But the buyback arrangement has nonetheless been very unpopular with most international businesses. On the one hand, such an arrangement gives the contractor no incentive to incur extra costs, thereby improving total returns for such a project, or to maximize the life of the field in question beyond the limited time-span of the contract. The terms of these contracts are also highly inflexible and cannot be renegotiated, even though this is particularly important if new oil and gas deposits are unexpectedly discovered, unanticipated technical problems arise or the price of oil suddenly changes. All sorts of other unexpected events could crop up – dramatic regional events or important changes in capital markets – that might place the overseas contractor under such immense financial pressure that they want to pull the deal. The rigid formula of the buyback is particularly ill suited to a project as complicated as the three-field Bangestan gas injection operation, for example, for which a great deal of field operational information is required if a detailed development plan is to be drawn up. In other countries a development plan for fields like this one would usually allow some degree of flexibility when the number of wells is assessed, whereas the Iranian model of contract only specifies a particular number, which is very time consuming and costly to renegotiate.

The buyback arrangement has other drawbacks. The relatively brief duration of the contracts – about seven years – also means that foreign contractors have little time to build up the spirit of trust and cooperation with the Iranians that their work requires if it is to be successful, and prompts them to ask how much they really have to gain when, at the end of the contract, they are obliged to transfer their up-to-date, highly valued technology into the hands of the Iranians, who currently lag far behind the outside world in technological terms. Such a sacrifice is worthwhile only if the contractor has longer to benefit from such a deal and when the technology used in the project has become more outdated. 'In buyback you develop fields and when it is finished you say goodbye to everything,' a Total official complained to a news agency at the Iran Oil Show in April 2006.[41] Any company that signs a buyback contract to explore a field, rather than develop its resources, also risks incurring massive costs before finding that the field is far less productive than originally expected and therefore offers no further lucrative contracts that the company would be well placed to bid for.

The Iranian government has recently made some moves to alleviate the concerns of international business. Although since 1999 NIOC officials have proclaimed their willingness to consider almost any kind of financing scheme that participants want to suggest,[42] there were few real signs that any such alternatives might be adopted until January 2004, when government officials announced modifications to the standard buyback model that included an extension of the contract term from a standard five to seven years to as much as 25 years, and would potentially allow foreign companies to continue their involvement in the field's development after its tenure was finished and ownership had reverted back to the NIOC. A few months later Kamal Daneshyar, head of the Majlis Energy Committee, announced that an ad hoc committee of Ministry of Petroleum members, industrialists and university professors would flesh out these skeleton proposals in order to encourage more oil tenders for contracts to explore 16 exploration blocks: the key feature of the revision was that whoever discovered any commercial oil or gas field would have the automatic right to develop the find, whereas under the earlier terms the licence holder would have to bid competitively to develop any commercial discovery. This announcement formed part of a wider 2005–2010 economic development plan, put forward by Iran's parliament, to lure international business into the oil and gas sectors.[43]

The importance of these reforms, like those of the foreign investment laws, should not be exaggerated, however. After signing the 1997 deal to develop South Pars, a Total vice-president pointed out that the buyback system had not weighed heavily against the deal and that there were comparable drawbacks in other countries that similarly were not insuperable: 'Iran's buyback contract system is characteristic of countries reopening their upstream sectors to foreign oil companies. The scenario is the same in Iraq and Kuwait. ... These countries have a long history of oil development and their own national oil companies.'[44] In narrowly economic terms there are in any case a great many other reforms that are much more important to international business. As one study has claimed, Iran needs above all to foster a prosperous private sector that would be more attractive to outside investors than a much less efficient state sector. This means that some radical steps need to be taken to encourage private institutions and individuals to buy shares and bonds in all major gas and oil sectors, even though, strictly speaking, Articles 44 and 45 of the constitution leave not more than 5–10 per cent of the economy open to the private sector.[45] By 2005 some initial steps had been taken in this direction, notably after October 2004, when one of Iran's constitutional watchdog bodies, the Expediency Council, overruled earlier constitutional decrees to block any bid to privatize the energy and other sectors.

All of these narrowly economic considerations are probably also less important than the wider framework of international politics. Only very few of the foreign business representatives who attended the November 1995 Tehran conference, for example, wanted their names and employers' details disclosed for fear of provoking US retaliation, whereas three years later, in July 1998, many international companies openly expressed interest in the 40

contracts – which included opportunities to develop 15 onshore sites – that
Oil Minister Zanganeh had offered to foreign investors: China's state-owned
National Petroleum Corporation, Cairn Energy in Edinburgh and Monu-
ment Oil and Gas in London all openly bid to develop the Balal offshore
oil field. The difference is essentially that, after the Clinton administration backed down over Total in 1998, the threat of US sanctions no longer
loomed so large, and while D'Amato was still privately warning the Cana-
dian company Bow Valley not to make a bid, his words no longer carried the
same weight as before.[46]

While most oil investors take a long-term view on their holdings, Iran is
generally regarded as much more risky than other rival markets because its
nuclear infrastructure might at some point be a future target for American
or Israeli military attack or for UN-imposed economic sanctions. Although
most Western businessmen in Iran have professed themselves to be uncon-
cerned by newspaper reports of US strikes as long as the EU has continued
negotiating over the nuclear issue,[47] commercial sensitivity to regional politics became clear on 16 February 2005 when financial markets panicked over
reports of an explosion in Bushehr province which was wrongly assumed to
be a foreign missile attack. Some analysts have also regarded the election
as president of the conservative hardliner Mahmoud Ahmadinejad in June
2005 to be a harbinger of domestic tension and unrest. Iran has also deterred
some investors in the past because it generally prefers commercial disputes to
be considered by Iranian courts rather than through international arbitra-
tion. What is more, the Iranian oil sector is particularly susceptible to these
pressures because of the degree to which it is closely controlled by the state
and therefore highly sensitive to political tremors: since the revolution, only
the oil minister, who is chosen by the premier, is eligible to be president of
NIOC. Also much more important than its foreign investor law would be
Iran's signing of the 1994 Energy Charter Treaty (ECT), a framework agreement intended to promote investor confidence in transnational projects.
Some moves have been made towards this, and in November 2003 the ECT's
Secretary General, Dr Ria Kemper, was invited to Tehran to discuss possible
membership.

The combined influence of these different factors – an increasing global
need for oil and gas as well as Iranian efforts to lure foreign investors – have
already merged to present American global power with a new and powerful
challenge. But there are of course a great many unknown factors in this
picture, and chief among them is the influence of Iran's newly elected president, Mahmoud Ahmadinejad.

The new Iranian president

It was said above that the hard, uncompromising line adopted by Ahmadinejad initially succeeded in alienating some of the international support that
he might otherwise have found. But although he might continue to alienate
this potential support, it is also possible that his harsh approach might force
international governments to make a much more stark choice between 'Iran'
and the 'United States' in a way that plays to Tehran's distinct advantage.
Such threats could not be easily dismissed because Tehran knows that it can
easily offer its highly valued contracts to other foreign contractors, notably
Russian or Chinese businesses, that are more willing to sacrifice their ties, if
they have any at all, with the United States.

A glance at Ahmadinejad's political manifesto and personal background
does suggest an inflexible individual who may be inclined to force such a
stark choice on the outside world. For when on 24 June 2005 the 49-year-old
presidential candidate won the second round of voting in the electoral race
by promising a pure 'Islamic government', he was well qualified to make such
claims. Having served in the Revolutionary Guard during the war with Iraq,
subsequently worked as a trusted regime official in a variety of positions
and acted as a conservative mayor of Tehran after the municipal elections of
2003, Ahmadinejad is part of a paternalistic, xenophobic and economically
interventionist tradition that contrasts sharply with the easy pragmatism that
most economists think Iran needs so badly. Evidence of this inflexibility of
attitude emerged within a few weeks of taking up office in August, when
his economic spokesman announced a reduction of interest rates that was
opposed by independent economists and which respected analysts, such as
Amir Mohebian, a well-known Iranian newspaper columnist, thought would
help the already bloated state sector to grow even more.[48]

Within weeks of becoming prime minister, Ahmadinejad had also given
the outside world a clue that he would take the hardline, uncompromising stance towards international investors that may in future force them to
make a stark choice between Washington and Tehran. In a clear warning
to the EU, he told the Iranian parliament in August that 'economic ties are
not irrelevant to political ties' especially with 'hostile' countries that 'fail
to recognize Iran's legitimate rights'. Industry observers also believed that
Ahmadinejad was unhappy about some of the links forged with Western
companies under the previous government, led by the much more moderate Mohammad Khatami, and the new president confirmed this hardline
attitude by cancelling a drilling contract struck with Kish Oriental, which
is linked to the giant US firm Halliburton, after an Iranian court accepted
charges that Kish Oriental officials had bribed Iranian workers.

The net result of all these different pressures – some that are internal to Iran, others either a consequence of American perceptions of Iran or else born of a sharply increasing global demand for oil – is the creation of a new challenge to American power. On the one hand, Washington is trying to pull its allies, non-aligned countries and rivals away from Tehran, while on the other their growing energy needs are pushing these countries towards it.

Of course this statement is one that requires some careful elucidation. What kind of 'power', in any case, is it that is now in real danger of being eroded?

US 'power'

'Power', as one leading American writer on international affairs, Joseph Nye, has defined it, is 'the ability to effect the outcomes you want, and if necessary, to change the behaviour of others to make this happen'.[49] This 'ability' can, of course, manifest itself in different ways, and it is clear that Iran is not currently posing any challenge to America's 'soft power' which Nye identifies when he writes that 'a country may obtain the outcomes it wants in world politics because other countries want to follow it, admiring its values, emulating its example, aspiring to its level of prosperity and openness'.[50] Other than in the Shiite areas of Iraq, there are few places in the world where people are clamouring for the strict Islamic values that were championed by the Islamic revolution in 1979 and which have since been resurrected, symbolically at least, by Mahmoud Ahmadinejad. By contrast there are many young people inside Iran who consciously emulate the fashions and manners, and admire the perceived lifestyle and values, that are held by many ordinary Americans: 'if the Americans opened a visa office in Tehran then there would be a queue ten miles long outside,' one Iran-based European diplomat once told me, 'and that in itself would be enough to bring the regime crashing down'.

Iran instead poses a challenge to America's 'hard power', which Nye defines as a country's ability to offer rewards and make threats. This type of power was traditionally always measured by a country's capacity to make war on its enemies, a capacity that was in turn dependent on factors such as its population, territory, natural resources, economic strength, military force and political stability. In the contemporary world, however, he argues that 'economic power has become more important than in the past, both because of the relative increase in the costliness of force and because economic objectives loom large in the values of post-industrial societies'.

'Hard power'

In every respect, the United States exerts considerable 'hard power' over other nations, giving them very strong reasons to follow its lead. It has, after all, a vast economic strength that flexes its muscle over other countries in a number of ways, not least because it generates resources that enable Washington to grant huge subsidies or loans, with political strings typically attached, if it so chooses. When economies like those of Indonesia, Brazil and Malaysia have approached a point of collapse, it is the United States above all that has played a fundamental role in rescuing them, often making emergency loans conditional on the implementation of domestic programmes of privatization and deregulation. It was the promise of economic aid to Serbia's devastated economy, for example, that in 2000 persuaded the government in Belgrade to change course and hand its leader, Slobodan Milošević, over to The Hague tribunal, while the leaders of Pakistan currently have to weigh the $700 million of aid they receive from the United States with the value of their trade with Tehran. The promise of material aid may not always prove irresistible – in March 2003 Washington's promise of a $15 billion aid package in return for support for the Iraq war could not tempt the Ankara parliament to allow the deployment on Turkish soil of 62,000 US troops and 250 planes[51] – but it is for most parties a very alluring one.

Of course the economic and financial benefits offered by Washington cannot just be weighed in narrow terms of aid and subsidy. This is partly because America's foreign aid budget is no longer as voluminous as it once was. While in 1948, for example, this budget amounted to around 6 per cent of its GDP, the figure today stands at only 0.17 per cent, or less than $17 billion. Even this figure is misleading because, taking aside military assistance and the $3 billion spent each year on supporting Israel, the real figure is much closer to an annual $8 billion.[52] In any event the benefits bestowed by such foreign aid are probably insignificant compared with those offered by trade with and investment from a country whose GDP in 2004 was measured at $10 trillion, making up nearly 30 per cent of the global economy. For any political enmity with Washington means the possible imposition of economic sanctions that can disrupt the flow of capital into and out of the United States, with perhaps disastrous consequences for the particular business or country involved.

The crucial importance of American trade and investment to other countries is well measured by its role as an inducement in alleviating mistrust and tension in global hotspots. In 1994, for example, North Korea agreed to halt its defiant bid to develop nuclear weapons in return for an American promise not only to arrange the supply of huge quantities of oil but also to bring down trade and investment barriers and restore 'the full normalization of political and economic relations' between the two countries. These relations had not been restored by 2001, however, as suspicions grew that Pyongyang had resumed its nuclear programme, but in September 2005 similar promises of economic ties between North Korea and the United States helped to broker a new agreement.

Also more important than Washington's foreign aid budget is its strong influence over international financial bodies, most notably the World Bank and the International Monetary Fund. To a large degree this influence is a consequence of American economic power: the US contributes more than any other country to the IMF, which receives 17.5 per cent of its funding from Washington, while by a long-standing, informal agreement the president of the World Bank is an American national, who is nominated by the Bank's US executive director. The importance of American influence on these bodies became clear during the Suez crisis in November 1956, for example, when the Eisenhower administration effectively imposed economic sanctions on Britain by using its influence in the IMF to block London's desperate request for economic assistance. Other international bodies and organizations over which, despite all their boasts of independence from outside pressure, the US exerts a strong influence are the United Nations and OPEC. In March 1999 OPEC's decision to raise production quotas perhaps partly reflected a strong American bid to influence its decisions: on 11 April, after he had made several high-profile visits to oil ministers of key OPEC countries before their conference in Vienna, and subsequently made repeated phone calls during their quota negotiations, US Energy Secretary Bill Richardson had claimed that 'the administration's diplomatic efforts should result in an immediate production increase of 1.8 million barrels per day'.[53]

Washington also has a strong influence over the United Nations, and India's ambition to gain a permanent seat in the United Nations Security Council helps explain its recent efforts to establish new ties with the United States. Washington had reportedly already sought to persuade New Delhi to deploy Indian troops to Iraq in return for this representation on the Security Council.[54]

A country's wealth is also both a symptom and a cause of its technological advances, since it is able to fund research into developments that, when discovered, also yield a competitive edge and help to sustain its economic pre-eminence. One country that has a clear head start in developing new areas of information technology, for example, can also establish itself in a global marketplace more quickly than its competitors, whose late arrival can be extremely difficult to recoup. So a government that sacrifices its ties with Washington can also risk falling behind with the rapid pace of technological advance that the United States has often set. When, in the winter of 2004, US Congress sought to deter the EU from lifting a proposed arms embargo on China, some members proposed placing restrictions on the transfer of US technology to their European allies, as well as other 'limitations and constraints'.[55] As one Congressman put it, 'in the mad dash to secure lucrative Chinese contracts, more thoughtful Europeans might want to assess the potential damage to transatlantic defence cooperation'. Such threats helped to ensure that by March 2005 the EU had abandoned any such plans.

Technological advances also yield a clear advantage on the battlefield, and any country that falls behind technologically can catch up, if at all, only at very great cost. In the post-war period, for example, France struggled to develop its own nuclear deterrent while Britain, enjoying close ties with Washington from 1957, shared US technical information on the production of nuclear bombs and bought the Polaris missile at a special knock-down price. Today the US-led campaigns in Kosovo, Iraq and Afghanistan have illustrated the importance of keeping pace with such advances, having demonstrated the might and sophistication of American military power, with its dependency on computers, satellites and 'smart' weapons, as well as its limitations and vulnerabilities. Of particular importance in this regard is America's contemporary role as a pivot on which the traffic of global communications rests: around 75 per cent of global internet traffic is today switched through the United States and handled at some point by US carriers, a legacy of the origins of the internet, which began as the internal network of the Defense Department's Advanced Research Projects Agency (ARPA).[56] The security of many countries in this regard is to some degree dependent on the United States, despite unsuccessful efforts by the Iranian government in November 2005 to transfer control of the internet into the hands of an independent UN body.

The importance of military technology in buying political support emerged in the summer of 2005 when Washington used its nuclear know-how as a bargaining chip to win favour in New Delhi (see Chapter 3). Although a political row ensued in Washington and elsewhere, the Bush administration offered the Indian government sensitive nuclear technology and highly sophisticated nuclear-capable weapons systems that would allow New Delhi to deter any possible Chinese military attacks comparable to those that were launched on India's northern borders during the Sino-Indian war of 1962. It is from just such military as well as civilian technology that any US ally risks being alienated if it refuses to toe the Washington line. This was the price that France risked paying when in the run-up to the Iraq war in 2003 its government refused to support frantic British and American attempts to secure a second United Nations resolution against Iraq, as President Jacques

Chirac announced that France would vote no, 'whatever the circumstances, because we do not think war is necessary to achieve the goal we've established' and because waging war without UN backing would set a 'dangerous' precedent.

American military strength is of course an issue not just of sophistication but of the sheer numbers that the country can afford to maintain, and it was this capacity to sustain a protracted war effort that Eisenhower had in mind when he once remarked that 'the foundation of military strength is economic strength ... a bankrupt America is more the Soviet goal than an America conquered on the field of battle'.[57] It is because of the size of the US military that, since the time of its entry into the Second World War in 1942, no country in the world, other than the neutral, could be indifferent to American influence. Even after the demise of the Soviet Union in the early 1990s, and with it the end of a perceived threat of Soviet expansion, no government could afford either to provoke America's enmity or to overlook the military and political benefits that it might reap from an alliance with a country that in 2004 spent $437 billion, or roughly half of all military spending around the world, and which had proportionately spent even more during the Cold War.

In some respects this is less true today than before. In raw material terms, the US military has looked much more vulnerable and overstretched ever since the invasion of Iraq re-exposed its susceptibility to protracted guerrilla war and made any large-scale intervention in the world both militarily impossible and politically unacceptable to an American public that has had to bear large and mounting casualties. Moreover since 2001 any close alliance with the United States has also brought new dangers and risks by making the other party a target for Al Qaeda terrorists: the perpetrators of the Madrid train bombings of 2004 and the London tube bombings in July 2005, for example, claimed to be 'retaliating' for their governments' support of the American invasion of Iraq. Finally some countries are now able to look away from Washington and turn instead towards rival defensive and political blocs that have emerged since the end of the Cold War, the most obvious example being the member states of the European Union, which have gradually forged a common defence policy over the past decade.

So in what ways, then, is America's 'power', as defined in all these different ways, now being eroded by the Iranian challenge?

How American power is being undermined

American power is already being undermined, or could perhaps one day be challenged, by the influence of Iranian oil in a number of different ways that lie outside the scope of this book. So although earlier on in this chapter the point was made that the global dependency on oil puts out of the question any suggestion of enforcing meaningful economic sanctions on Iran, this limits not just American power over Iran but that of any other country that wants to change the behaviour of any oil-producing state. Moreover while any UN resolution against Iran would in all likelihood be vetoed by China – and perhaps too by Russia – which is increasingly dependent on Iranian oil, this is clearly a reflection not of any Iranian challenge but of the weaknesses of the voting system in the UN Security Council, whose perceived inequities the Bush administration has made efforts to reform: Beijing and Moscow had, after all, also vetoed American moves to sanction North Korea in early 2003 after the Pyongyang regime expelled international weapons inspectors and broke out of the Nuclear Non-Proliferation Treaty.

Other possible Iranian challenges to Washington's pre-eminence are too speculative to lie within this book's ambit. When in July 2005 the head of the board of directors of the Stock Exchange Council in Iran, Haidar Mosta-khdemin Hosseini, said that the council had agreed in principle to establish a new oil exchange on Kish Island that would be the first of its kind in the Middle East, eyebrows were quickly raised. Because this new body would deal only in euros, it seemed quite possible that it might eventually start to challenge the market dominance of the world's two existing financial exchanges – London's International Petroleum Exchange and New York's Mercantile Exchange – which are both owned by US companies. Some experts reckoned that if vast quantities of oil sales were ever traded in euros, then global demand for dollars would wane, creating big trouble for a heavily indebted American economy that greatly depends on such a demand. 'At this point it's really to poke their finger in the eye of the US,' an analyst at Columbia University told one American newspaper, 'and certainly part of their idea is to weaken American economic hegemony.'[58] But most analysts are agreed that such a scenario would present only a very long-term threat and presents no short or even intermediate-term challenge to American interests, even if the exchange, which was licensed in May 2006, soon opens. By contrast, Washington's international influence is already being challenged by the impact of Iranian oil in three other ways.

On the one hand, Washington's strategic rivals, notably China, are being economically fuelled by Iranian resources, which are therefore augmenting the challenge to US interests posed by these countries. What is more, within Iran the foreign exchange earnings of oil and gas exports are buttressing the Iranian regime, a chief US rival and enemy in the Middle East, thus allowing it to pursue a nuclear programme, one that is widely deemed to hide a covert weapons programme, and to buy off its political enemies.

The next chapter looks at the way in which some of America's existing allies, as well as non-aligned countries, are being increasingly tempted to break ranks with Washington and instead build economic ties with Tehran. A glimpse of what this divide may resemble in the future appeared after Total signed the contract in 1997 to develop South Pars, thereby beckoning the threat of American sanctions under ILSA. The chairman of Total told *Le Monde*, with good reason, that in signing the deal he 'had the backing of the French government', whose spokesmen also joined EU officials in condemning the American threat as 'illegal and unacceptable'. Sir Leon Brittan, the vice-president of the European Commission, said of ILSA that 'such legislation is contrary to international law. It is also counter-productive in political terms since it creates tension between Europe and the US, which makes it more difficult to work together to achieve shared political objectives in Iran. It plays into the hands of hardliners in Tehran.'[59] His condemnation was echoed by the EU's ambassador to Washington, who had written to US Congressional leaders the previous year to express his opposition to the proposed legislation, while at the same time EU officials had implied, by asking for consultation under the auspices of the WTO, that they would consider the enactment of third-party sanctions to be a violation of international trade agreements.[60] The White House doubtless had such a furious reaction in mind when in February 2004 an internal report argued that steps to enforce ILSA could 'lead to serious strains with some of our closest allies, with negative consequences across a very broad range of issues'.

Of course Iran's challenge to the United States is not in any way dependent on ILSA. Even if we just suppose that some long-term compromise over the nuclear issue was found and that this piece of legislation was not subsequently renewed by President Bush in August 2006, then there would still be a stark contrast between America's position on the one hand and those countries that do have some economic interests inside Iran. Japan and the European governments, for example, would still have the incentive to do their own thing and give Tehran more flexibility on foreign policy issues, instead of toeing the Washington line. So at the heart of this issue is not the Iran–Libya Sanctions Act but America's own economic isolation from Iran, however much this piece of legislation exemplifies and heightens this contrast.

These are the various challenges to American political supremacy that Iran's natural resources now pose. The relations between Washington and some of her various allies is considered in the next chapter.

CHAPTER TWO

Breaking US Alliances

The European ambassador who, in early November 2004, was spearheading the diplomatic effort to resolve the Iranian nuclear issue had met and dealt with some very difficult individuals in the course of his distinguished 30-year career. But although there had been some particularly tense moments when diplomatic discussions had become somewhat heated and tempers a little frayed, he had never before been shouted at by one of his opposite numbers. Yet now, as he met US diplomats in a large conference room in Vienna, his American counterpart, Kenneth Brill, suddenly became highly agitated before exploding with furious anger in front of all his amazed colleagues. 'I'd heard about this sort of thing happening in the Khrushchev days of the Cold War,' the European envoy told me a year later, 'but I'd never before seen any foreign diplomat, let alone one representing our key ally, acting like this.'

Causing such tension was the question of how to respond when, two weeks later, the IAEA board would meet to discuss the Iranian nuclear issue. The Americans were pressing for Iran's referral by the IAEA to the UN Security Council, and pressing so hard that a mild riposte by the EU envoy had now prompted this belligerent reaction. 'I'd merely asked Brill to be more specific about why this referral would be necessary. Why were some of the incidents between Iran and us a cause for this? I think that Brill was under so much pressure from Washington to get the EU on its side that he just exploded,' recalled the ambassador.

This small incident is a symptom of how the loyalties of some of America's key allies in several different parts of the world are today being torn more than ever before by the lure and temptation of Iran's natural resources. For at the same time that Washington is putting ever greater pressure on its allies to withhold unnecessary trade and investment in Iran, these governments are finding such ties both more lucrative and increasingly necessary. To date some of these governments have been able to dance to both tunes and have just about succeeded in appeasing Washington's pressure while still reaping Tehran's economic rewards, but the benefits of building and sustaining economic ties with Iran are so considerable that some of Washington's allies have already been tempted to openly break ranks with American policy and instead do deals with the Tehran regime. In the future, it also looks likely that these governments will be forced to make some harsh choices about whose wishes they will respect and the direction they wish to turn towards.

The American 'allies' with which this chapter is essentially concerned are the European Union – particularly the three member states, Britain, France and Germany, that form its diplomatic front with Tehran (the 'EU3' or E3) – and Japan and Pakistan. Their governments have at times been motivated by the economic rewards offered by Iranian natural resources to defy American pressure and deal with Tehran in a way that Washington strongly disapproves of. More speculatively, this chapter also looks briefly at how a similar divergence may in future emerge between Washington and other countries that may be loosely labelled as 'allies'. These include Iraq, South Korea and Canada, whose trading links with Iran are either already considerable or else rapidly growing.

Although this divergence has come about because Washington's allies are increasingly tempted to prioritize their own interests instead of America's, this is just one of two quite different ways in which American political influence is now being undermined. For in a situation like this, not only does Washington exert less leverage over its allies but also over other countries, most obviously Iran. This is because no government, even one that exerts the unrivalled global power that the United States has enjoyed since the demise of the Soviet Union in the early 1990s, is likely to be willing to speak in an isolated voice. On the eve of the American assault on Iraq in March 2003, at a time when US military power seemed invincible and the Bush administration made little secret of its unilateralist leanings, Washington was still extremely keen to enlist the support of other countries – notably Britain – and to get the backing of a UN resolution in a bid to portray the invasion not as an imperialist adventure, as its critics claimed, but as a necessary war of self-defence. So Washington's efforts to pressurize Iran into surrendering its nuclear programme have been impeded by its differences with EU governments, whose more conciliatory line has created a fissure that the Iranians have sought to exploit, and sometimes succeeded in exploiting very adeptly. And occasionally, transatlantic differences over Iran have also undermined Washington's influence not just over Iran but other countries too. Tension between Tokyo and Washington, for example, has at times divided the united front that both sought to build against North Korea during a protracted series of negotiations over Pyongyang's nuclear programme.

As Chapter 1 pointed out, the force that is driving this wedge between allies is most obviously Iran's capacity to supply vast quantities of oil and gas that are of indispensable value to the functioning of their economies. But Iran's burgeoning energy sector also offers foreign governments vast opportunities in a more subtle way. On the one hand, NIOC requires considerable international expertise to explore and develop its oil and gas deposits and to build, mend and update its own outdated, inadequate infrastructure. And in a more indirect way, the sale of vast quantities of its oil has in recent years earned Iran huge quantities of foreign exchange, thereby helping to generate market demand that offers lucrative opportunities for international business. So if the international trading of oil and gas represents Iran's most obvious temptation to the outside world, then these business opportunities to invest inside the country are what might be termed its 'wider' energy market.

This of course prompts an obvious question. Although these wider commercial opportunities have an obvious benefit to a businessman or shareholder, why should they interest any foreign government? Why, in particular, should a government perhaps be willing to sacrifice its alliance with the United States so that their businesses can make the most of these openings?

Iran's economic temptations

Importing Iranian oil and gas

One reason why a foreign government may sometimes have much to gain from promoting the interests of its national enterprises in this 'wider' market is that any deal of any sort in the oil and gas sector can help secure supplies of its highly valued natural resources, or at least their importation on more favourable terms than a competitor may be able to do. This was of course one reason why the British government had such a strong interest in the Anglo-Persian Oil Company after its foundation in 1909: by buying out 51 per cent of the company almost as soon as it was formed, the British government was able to secure the supplies of oil it needed not just for its economy as a whole but for the Royal Navy in particular, which bought the APOC's oil at a specially discounted price.

These days things are done slightly differently. If an oil or gas company is state-owned, then a government can link the terms of one contract with another wholly separate deal to secure oil or gas supplies. So when in October 2004 the Chinese oil giant Sinopec signed a $70 billion deal with the National Iranian Gas Exporting Company (NIGEC) to develop Iran's massive Yadavaran oil field, the head of China's National Reform and Development Commission in Beijing was able to link this contract with a promise by the Tehran authorities to export not only 150,000 barrels of oil every day at market prices after the field had been developed but also another 10 million tons of liquefied natural gas each year. Beijing's desperation to secure long-term sources of supply had already become clear six months earlier, when the state-owned Chinese oil trader Zhuhai Zhenrong announced that it had struck a separate deal to import more than 110 million tons of gas over the next 25 years

But if a company is privately owned, then its contract to develop or explore an oil or gas field can still allow a government to obtain energy supplies in a more indirect way. This is because a standard buyback contract to develop an oil or gas field will allow the contractor to take possession of an agreed quantity of Iranian oil or gas that allows them to recoup the expenses they have incurred on the project. Although the contractors or their agents are then free to sell this wherever they like, it is usually the contractor's domestic market back home that is particularly likely to benefit. The reason for this is simply that the contractor's refineries, and the network that takes the refined oil to the high-street petrol pumps, are likely to be based in its country of origin. So when in February 2004 Tehran granted a Japanese consortium the exclusive negotiating rights to develop the massive South Azadegan field, the government in Tokyo was also able to secure much of the oil that the field would eventually produce. For under the terms of the buyback contract, the consortium partners could recoup their expenditure in the course of six years following the completion of the project by taking delivery of its supplies, which the partners were then able to sell straight into the Japanese market and thereby reimburse their creditors in Tokyo who had funded the project from the outset. Since Japan is already a big importer of Iranian oil, the Azadegan project was always viewed by Tokyo as a way of securing future supplies. Japanese efforts to link exploration and development contracts inside Iran with the subsequent supply of its oil had already come to fruition three years earlier, when in November 2000 a preliminary deal between the two countries over the Azadegan field had given the Japanese exclusive negotiating rights for a specific area of the field as well as securing an Iranian promise to export $1 billion worth of Iranian crude oil over the next three years.

Tax and employment

There are other reasons why a government should want to promote the interests of its own national enterprises. The sheer size of Iran's massive oil and gas deposits, which the Economist Intelligence Unit estimates has attracted between $15-20 billion in combined foreign investment over the past decade, clearly promises international companies and businesses large profits if they win contracts to develop them. From these profits their respective governments can reap a perhaps huge taxable harvest, while on these contracts a very significant number of jobs may perhaps also depend.

Although the financial reports of European oil giants generally do not break down their overall turnover by giving details of the particular regions they are involved in, even a quick glance shows why their respective governments take such an interest in acquiring new markets. So one company that has previously had a large stake in Iran, for example, is the Royal Dutch Shell consortium, whose taxable profits in the first quarter of 2006 were $12.3 billion, from which tax collectors reaped a colossal $5.3 billion.

This is also true of the wider Iranian domestic consumer market. In recent years, sharp increases in the price of oil have caused an influx of foreign exchange from which a small but sizeable minority have particularly benefited. This has created a curious paradox: while on the one hand Iran is undoubtedly economically stricken and afflicted by a rapid rate of inflation and large-scale unemployment and underemployment, a new middle class has nonetheless also emerged in recent years, whose presence and whose taste for Western-style consumer goods is unmistakably visible in the fashionable and fast-growing districts of north Tehran. Without American competition, overseas businessmen and their governments know that Iran offers vast opportunities and huge profits that are ready for the taking. This includes the British government, which derives considerable income from the growing volume of bilateral trade transactions between the UK and Iran, and knows that a good many jobs are dependent on this commerce. In 2004 Britain's direct trade with Iran stood at around £450 million, with another £700 million or so of indirect trade also going through Dubai, the main areas of cooperation being transportation, housing, pharmaceuticals, mining and the provision of banking and insurance services. The following year the director of the Middle East Association in London, Michael Thomas, still described trade between the two countries as 'excellent', with Dubai-based commerce estimated to be closer to the £1 billion mark, even though the election as president of Mahmoud Ahmadinejad, who took such a hard line on the ongoing nuclear dispute, threatened to disrupt these fast-growing relations.[1]

Political donations

Occasionally there can also be other, less obvious, reasons why foreign governments are willing to lobby hard on behalf of their national companies in the battle to win a share in Iran's 'wider' energy market. Sometimes a government can hope to win substantial donations from companies whose business interests they have advanced, and just such a relationship has at times been alleged to exist, for example, between Britain's Labour Party and

British Petroleum, which has in recent years made several bids to acquire a big stake in Iran's energy sector. 'The connections [between them] are probably more extensive than with any other UK company,' says Norman Baker, a Liberal Democrat MP who has closely investigated the ties between BP and the Blair government.[2] In January 2005 BP chairman Lord Browne declared that 'right now it is impractical for BP because 40 per cent of BP is in the US and we are the largest producer of oil and gas in the US ... politically Iran is not a flyer'. But until then the company had actively pitched the Iranian oil and gas markets. In 2001 it formed a joint venture with India's Reliance and NIOC to form Iran LNG, one of four companies licensed to export Iranian natural gas, which has made bids for many major contracts. In January 2003 the official Iranian news agency, IRNA, announced that BP was one of six companies, along with Total, Statoil, Norsk Hydro, Petronas and Russia's Tatneft, that was involved in discussions about enhanced recovery programmes for Iranian oil and gas fields, while in May 2004 it was also one of several European companies, alongside Total, Petronas, ENI and Statoil, that made a bid (as part of Iran LNG) for a $1.2 billion project to develop Phase 11 of South Pars. The British energy giant had also showed particular interest, along with three other rival firms, in a contract to undertake gas injection in Iran's much-prized Ahwaz-Bangestan field, a deal that was eventually awarded in December 2004 to Petropars, a domestic firm.

So these are the economic incentives that might drive a government, not just its national businesses, into the arms of the Tehran regime. And though there are a number of other influences that also help create EU foreign policy towards Iran, the interest of European governments in Iran's hydrocarbons have played an important part in driving a transatlantic wedge and undermining American political power and influence.

The US and the EU: Iran, oil and the nuclear issue

European governments have a strong economic interest in Iranian oil and gas that has accentuated sharp differences with the United States over the difficult issue of formulating an international response to Iran's nuclear programme. Not only has this loosened Washington's political grip over European governments but it has also undermined American leverage over Tehran by allowing the Iranians opportunities to deflect international pressure and instead pursue their enrichment programme, opportunities that would have been missing if Washington and the European capitals had always spoken with one voice.

The size and seriousness of this transatlantic divide has of course ebbed and flowed. From the summer of 2005, for example, there seemed at first sight to be few obvious signs of any serious disunity when European and other governments echoed Washington's call to refer Iran to the United Nations and then impose diplomatic sanctions against a government that appeared determined to press ahead with uranium enrichment and thereby dash hopes for a diplomatic compromise.[3] Yet disagreements had often lurked below this superficial appearance of unity, and over the preceding two years the US administration had frequently strongly disapproved of the efforts made by EU ministers to strike a conciliatory deal with Tehran over the nuclear issue. These disagreements have also scarcely gone unnoticed by the Iranians, who have been quick and ingenious in their bid to exploit them.

In what ways, then, has EU policy diverged from Washington's preferred approach, and to what degree have the European governments openly defied American pressure to adopt a different course? How far, in any case, has EU policy been determined by the lure of Iranian natural resources, and in what ways has the transatlantic divide played into Iranian hands?

The transatlantic divide

One cold morning in March 2003 weapons inspectors of the IAEA were in the course of examining a large factory site on the southern outskirts of the capital when voices were suddenly raised. For despite the inspectors' insistence that they take a look inside, the Iranian officials who escorted them refused permission to enter one of the workshop buildings, changing their story until eventually claiming that the building was used for storage and that no keys to the building were available.

The place in question was the Kalaye Electric factory, and this was the first of two particular incidents that now caused serious alarm among the watching world. The other incident took place a few weeks later when the IAEA had requested permission to take environmental samples at the same workshop, where the Iranians had admitted to constructing components for centrifuges designed for enriching uranium but where a dissident source had claimed that something illicit was going on. Although officials in Tehran had initially indicated that they would allow the IAEA team to take samples at Kalaye during their 7-11 June inspections, they then refused to allow the team to take them, prompting the inspectors to pack up their bags and leave Iran soon afterwards, on 21 June.

By denying UN inspectors permission to take samples from the Kalaye Electric Company, the Iranians were not technically violating any of their obligations under the Safeguards Agreement, but such an obstinate denial hardly allayed the outside world's suspicions either of Tehran's nuclear ambitions or of its willingness to deal with the IAEA. And when in August inspectors were finally permitted to enter the factory and take dust samples, they found that the plant had been substantially rebuilt in order to hamper their detective work and to 'sanitize' the factory.

It was at this point, a year after the size and sophistication of its nuclear programme had been unmistakably exposed by a dissident organization,[4] that the Tehran regime's continuing defiance of the outside world brought underlying transatlantic divisions unmistakably to the surface, a division based on two different approaches towards the Iranian nuclear issue that were sharply contrasting. On the one hand the British, French and German governments that led the European Union's diplomacy advocated a policy of negotiation with Tehran and urged the regime to sign the Safeguards Agreement's Additional Protocol that would give more powers to the IAEA inspectors and thereby reassure the outside world that the nuclear programme really was, as Tehran had always claimed, purely for peaceful purposes: as a signatory of this protocol the Iranians would have been obliged, for example, to let the weapons inspectors into the Kalaye factory without the prior warning that the Safeguards Agreement obliged the IAEA to give. This EU approach was part of a wider engagement with Tehran that some of the European governments had pursued, off and on, ever since the 1979 revolution: 'the UK and EU have a policy of constructive engagement with Iran, but a policy that is open-eyed,' the British Foreign Secretary, Jack Straw, claimed in 2003, 'and we are all very concerned to see progress and particularly for Iran to better cooperate with the IAEA.'[5]

While the sharply contrasting approaches adopted by American and European governments have often been labelled as a deliberate policy of 'good cop, bad cop' that is designed to maximize pressure on the Tehran regime, such a label disguises not just its accidental quality but, more specifically, also the strength of the political disagreements between the different capitals. But although the strength of such disagreements has long been regarded on both sides of the Atlantic as a serious obstacle to progress on the Iranian issue, efforts to heal them have not proved either fruitful or lasting. Former British Foreign Secretary Robin Cook had tried long before the Iranian nuclear issue erupted in earnest to find a common US–EU approach towards Iran – declaring his ambition to do so during Britain's presidency of the European Union in 1998, for example – but singularly failed to succeed.

The contrast between this conciliatory approach and the much more hawkish line taken by successive Washington administrations emerged unmistakably in the months that followed the dispute over the Kalaye Electric factory. Up until this time, the Americans had not only been too preoccupied with the invasion of Iraq to launch any diplomatic offensive but also knew that there was just not enough evidence to stand any chance of indicting Tehran of violating its nuclear obligations. The Kalaye incident was just one fitting what Washington called 'a pattern of Iranian behaviour' that was inconsistent with those obligations, but worse was to follow for Tehran when in September the IAEA revealed that their inspectors had discovered traces of weapons-grade uranium both at the Natanz complex and at Kalaye. Although Iran immediately counter-claimed that this uranium had been brought into the country on imported equipment that had already been contaminated in its country of origin – a counter-claim that was later judged by the IAEA to be the likely truth – they were immediately pushed on to the back foot. 'We felt sure that the Iranians genuinely didn't know about the uranium contamination,' a very senior EU negotiator in Vienna later told me, 'and thought that its discovery made things look very black for them.'

It was at this point, in September 2003, that the United States did not merely push the case for more EU–Iran negotiations but instead made explicit threats of punitive diplomatic sanctions and dropped hints that it was prepared to consider undertaking military action. Initially Washington urged the IAEA's board to make the formal, condemnatory resolution that has to be passed before there is any realistic hope of obtaining a declaration that any country has failed to comply with the NPT, a step that could then perhaps lead to its referral before the UN Security Council. Washington needed the support from the 35-nation IAEA board to get such a resolution, and although by 21 October this had not been forthcoming, administration officials waited patiently, and vainly,[6] for the emergence of another 'killer fact', even more damning than the discovery of enriched uranium, that would firmly seal Iran's fate.

But the European powers did not share Washington's hawkish approach, and the transatlantic contrast now became particularly evident.

The October 2003 deal

The European approach appeared to bear fruit in October 2003 when the British, French and German foreign ministers visited Tehran and persuaded regime officials to bow to international pressure, knowing that unless the Iranians did so then a major international crisis was certain to erupt. Unnerved by the discovery of heavily enriched uranium at Kalaye and Natanz, Tehran suddenly complied, and on Tuesday 21 October issued a declaration that firmly renounced any ambitions to build a nuclear bomb and accepted the Additional Protocol. The Iranians also agreed 'to cooperate with the agency in accordance with the protocol in advance of its ratification', and promised to 'engage in full cooperation with IAEA', offering the inspectors 'full transparency' when doing so.

But after the signing of the October deal, US administration officials continued to strike an overwhelmingly sceptical note, emphasizing that Iran had only agreed to a temporary suspension of uranium enrichment and that it had a long track record, stretching back nearly two decades, of serious duplicity over the nuclear issue.[7] For John R. Bolton, then the hawkish Under-Secretary of State for Arms Control, Tehran's pledge to halt its enrichment activities was plainly bogus: 'there's no doubt in our mind that Tehran continues to pursue a nuclear weapons programme,' he announced four months later, since the Iranians 'have not yet, in our judgement, complied even with the commitment they made in October to suspend their enrichment activities.'[8] American intelligence chiefs also remained convinced that Tehran was shielding a lot from the inspectors' eyes, making UN referral inevitable sooner or later: 'there is no doubt in our mind that the Iranians have a lot that the IAEA does not know about,' one official told a British newspaper, 'and have a military programme that the IAEA has never set eyes on.'[9] This seemed particularly likely because the Iranians had taken possession of drawings of the highly sophisticated P2 centrifuge in 1995 but had not 'officially' done anything with them. Diplomats were puzzled, and felt that this made no sense unless the designs had been worked on under a secret nuclear programme.

A very senior European diplomat later recalled the strength of transatlantic disagreement over the Iranian nuclear issue. 'The Americans felt very uncomfortable about the October deal and had really set their hearts onto Iran's UN referral as soon as news of the HEU contamination at Natanz and Kalaye broke. They saw this agreement as scuppering their plans.' The diplomat had felt sure that John Bolton was 'particularly determined to take things before the Security Council' and was now a very powerful influence in pressuring the E3 to take its side.

The November 2004 deal

As the October deal unravelled during the spring and summer of 2004, the international controversy over Iran's nuclear programme once again flared up. But in November, after months of defiance, Iranian representatives struck another note of compromise with EU diplomats and now signed a new agreement, this time brokered in Paris, that seemed to alleviate Washington's concern and render unnecessary American demands to refer Iran to the UN Security Council in retaliation for its alleged breaches of both the 2003 deal and its wider obligations under the 1968 Treaty. But Washington still pulled in a very different direction from the European governments, and transatlantic disagreements immediately came to the fore.

Under the Paris Accords, Iran agreed to bring an immediate halt to 'all enrichment-related and reprocessing (of uranium) activities'. This suspension was now defined much more precisely than the earlier EU–Iran agreement, and was now intended only 'as a voluntary confidence building measure ... while negotiations on a long-term agreement are underway'. These further EU–Iran negotiations, which began the following month, did not deny Iran the right to pursue its own nuclear programme *per se* but instead sought to provide 'objective guarantees' that such a programme 'is exclusively for peaceful purposes', not a military programme, and sought to promise Tehran a package of economic rewards in return for cooperation. Typical of such an arrangement, for example, would have been an Iranian renouncement of its own enrichment programme in return for guaranteed imports of enriched uranium fuel that would be carefully monitored by international inspectors to prevent their diversion away from the main energy reactor at Bushehr.

All of these negotiations had been watched in Washington with just as much hostility as the deal struck the previous October: 'the Americans made a lot of difficulties over our draft resolution,' recalled the same European envoy who had been confronted by such an angry Kenneth Brill a few days before the deal was struck. Just days after it was signed and sealed, this sharp divide between the more moderate EU3 position and the much less conciliatory American stance became public knowledge, and looked serious enough to cast a dark shadow over the long-term prospects for a lasting deal. At a press conference on 17 November, for example, the outgoing Secretary of State Colin Powell claimed that the Iranians 'had been actively working on delivery systems' of ballistic missiles to carry a nuclear warhead, a programme that would seem inconsistent with any renunciation of its nuclear ambitions. Powell's remarks were important because they manifested a strong American scepticism towards Iranian intentions. Announced just three days after the deal had been struck, and only a week before an important IAEA resolution on Iran, his comments could not fail to bring into disrepute a new deal that was based on mutual good faith. But the nature of the 'intelligence' cited by Powell also seemed to vindicate fears that Washington was determined to find fault with almost any deal the EU might strike. His comments appear to have been based on information from a single, unverified source whose claims chimed conveniently with the views of hawkish administration officials strongly antipathetic to and mistrustful of the Iran regime, raising concerns that US intelligence on Iran could be 'skewered' for political ends in the same way as information on Saddam Hussein's weapons of mass destruction was similarly distorted.

This initial reaction in Washington reflected much wider transatlantic differences towards the Iranian nuclear issue that quickly became apparent in other ways. Before the first round of EU–Iran negotiations even began, the US administration continued to assert its familiar uncompromising approach by demanding a full Iranian renunciation of the right in principle to pursue an independent civilian nuclear energy programme, even denying Tehran the same light-water reactors that it had previously allowed another pariah regime, North Korea, to operate. The US also lobbied hard for the IAEA resolution of 26 November to include a 'trigger clause' that would immediately penalize any breach of the deal by hauling Tehran straight before the UN Security Council.

By contrast the Europeans continued to follow their more flexible line toward Iran, using dialogue and offering concession in exchange for 'objective guarantees' that a peaceful nuclear programme was not to be used for military ends. 'We try to engage them as far as we can,' Joschka Fischer has said, 'and if the Americans joined us, that would make it much more powerful.' But in practice the Europeans have at times entertained suggestions that Iran retain something of its own independent nuclear fuel cycle to enrich uranium, a suggestion that has in principle always been unacceptable to the Americans. The Europeans have also long entertained proposals that Iran retain its own light-water reactor, for example, from which weapons-grade plutonium could not conceivably be derived.

It was not until the following February that the different European and American approaches showed signs of converging. This was partly because Washington adopted a more moderate line after a re-elected President Bush and his new Secretary of State, Condoleezza Rice, had made reconciliatory tours of Europe aimed at restoring the relations that had been badly strained by the Iraq war. In the weeks that followed, Washington formulated a change of approach and on 11 March administration spokesmen announced a shift of policy, offering to support the November deal by promising not to block Iran's entry into the World Trade Organization and to sell some spare parts for Iran's ageing civilian aircraft. In practice these were largely meaningless gestures, since the Iranians had in any case already been able to obtain the spare parts, albeit at a high price, and since membership of the WTO would have required some radical alterations to its economic infrastructure that the regime would have been most unlikely to agree to. Yet they were nonetheless a sign of relative moderation and multilateralism on the part of the Bush administration.

Washington's *quid pro quo* for assisting European diplomacy was to secure a promise that if its efforts did eventually prove fruitless the EU3 would unreservedly back an American bid to refer Iran to the United Nations Security Council. Nine months after the Paris Accords were struck, it appeared increasingly likely that such a clause might have to be invoked, as European diplomacy appeared to be at the end of the road and the EU governments looked set to fall into line with Washington. For in early August the mullahs dismissed the EU's proposed package of economic and political incentives as inadequate and, less than 48 hours later, announced their decision to resume a part of the enrichment process.

The crisis from summer 2005

In one sense, Iranian intransigence healed the transatlantic rift that had kept European capitals apart from Washington over the nuclear issue in the course of the preceding two years. Tehran's rejection of the trade package, its threats to resume enrichment and a very belligerent speech before the United Nations by President Ahmadinejad in September prompted European capitals to make forceful criticism and threats of UN referral with a vehemence that took Washington hawks by surprise. But even at this point, the degree of EU–US unity should not be exaggerated.

This is partly because reports emerged of deep splits within the European Union over how to deal with Tehran. At a conference of EU foreign ministers that was held in Wales in early August, a few weeks before a crucial new meeting of the IAEA board, signs of dissension had emerged. 'I'd never before seen the Spaniards or Italians look ill at ease with the E3's approach to Iran,' one envoy who was present told me, 'but at this meeting there was suddenly a lot of unrest about what would happen, and for the first time their representatives made a request to be involved in the diplomatic process with the Iranians and actually help draft an IAEA resolution against them. All of a sudden we had to spend a lot of time discussing the issue to reassure them.' Some EU governments were reported to be wary of possible retaliatory measures by Tehran and looked ready to oppose an immediate referral to the UN Council: 'countries like Italy and Austria are afraid for their exports,' one European diplomat told CNN during the flurry of diplomatic activity in early September, when the Vienna government was also said to have suddenly taken a critical line towards the E3's posturing.

Faced with these disagreements, EU diplomats adopted a note of compromise and said that they might not insist that the IAEA board vote on the resolution that would be introduced at the 19 September meeting, despite US insistence that they go for a quick vote.[10] Ahead of the board meeting, French, German and British officials also met with colleagues from other EU countries who reportedly insisted that only the bloc as a whole should agree any resolution and strategy.

There is other evidence that by the autumn of 2005 there was a sharp EU–US divide underneath a superficial show of unity. Above all, European diplomats were more willing than their American counterparts to lobby not for the immediate imposition of UN sanctions against Iran but only for a

Security Council resolution demanding an immediate freeze of Iran's entire uranium enrichment programme. It was to this end that on 20 September the Europeans circulated a draft resolution referring the case to the Security Council and asking the IAEA 'to report to all members of the Agency and to the Security Council and General Assembly of the United Nations ... Iran's many failures and breaches of its obligations to comply with its NPT Safeguards Agreement'. The resolution, entitled *Iran: Elements for an IAEA Board Resolution*, cited 'the history of concealment of Iran's nuclear activities' as one of the reasons why the Security Council now needed to take up the matter.

As the lobbying effort to win the support of China, Russia and non-aligned countries such as India[11] gathered pace, the Europeans then changed tack again and advocated an even more moderate line that did not demand Iran's referral to the UN or even make any explicit threat of doing so but merely raised the possibility of making such a referral at some point in the future. On 24 September the IAEA board of governors adopted a resolution, approved by a 22–1 vote with 12 abstentions, that accused Iran of breaching the Safeguards Agreement by undertaking activities that 'have given rise to questions that are *within the competence* of the Security Council, as the organ bearing the main responsibility for the maintenance of international peace and security' (italics supplied).

Iran's referral to the UN Security Council 2006

As the Iranians restarted their uranium enrichment programme in earnest, in January 2006, after a two-year suspension, the E3 struck a strong note of harmony with the US, calling for an emergency IAEA session that could refer Tehran to the UN for possible punitive sanctions. But even then cracks were appearing underneath the superficial unity. In January Germany's Deputy Foreign Minister, Gernot Erler, appeared to break ranks when he predicted that UN sanctions could rebound on the West. 'We have a global situation in the energy sector where we are seeing desperate measures by Asian countries, mainly from China, India and others, to get hold of energy resources,' he told Inforadio Berlin. 'For them, Iran is a partner they can't do without.' Adding that 'we are still very far away from any concrete sanctions', Mr Erler went on to say that imposing trade restrictions was a 'dangerous path' that 'could hurt one's own side more than the other side'.[12]

During the diplomatic wrangling that ensued in the United Nations over the months that followed, transatlantic disagreements broke out not only over the issue of military action – British Foreign Secretary Jack Straw's insistence that such a possibility was 'not on the table' was rumoured to have cost him his job in the ministerial reshuffle of May 2006 – but also about how to reward and penalize a recalcitrant Iran. For in May splits emerged over European proposals to bargain with Tehran by offering a generous package of incentives in return for the cessation of uranium enrichment. According to European diplomats, Washington's serious reservations about these proposals were the cause of the first serious split in the transatlantic alliance since Iran's referral to the UN, as the Bush administration was deeply unhappy about offering Iran any reactors and was loath to ask Congress to exempt EU firms from US penalties for nuclear deals with Iran. The draft proposals also offered Iran a kind of security guarantee, saying that the EU would work towards the 'recognition of territorial integrity' of Middle Eastern countries, but US hardliners were not happy with the idea of any security pledges for Iran as long it continued to threaten Israel and supported regional 'terrorism'. On 20 May Secretary of State Rice rejected the proposal for 'security guarantees'.[13] American officials had already said that it was no secret that Vice-President Dick Cheney and Defense Secretary Donald Rumsfeld were in any case deeply distrustful of the European effort, and much preferred to support efforts to topple the Iranian regime from within, rather than through military action.

Since 2003, then, there have been important and sometimes large transatlantic differences over the Iranian nuclear programme. But what has stopped the Europeans from firmly taking sides with their American counterparts and taking a hard line against Tehran? How far has such divergence from the Washington line been a product of European interest in Iranian hydrocarbons?

Hydrocarbons and the formation of EU policy

European leaders officially deny that their policy towards Iran over its nuclear programme is in any way determined by their interest in Iranian resources and argue instead that dialogue offers the only real chance of resolving the issue: to admit to any material interest would of course render them vulnerable to highly damaging charges of prioritizing profit over national security. Yet a glance at the strength of European economic interest in Iran at the time when the EU negotiations with Tehran were incurring strong American displeasure suggests that such motives were likely to have been powerful ones.

So the efforts of EU3 diplomats to seek a nuclear compromise with Tehran in October 2003 coincided with the quest of the French and British oil giants Total and BP to win a very large contract to upgrade a huge and highly prized Iranian oil deposit at Bangestan, which is comprised of the Ahwaz and Mansouri fields off the coast of Khuzestan. At the same time, Total was leading an international consortium to develop parts of the massive

South Pars gas field, at a cost of around $2 billion,[14] and had subsequently formed 'Pars LNG', a joint gas development venture along with Petronas and the National Iranian Oil Company, that operated as one of four Iranian gas companies.

In the preceding weeks Iranian leaders had also dangled another carrot in front of European businesses when, at the end of August, several European and Asian countries were formally invited by the Ministry of Petroleum to hear a presentation about another great Iranian energy prize, the Azadegan oil and gas complex, and to attend an international conference on the site's development that was due to be held in Tehran on 16 September. Although a Japanese consortium had been earmarked to develop this field, the Iranian authorities were now busily wooing other companies from across the globe at a particularly convenient time.

There were numerous other deals, or potential deals, that were relatively low-key but towards which European governments, for reasons stated at the beginning of this chapter, could not afford to be indifferent. In late 2001, for example, Shell had bought part of the $800 million Soroush–Nowruz development, which was expected to produce about 190,000 barrels per day by 2006, while until 2004 the Spanish firm Cepsa was still developing the Cheshmeh Khosh field. In October 2002 Norway's Statoil had also signed a $300 million deal with Iran's Petropars to take on the operation and to participate in the offshore development of Phases 6, 7 and 8 of South Pars, having already submitted to NIOC a detailed recovery plan to increase the rate of national oil extraction. Two months later, in December 2002, Italian-owned Edison International had acquired a 40 per cent stake, worth $40 million, in the licence to explore the Munir block, while another Italian company, Eni, had in July 2001 already signed a $1 billion contract to develop the Darquain onshore oil field development. In September 2002 a $25 million contract had also been awarded to a local subsidiary of Aberdeen's Abbot Group for a five-well exploration programme on the Anaran exploration block that was heralded by Alistair Locke, Abbott's executive chairman, as 'a significant contract which increases substantially our group portfolio of work in Iran'. The same subsidiary, KCA, was also involved in developmental drilling work in the Doroud field on behalf of Total and in offshore drilling for the Petro-Iran Development Company.

Some Western companies had also signed important deals to develop Iran's fast expanding petrochemicals sector. In 2001 Iran had awarded a contract to a consortium of Italy's Sondel and Germany DSD to develop a plant at Par-e Sar on the Caspian coast, while in August the following year NPC and the Spanish-owned Intecsa-Uhde construction group signed a €140 million contract to supply a petrochemical plant at Assaluyeh. Other important petrochemical contracts were awarded to the Paris-based Technip-Coflexip, which in September 2002 signed a €330 million deal to build part of the Olefins 10 complex, to Germany's Hansa Chemie and to France's Sofregaz for the conversion of a natural water reservoir into a gas storage facility to serve the Tehran area.

With such strong business interests inside the country, European governments had good reason to fear possible retaliation against any move they made to haul a defiant Iran before the UN Security Council. These concerns appeared well grounded when in late September 2005, just after the IAEA board had passed a resolution that was highly critical of Iran, chief negotiator Ali Larijani struck a strongly vindictive note when speaking about the countries that had voted against his country. 'Some countries with economic interests especially in oil do not show any feelings of responsibility,' argued Larijani in words and tone that would have chilled even the most resilient shareholder, 'and the Supreme National Security Council is determined to create a balance and provide the ground for their participation [in energy projects] accordingly.'

The fears of European business leaders were hardly allayed by a previous pattern of Iranian behaviour, for when tension over the nuclear debate had suddenly increased the previous year the Tehran regime had sometimes showed a vindictiveness that was as unhesitating as it was ruthless. On 12 March 2004, just after the IAEA governing board had issued a resolution that was critical of Iran's nuclear record, the mullahs imposed a month-long delay of official inspections of their installations that agency personnel had been due to make a few days later. Although the Iranians claimed the delay was 'due to the practical reasons such as unavailability of personnel', it was widely thought to be a way of showing vindictive displeasure at the agency's criticisms. Three months later, as the international furore over Tehran's right to enrich uranium heated up, eight British soldiers and their patrol boats were seized by Iranian soldiers at gunpoint and held captive during a week-long ordeal that allowed the mullahs to send a clear message to a watching world: if America and its allies make life difficult for Iran over the nuclear issue, then Iran would do the same to them in Iraq. And the following year, as tension over the nuclear issue mounted further, the Iranians hit back against British allegations that Tehran had been supplying Iraqi insurgents around Basra with highly sophisticated remote-control bombs. Days later, regime spokesmen made absurd allegations that the British had been supplying their own terrorists with explosives that had been used to kill six civilians in Ahwaz on 15 October, and announced they had foiled a 'plot' by 'British spies' to blow up the oil refinery in Abadan, 'using five Katyusha rockets with a timer on them'.

Larijani's remarks in the autumn of 2005 immediately wrote a large question mark over many existing and future contracts, particularly the multi-billion dollar deals that Royal Dutch Shell, Repsol and Total had signed to develop South Pars but which were still awaiting final approval before they could proceed. Even before the nuclear talks with the EU had broken down during the summer, some of Iran's parliamentarians had sharply criticized the earlier policy, practised by Khatami's administration, of selling gas to any foreign markets, and arguing that it should instead be injected into domestic oil wells to increase recovery. Now, after the IAEA vote, these voices grew louder still. This meant that although Akbar Torkan, the managing director of the state-owned Pars Oil and Gas Company which oversees the South Pars operations, had said a short time before that the contracts could be signed once engineering work and financial discussions were completed, other officials suddenly seemed much more pessimistic that the deals would ever be given the go-ahead if the nuclear stand-off continued.

The worst fears of European governments and businesses also appeared to be vindicated when on 26 September the Majlis National Security and Foreign Policy Commission called on the government to present a report on the volume of Iran's trade exchanges with Britain, France and Germany: 'if such a report is presented to Majlis, an appropriate decision will be made on the continuation of economic cooperation with the three European states based on the stance of the EU3 and other countries which voted in favour of the resolution,' the head of the parliamentary commission, Alaeddin Boroujerdi, told reporters. Such a gesture was a typically well-timed bid to manipulate the fears of Iran's critics over the nuclear issue.

In the same way, European governments had also had a great deal to lose in the autumn of 2004, at the time the Paris Accords were signed. The striking of the new EU–Iran nuclear deal in November followed just weeks after Shell and Repsol had formed a consortium, Persian LNG, that then bid to develop an area of South Pars and which had then signed a framework agreement to begin work on this $4 billion programme. Shell was also very interested in winning the contract to develop the next phase of the South Pars field, while other contracts were also looming on the commercial horizon: the Japanese consortium contracted in February to develop part of the giant Azadegan field, for example, had subsequently announced that it expected to seek a European partner to replace a company that had been signed up before being forced to drop out of the deal.[15]

Numerous other highly lucrative contracts had already been struck with European companies that year. In October Repsol had signed a contract with NIOC to explore the offshore Iran Mehir and Ferrouz tracts, a deal that would also enable it to negotiate exclusively with NIOC to develop any reserves that were found. During the summer, newly offered development projects in the Kushk and Hosseinieh oil fields (renamed Yadavaran) had generated serious interest among many international oil companies, including Shell, Total, Petronas, Repsol, Sinopec and ONGC, especially when it emerged that Petronas and other non-European companies had been asked by the Iranians to involve a Western partner in their existing contracts. And in September, as the nuclear debate hotted up, six international oil companies made their bids for an engineering procurement and construction contract to develop Phases 15 and 16 of South Pars: South Korea's Hyundai; LG, the British subsidiary of US firm Foster-Wheeler; France's Technip; Norway's Aker Kvaerner and the Zurich-based ABB had all teamed up with Iranian partners in order to place their bids.

Since the nuclear accord of 21 October 2003, European businesses had also been busy signing other important deals to develop the petrochemical sector. In July 2004 Danish company Haldor Topsoe had signed a contract with a subsidiary of NPC to develop a petrochemical plant that manufactured dimethyl ether, while at the same time Germany's Lurgi set up another similar project at Assaluyeh. In Vienna on 16 September, Repsol and Shell also signed a preliminary agreement with NIOC for a proposed liquefaction and export plant in Iran, while the British firm Simon-Carves negotiated a £182 million contract to build a polyethylene plant that was eventually signed in January 2005.

Iran's burgeoning petrochemical sector is also creating highly profitable opportunities for the banking sector that European businesses are increasingly keen to take. A few European-based banks have already begun funding companies involved in the wider Iranian oil and gas sectors, anxious to establish themselves in such a large and lucrative market. Their confidence has also been given a boost by some initial moves that the Iranian authorities have made towards the privatization of the oil and gas industries, and by the issuing in July 2002 of sovereign Eurobonds, which was the first such bond sale in the country since the revolution but one that nonetheless proved highly successful. In October 2000 business ties with Britain were also made more secure by the resumption of medium-term cover for the Iranian market by the UK Export Credits Guarantee Department (ECGD), which helps to provide insurance and cover on the equity or loan investment that British companies make in overseas concerns.

One of the Western banks with a particularly strong presence in Iran is the London-based HSBC group, which began its operations in earnest in 1999. In February 2002 representatives of the HSBC Project and Export Finance Department signed a $34 million export credit to Iran's Bank Tejarat, guaranteed by the ECGD, to help finance the construction of a

petrochemical plant at Bandar Iman, and the following month made a deal
to co-finance a $155 million export credit facility with the Japanese Bank for
International Cooperation and Iran's Bank Mellat to finance other operations in the petrochemical sector. Soon afterwards the bank made available
a $33.6 million export credit loan facility, also guaranteed by the ECGD, to
finance a carbon monoxide plant that was being built by Italy's Snamprogetti
on behalf of the NPC. But while the bank has subsequently funded several
other similar schemes, by far its most important project has been to help
provide a subsidiary of Iran's National Gas Export Company (NIGEC) with
financing of around $2 billion to form a joint venture that could supply Asia
and European markets. The two other LNG joint-venture projects in the
country – Pars LNG and Persian LNG – are currently in the early stages of
financing and are widely said to offer Western banks lucrative opportunities:
at the time of writing, Persian LNG has appointed Société Generale as its
financial adviser, while Pars LNG is at the same time preparing to appoint
its own.

Thus transatlantic disagreements over the difficult question of how to
deal with the Iranian nuclear challenge had not appeared suddenly from the
summer of 2002 but instead merely aggravated sharp differences between
Washington and European capitals that were long standing. These differences can to an important degree be explained by the strength of European
business interests in a country whose oil and gas resources offered highly
lucrative opportunities.

Oil, trade and the formation of critical dialogue

There has been tension between the USA and the European Union over
Iran ever since the early 1990s when, for the first time since the Islamic
revolution, EU leaders made moves to open up multilateral diplomatic
contact with Tehran on behalf of the EU members as a whole. Although
Iran had continued to negotiate with particular countries on a bilateral basis
ever since the 1979 revolution, European diplomats now wanted to forge a
more collective approach towards Tehran, and in 1992 representatives of
the Brussels-based European Commission held several rounds of talks with
the Iranians aimed at 'assisting [Iran's] economic reconstruction', 'negotiating a free trade agreement between the EC and Iran' and 'advocating ... the
liberalization of trade between the Gulf Cooperation Council (GCC) and
Iran'. These initial efforts ended without agreement but were soon followed
by a new approach, heralded at the Council of Ministers in Edinburgh in
December 1992 as 'critical dialogue', that would seek to soften Iran's policies
on matters of concern – the Middle East peace process, international terrorism and production of weapons of mass destruction – while also seeking to

strike a new commercial agreement. This 'critical dialogue' was intended to be a precursor to a more formal 'political dialogue' that would eventuate if the mullahs changed tack in the way the Europeans hoped they would.

Over the years that followed, EU–Iranian multilateral talks have blown hot and cold, depending on the wider economic and political climate. The dialogue was suspended in April 1997, for example, after a Berlin court held that Iranian leaders had instigated the assassination of Kurdish dissidents in Germany five years previously, but a new round of negotiations – now labelled as 'constructive dialogue' – recommenced in July 1998, a year after the election of the reformist President Mohammad Khatami had thawed relations with the West and seemed to herald a new policy of détente. But because the European governments were willing to expand trade and cooperation with Iran without first obtaining the firm concessions on terrorism and nuclear proliferation that Washington wanted, a transatlantic rift immediately reopened. In June 1993 US Secretary of State Warren Christopher tried unsuccessfully to persuade EU ministers to impose a joint economic embargo on Iran, although he did obtain an agreement to ban the export of 'dual-use' technology that could have been used in a covert nuclear weapons programme. Washington also helped to block the joint rescheduling of Iranian debts by the so-called 'Paris Club' of international bankers, thereby forcing several governments to strike their own bilateral agreements instead: the French, German, Italian and Japanese governments eventually made separate moves to reschedule the $15 billion that Iran owed.

Although Washington has publicly and privately ventured such criticisms throughout the years of EU–Iranian dialogue, there have been times when a particularly strong political furore has erupted. When on 17 June 2002, for example, EU ministers authorized the European Commission to pursue closer trade links with Iran, the Bush administration voiced a vociferous protest. Two days later Alan Larson, Under-Secretary for Economic Business and Agricultural Affairs in the State Department, told the House of Representatives International Relations Committee that 'we have pressed strenuously the view that the European Union should make counter-terrorism and fighting against weapons of mass destruction a central element of their dialogue with Iran, and make future economic cooperation with Iran conditional on satisfactory results. We know that Europe has a different opinion than we do ... the Secretary of State and other administrative officials have worked hard to sensitize our friends and allies about the depth of our concerns [although] some of our allies don't agree with our focus in the energy sector.'

Washington's protests were just as strong when a first round of EU–Iranian negotiations opened on 12 December 2002 and senior EU diplomats such as Peter Lysholt Hansen, a Danish foreign minister, and Christian Leffler, a director of the European Commission, met their Iranian counterparts in Brussels. Richard Boucher once again expressed his concern and disappointment, emphasizing that the administration had 'grave concerns about Iran's behaviour ... [and] it has been our understanding that any economic incentives for Iran would be linked to an improvement in Iranian behaviour in these areas of concern'. Boucher also dropped a heavy hint that ILSA might be invoked when he stated that 'we will continue to consult closely with EU officials regarding Iran policy and would have to look at, of course, any actual business developments in terms of US law'.

It is also just as true to say that there have been times when European governments have sharply denounced Washington's harsh line towards Tehran. When President Bush, delivering his State of the Union address in January 2002, condemned Iran as standing alongside North Korea and Iraq as a member of the 'Axis of Evil', his remarks provoked fury from some European quarters. In Germany the Deputy Foreign Minister, Ludger Volmer, warned that the US should not accuse Iran of terrorism just to pay off old scores and should instead seek to engage Tehran. Similar views were also voiced by the Spanish government, which at that time held the chairmanship of the European Union. The most striking denunciation came from Paris, however, where Foreign Minister Hubert Vedrine used almost exactly the same words as his Iranian counterpart, Kamal Kharrazi, to criticize the Washington line: 'we are threatened today by a new simplism which consists in reducing everything to the war on terrorism,' he argued. 'We cannot accept that idea. You have got to tackle the root causes, the situations, the poverty, the injustice.' [16]

But how far is a concern for oil, and for the wider business opportunities in Iran that the proceeds of oil sales help to create, a driving force in the formation of critical dialogue? European diplomats involved in the negotiations generally reply that trade and investment have always been just one of their many interests and that their essential aim is to foster a spirit of international cooperation and to improve the plight of ordinary Iranians. But economic interests undoubtedly stood at the heart of this dialogue, even though the architects of the policy certainly had a number of other motives and have always emphasized how 'critical' of Tehran their approach really was. After all, it was no coincidence that the staunchest advocates of dialogue – France, Germany, Italy and the United Kingdom – are those that have had the strongest economic ties with Iran, while the country advocating breaking off contact, Denmark, on the grounds that it was achieving nothing, is also the one country that in commercial terms has much less to lose.

One key driving force behind the dialogue was the French government, which had renewed its own bilateral diplomatic relationship with Tehran in late 1988, more than three years before the EU's multilateral dialogue was formally initiated. These ties were renewed just months after the end of the Iran-Iraq War heralded new opportunities for foreign businesses, particularly in the oil sector, which had previously been far too vulnerable to military attack by the Iraqis and, in the latter stages of the war, by the Americans to attract any international investment. By the end of 1988 the temptations of Iran's oil sector also seemed all the greater because the French oil giant Total had shortly before made a breakthrough in a long-running dispute that concerned its right to compensation for the seizure and nationalization in the early post-revolutionary years of its assets in the shah's Iranian Oil Consortium. The offer of compensation was widely viewed as a highly conciliatory gesture towards foreign oil companies that, after the ceasefire with Iraq, would now have much to gain. After the resumption of diplomatic relations between Paris and Tehran, the Total Group quickly renewed its commercial ties with Iran, making regular purchases of crude oil, selling motor fuels and lubricants and gradually increasing its participation in the industrial projects of a country it felt sure was set to play a key role in meeting the world's future energy needs.

Germany has been another leading European exponent of critical dialogue, and it is often claimed that this policy grew out of a special German-Iranian relationship that by 1992 had already been a long-term affair. The Germans had been almost alone among European countries in keeping open a political dialogue with Tehran after 1979 as well as maintaining a number of other cultural and academic contacts between the two countries throughout the difficult years of the 1980s. German leaders were also unusually bold about making official visits to Tehran: in 1984 Foreign Minister Hans-Dietrich Genscher became the first Western official to visit post-revolutionary Tehran, while in 1997 Foreign Minister Klaus Kinkel wasted little time in meeting Mohammad Khatami, elected as Iranian president the same year, and calling for Germany and the outside world to 'deal openly with the apparently more liberal government'.[17] After Khatami gave an electrifying interview to America's CNN Television in 1998, in which he called for a 'crack in the wall of mistrust' between the USA and Iran and proposed new dialogue, Kinkel was also quick to reiterate his calls for a 'resumption of contacts' and to declare that Germany 'wanted to resume closer economic cooperation'.[18]

The German government certainly had strong economic motives to build such ties. In 1992, as the policy of critical dialogue was formulated, Germany was exporting $5 billion of goods to Iran, nearly 50 per cent of the European Community's total of $10.7 billion, and throughout the 1990s German trade with Iran always made up between 25–50 per cent of this overall European figure. Not surprisingly the strength of these ties had often provoked American and Israeli anger, and when in 1995 the German government sent an economic delegation to Iran and decided to offer credit guarantees of DM150 billion to revitalize economic relations, its actions caused a storm in Washington and Tel Aviv, even though they were in themselves arguably of no particular material significance.

Such commercial pressures also help to explain the same transatlantic divergence that has also emerged over a much more hypothetical issue – a pre-emptive military strike on Iranian nuclear or wider political infrastructures by American warplanes or missiles. Some British ministers have stated that they would not support any such American military action against Iran, striking a clear contrast with Saddam's Iraq, where there were no comparable British economic interests. Foreign Secretary Jack Straw argued in September 2005 that the Iranian nuclear crisis would 'not be resolved by military means' and that 'the truth is, as Condoleezza Rice has said, military action in respect of the Iran dossier is not on anybody's agenda. ... All United States presidents always say all options are open. But it is not on the table, it is not on the agenda. I happen to think that it is inconceivable.'[19] Particularly strong criticism of American threats of military force against Iran also came from former German Chancellor Gerhard Schroeder, who publicly argued before a crowd in Hanover on 13 August 2005 that he wanted to 'take the military option off the table. We have seen it doesn't work.'

Another of Iran's strong trading partners, Italy, has also taken a slightly different approach that is even more adverse to Washington's hard line. While this approach has always involved dialogue, Italy's bilateral dialogue has often been somewhat less 'critical' of Iran than that of other European governments.

So in 1998, when Italy was exporting $848 million worth of goods to Iran, Italian Prime Minister Romano Prodi visited Tehran, the most influential European statesman to do so since 1979, and held talks with Khatami that were reported to be 'focused largely on trade issues' and to be playing down the importance of human rights issues, which were dismissed as 'a problem of any one country'.[20] At the other end of the spectrum, Europe's leading antagonist of engagement has been a country that has had much less commercial interest in the Iranian market. In August 1996 Denmark decided to end the critical dialogue with Tehran on the grounds that it wasn't achieving anything, and instead opened up talks with Iranian dissidents. But in 1995 the Danes had exported only a relatively small quantity of goods to Iran, worth in total $83.5 million, and imported only $17.6 million.[21]

Of course disagreements about how to deal with Iran both reflect and accentuate a much wider transatlantic divide that has in recent years emerged unmistakably over many other issues. During the run-up to the Iraq war, when all of the EU governments were insisting that any action against Iraq would need some mandate from the UN Security Council, Javier Solana, the EU's High Representative for Common Foreign and Security Policy, noted that while the Americans tended to emphasize military solutions, the Europeans tended to regard military operations only as a last resort: 'the EU has a specific culture based on conflict prevention through dialogue and sensitivity to the economic and social roots of violence,' he claimed.[22] Such differences have also become much more pronounced over the last decade as the European Union has begun to forge a common security and defence policy that poses a sharper challenge to Washington's position than ever before. As this policy began to take shape in the late 1990s, it prompted serious concern in some political circles across the Atlantic. Senator Jesse Helms attacked the 'Euro-army', calling it a 'dangerous and divisive dynamic within NATO' with a note of alarm that was shared by, among others, Madeleine Albright, the Secretary of Defense William Cohen[23] and the editor of the influential *National Review*, John O'Sullivan, who also warned of Europe's 'drift to a rival and hostile set of policies'.[24]

But besides dissolving America's grip over its European allies, there is another reason why this growing transatlantic gulf also matters. And that is the effect it has on the Iranian regime itself.

Undermining US leverage over Iran

One reason why diplomats on both sides of the Atlantic have sought without success to bridge the gulf over the Iranian issue is that such sharp transatlantic differences play into the hands of the mullahs, who have proved adept at identifying and exploiting such divisions. This tactic has at times left Washington isolated and as a result less able to exert pressure on Tehran.

In one sense of course, these Iranian tactics have undermined European as well as American political power because they allow Tehran to pursue a nuclear programme, peaceful or otherwise, that has alarmed governments on both sides of the Atlantic and elsewhere. But they pose a particular challenge to Washington because the European governments, being more conciliatory, have not typically made claims as ambitious as those of their American counterparts. So Tehran has at times been able to meet some European demands while often falling far short of Washington's. In the summer of 2005, for example, the Bush administration called on Tehran not just to renounce its ambitions to enrich uranium but also to dismantle completely Iranian facilities at Isfahan and Natanz, whereas the EU3 had proposed that they work with

Tehran 'to establish a group to identify alternative uses' for the installations.

The Iranian tactic of identifying and exploiting transatlantic differences has been apparent ever since the international crisis over its suspected nuclear weapons programme really began, in the summer of 2002. So after the striking of the deal of October 2003, for example, some US and European diplomats questioned whether Iran's intent was really just to isolate the United States diplomatically while buying more time to pursue weapons surreptitiously: 'it may well be a clever device, a way to divide Europe and America while giving the Iranians a public relations coup,' one Western diplomat, closely associated with the negotiations, told an America newspaper.[25] Within months it seemed likely that their predictions had come true when Tehran found loopholes in the October deal that, if exploited, were certain to kick up a huge political storm.

The main area of ambiguity was the definition of 'uranium enrichment', which the Iranians claimed referred only to the introduction of gas into centrifuges and not to the building and testing of these machines. This dispute seemed to be solved when the Iranian negotiators struck a 'Brussels agreement' the following February that defined 'enrichment' in the more encompassing terms the Europeans had always wanted, but when on 29 July they announced their intention to 'revise their policies on nuclear activities' by resuming the construction and testing of the centrifuges, transatlantic differences immediately surfaced. While EU diplomats continued to negotiate, meeting their Iranian counterparts at a series of secret meetings in Paris, Washington once again reiterated its calls to refer Iran to the UN Security Council for possible sanctions: for the hawkish John Bolton, Tehran's actions 'underline why we continue to believe that the Iranian nuclear weapons programme must be taken up by the UN Security Council, falling as it does within the Council's mandate to address threats to international peace and security ... the time to report this issue to the Security Council is long overdue.'[26] Bolton echoed the hard line of National Security Adviser Condoleezza Rice, who had told Fox News two weeks earlier that 'the Iranians have been in trouble for a very long time. And it's one reason that this regime has to be isolated in its bad behaviour, not quote-unquote, "isolated".'

The state of transatlantic disunity created by this limited 'enrichment' gave the Iranians an opportunity to progress with their enrichment programme that would have been missing if European governments had spoken in a single, united voice with Washington. For without the support even of its European partners, the US administration had no chance of obtaining an IAEA resolution condemning Iranian behaviour. Yet without American support, EU negotiators knew they could not offer Iran any really tempting incentives. Instead transatlantic disunity only allowed the Iranians a chance to accelerate their enrichment programme, and almost as soon as the Paris Accords were struck on 14 November 2004 Western diplomats were informed by IAEA inspectors that the Iranians were 'going flat out' to convert tonnes of uranium concentrate into uranium hexafluoride gas, a key ingredient used in the enrichment process. This did not technically violate the agreement, which did not come into effect until 22 November, but illustrated how adept the Iranians were at creating and exploiting opportunities to maximum effect.

The Iranian premier, Mahmoud Ahmadinejad, also tried splitting international opinion in May 2006 by writing a letter, completely unexpectedly, to President Bush. The 18-page document, the first direct contact since 1980 between the leaders of the two countries, sparked intense interest because it seemed to offer an opportunity of negotiations between the US and Iran that might resolve the nuclear crisis. But the letter was carefully timed, coinciding as it did with a meeting of international ministers at the UN Security Council that was designed to hammer out a common position over Iran after weeks of deadlock. By penning his letter, Ahmadinejad hoped to appear moderate and conciliatory and make Washington look inflexible, thereby finding new support in New York.

But the lure of Iranian natural resources has not just created fissures between Europe and the United States. Washington has in recent years also had to watch a rift emerging with Japan, another global ally with growing energy ties to Iran.

Iran, America and Japan

Since 1945 Japan has been a particularly close and trusted American ally. In return for very generous economic assistance, Tokyo continues to allow American military bases on its soil and effectively lets Washington take command of its overall defence policy. This allows the United States to pose as its protector, guarding its territory and interests from the aggression of rivals such as North Korea and China, and to expect Japanese support in the event of any regional conflict over flashpoints such as Taiwan.

But the strong relationship between the United States and Japan is already being challenged by the lure of Iranian resources. For although Japan needs American military protection against a nuclear-armed North Korea as well as access to the US domestic market, these considerations are beginning to be outweighed by its massive and growing energy requirements and by the sheer size of some of the contracts that Japanese companies have already been awarded to develop Iran's energy infrastructure. This temptation is not only challenging America's grip over Japan but also over other countries towards which they need to show a united front, including Iran and to a lesser extent North Korea.

Lying behind these growing disputes over Iran lies not so much any increase in the energy requirements of Japan, whose economy has for some years been the world's second largest and whose population is not growing at any unusually high rate, but the increasing difficulties of meeting them. With no real indigenous sources of oil and gas, it has only limited options.

Partly to cut its emissions of carbon dioxide and thereby meet its obligations under the Kyoto Protocol on global warming, the Tokyo government had at one time sought to meet its domestic energy requirements with nuclear power, and to this end it planned to build up to 12 new nuclear reactors by 2010. But these plans not only met serious public opposition in a country still affected by memories of Hiroshima and Nagasaki but also encountered serious technical problems. In mid-October 2002, for example, Japanese providers had been forced to shut down 9.8 Gw of nuclear power generation capacity for unscheduled repairs and thereby prompted electric utilities to increase their intake of fuel oil, crude oil and LNG.[27] The previous month Tokyo Electric Power had also halted operations at seven of its eight nuclear reactors for emergency inspections following the discovery, during annual maintenance, of cracks on equipment in the reactor units. This discovery prompted other providers of nuclear power, the Chubu and Tohuku Electric Power Companies, to follow suit and close their own plants for several weeks.

The uncertainty over the future of nuclear power in Japan has some huge implications. According to a report by a highly respected independent consultancy, Japan's 13 nuclear reactors have a combined generating capacity of 12.3 Gw for which conventional fossil-fuel-fired stations would require feedstock amounting to either 411,000 b/d of crude oil, 395,000 b/d of fuel oil or a mixture of the two. In May 2004 another report argued that uncertainty over the future of Japan's nuclear energy programme would help ensure an average annual increase of 1.13 per cent in the amount of liquefied natural gas that would need to be imported between 2002 and 2015: 'we expect all gas imports will be in the form of LNG at least until 2015,' ran the report, 'thus Japan's LNG demand is forecast to reach 62.5 million tons in 2010 and 66.9 million in 2015.'[28]

Without a nuclear power programme to rely on, the Japanese are anxious to secure reliable sources of fuel that will render them less vulnerable to oil-price shocks. Such vulnerability has been highlighted by ministers in Tokyo, who have estimated that their economy's GDP growth would be lowered by between 0.3 and 0.4 per cent for every $10 that a barrel of oil rises by, while also emphasizing that this calculation does not take into account the impact of higher LNG and coal prices, which would also have a very negative effect.[29] 'If $50 per barrel oil prices continue for three months then there is no problem but if they are sustained for between three and four years then that becomes a heavy burden,' one minister told Asahi TV on 22 August 2004. The former chairman of the US Federal Reserve, Alan Greenspan, has also singled out Japan as a country that is particularly vulnerable to sustained high oil prices, telling the US Senate in a letter of 25 August 2004 that 'the recent run-up in oil prices, if sustained, may exert a significant drag on Japanese economic activity'.

Japan's main source of imported oil has always been the Middle East, which has supplied about 90 per cent of its needs. But although Saudi Arabia and the United Arab Emirates had always been the key exporters into the Japanese market, by the beginning of the millennium these sources of supply had become much less secure. In February 2000 the Tokyo-based Arabian Oil Company (AOC) was not allowed to renew its 40-year concession to develop the Khafji oil field on the Saudi side of the Neutral Zone between Saudi Arabia and Kuwait, sending shockwaves through a Japanese government that had regarded the concession as its prime source of supply. At this point the AOC had only one remaining foreign interest in crude oil, which was another concession in the Neutral Zone, this time granted by the Kuwaiti government. Yet this was due to expire in January 2003 and the company had been informed by Kuwait that constitutional restrictions would prevent this concession from being renewed as well.

The loss of the Saudi concession in 2000 galvanized the Japanese into searching for alternative suppliers of crude oil, and one obvious source was Iran. In May 2000, prior to a visit by President Khatami to Tokyo, the Japanese Minister of International Trade and Industry (MITI), Takashi Fukaya, announced that he hoped to soon open wide-ranging talks with Iran on cooperation in the energy sector. When they did begin soon afterwards, these negotiations heralded the opening of a new chapter in Iranian–Japanese cooperation, and within two years Iran had become Japan's third largest oil supplier, providing some 576,000 b/d, while Japanese companies also became heavily involved in developing the Iranian energy infrastructure: some notable deals took place in January 2003, for example, when Shell Exploration sold a 20 per cent interest in a deal to develop the Soroush–Nowruz fields to a Japanese consortium for a sum thought to be around $220 million, and in May 2004 when Japan's JGC and the National Iranian Oil Engineering and Construction Company (NIOECC) signed a $25 million agreement for the upgrading of the Arak refinery over five years which gave JGC a 49 per cent share in the project.

This commercial relationship has since continued unabated and has allowed Japanese companies to strike some particularly lucrative deals in the petrochemical sector. In May 2001, for example, Iran's NPC awarded a $205 million contract to a Japanese consortium of Toyo Engineering for the construction of a major new plant at Bandar Assaluyeh, while the following year Kawasaki Heavy Industries and Tomen were chosen to build a huge petrochemical plant at Kermanshah, and Mitsui was awarded a $225 million contract to build another high-density polyethylene plant. In May 2004 the deputy governor of the Japan Bank for International Cooperation told a forum in Tehran that the bank was currently providing financial backing for Japanese firms that had been contracted to build three major petrochemical plants to the value of $573 million and also regularly 'received many inquiries from Japanese firms interested in doing business in Iran'. And in May 2005 the giant Itochu Corporation announced that in 2008 it would launch a partnership with two Thai firms, the Siam Cement Public Company and the state-run PTT group, for a 25 billion yen investment to produce polyethylene in Iran. This investment would not violate American law, or so Itochu and its partners claimed, because petrochemical investments are not strictly 'oil-related' and therefore fell outside ILSA's scope.

Yet despite such efforts to placate Washington's concerns, the rapidly emerging accord between Tokyo and Tehran could hardly fail to raise American eyebrows. At the time of the Tokyo talks in the summer of 2000, a senior State Department official stated that such moves were bound to worry the US administration, although he added that American policy towards Iran was 'in a state of flux at the moment as we try to put relations on a more normal footing. That means that how we would react to closer economic ties between Japan and Iran is an open question. However, we are also well aware of Japan's precarious energy situation.'[30] Yet this moderate tone quickly hardened when, in the autumn of 2000, Tokyo acquired one of the greatest of Iran's energy prizes – a big stake in the Azadegan oil field.

South Azadegan

From the time it was discovered in March 1998, the huge Azadegan complex has sorely tempted international oil companies and their governments with visions of vast rewards. Located only 25km from the edge of Iraq's giant Majnoon field and 100km west of Iran's major producing region at Ahwaz, it covers an estimated 520 square kilometres and is reckoned to have reserves amounting to not less than 35–45 billion barrels of oil that can potentially produce a daily output of not less than 400,000 barrels. As the largest onshore project in Iran since the revolution, its exploration and development have not surprisingly attracted interest from companies the world over, including the American giants ExxonMobil and Conoco.[31]

Japan first got a firm foothold in the Azadegan project on 1 November 2000, when a new deal was signed in Tokyo between Takeo Hiranuma, the Japanese Minister of International Trade and Industry, and the Iranian Oil Minister. In a subsequent statement, the two parties announced that a consortium comprised of two Japanese-owned companies would be granted exclusive negotiating rights with NIOC to develop a 'specific area' of the field, although this did not prohibit them from signing up companies from other countries. One member of the consortium was the Japan Petroleum Exploration Company Ltd (Japex), of which the Japanese National Oil Company (JNOC) owns 65.7 per cent, while its partner in the venture was Indonesia Petroleum Ltd (Inpex), half of which is also owned by JNOC. Besides granting exclusive negotiating rights, the deal had other terms: in particular, NIOC also decided to 'encourage and support' the participation of Japanese companies as minority partners in the development of 'other oil and gas fields such as Ahwaz-Bangestan and South Pars', while the Japanese also agreed, as noted above, not only to buy $1 billion of Iranian oil each year for the next three years but also to pay Iran in advance.

Over the next three years extensive negotiations between Japanese and Iranian representatives followed. In June 2001 the Japanese consortium formally submitted their plan for the development of the field, while the following month NIOC and JNOC secured a deal to fund a $20 million survey. But it was not until 18 February 2004 that the consortium, which now also included the giant engineering corporation Tomen, finally concluded a $2 billion deal with Tehran officials. Under the terms of this agreement, the consortium would hold a 75 per cent interest in the licence and act as a development operator, while a marketing arm of NIOC, the Naftiran Intertrade Company (NICO), would hold the remaining 25 per cent. The development would then progress in two phases – the first increasing production capacity up to 150,000 b/d and the other extending it to 260,000 b/d – until, after 40 months, the field was finally fully operational. The contract also stipulated the drilling of 36 wells in the course of the first phase and 39 in the second, along with the construction and installation of oil and natural gas production facilities, the laying of oil and gas pipelines for export, and the injection of water and gas to maintain the right amount of pressure in the field.

To help fund the development, the state-run Japan Bank for International Cooperation announced soon afterwards, on 25 March, that it would join forces with four major banks to fund oil development by extending a $1.2 billion syndicated loan to the contractors. Under this arrangement the bank would provide 85 per cent of this amount while the remainder was to be divided among Mitsubishi Tokyo Financial Group, Mizuho Financial

Group, Sumitomo Mitsui Financial Group and UFJ Holdings. Overall this was a nine-year deal, during which time Iran was obliged to make an effort to increase its crude oil supplies to Japan in the event of a crisis or emergency situation in the Middle East. The five banks had already joined forces three years previously, in March 2001, having agreed to pay in advance for $3 billion worth of Iranian oil that Japan agreed to import over the next three years as part of the initial deal.

The new agreement was heralded triumphantly in both Tehran and Tokyo, where a joint statement was issued declaring that 'the parties do hope this project will be successfully conducted, strengthen the economic ties between the Islamic Republic of Iran and Japan, and contribute to further development of relationships between the two countries'. And during a later visit to Tokyo by Hassan Rowhani, the Japanese premier Junichiro Koizumi reiterated his confidence in the future of Japan's growing relationship with its new partner: these relations, he claimed, 'have been strengthening as seen in the agreement to develop the Azadegan oil field and I very much hope this will go farther'. But by striking such a deal, the Japanese inevitably provoked American wrath and invoked the spectre of ILSA, which now threatens to haunt them with a vengeance.

The US and Japan

In one sense, of course, the signing of the Azadegan deal was an important blow against a Washington administration that was extremely keen to starve Iran of the foreign exchange that subsidized its nuclear programme and its support for terrorism. As the deal was signed, the State Department's Richard Boucher declared that because 'our policy has been, with respect to Iran, to oppose petroleum investment there ... we remain deeply concerned about deals such as this and disappointed that these things might go forward. We have laws that affect our attitudes towards those investments. And we will have to look at those laws appropriately.' A Japanese official brushed aside the criticism, however: 'of course the US had to say they were "disappointed" with the deal due to their strong attitude against Iran, but we have continually kept them informed and updated on the Azadegan situation.' State Department officials had made little secret of their disapproval in the preceding few months, and at the end of June 2003 a British newspaper had cited an unnamed US official and sources close to the negotiations who 'confirmed that the administration of President George W. Bush is pressing Japan not to send the "wrong message" to Iran'.[32]

But although the deal was a rebuke to Washington's influence, it was far from a clear renunciation of American power because Tokyo was able to plausibly claim that, by February 2004, the Iranians had alleviated international concern over its nuclear ambitions and were by this stage cooperating with the IAEA. Within days of the deal, Japanese officials also made moves to placate Washington by inviting Rowhani to Tokyo to discuss his country's nuclear activities, its willingness to ratify the Additional Protocol, and its 13 March decision to shut out IAEA inspectors in protest at a resolution that 'deplored' Iran's failure to disclose its P2 centrifuge. When on 17 March Rowhani assured Koizumi that Tehran 'will continue cooperating with the IAEA so that the international community will have no concern over Iran's peaceful use of atomic energy', the Japanese premier felt able to reassure the watching world. 'Iran is trying to respond sincerely to the IAEA resolution,' he argued, and Rowhani's efforts to do so 'are very important for developing ties between Japan and Iran'.

By paying lip service to American concerns, Tokyo was able to give some reassurance to the Bush administration. During negotiations with Kamal Kharazi the previous summer, the Japanese Foreign Minister, Yoriko Kawaguchi, had initially appeared to ignore such concerns when she told reporters in Tokyo on 27 August that Iran's dealings with the IAEA would not hinder negotiations on the multibillion-dollar deal to develop the massive oil field, regardless of the nuclear issue. 'These are two separate policy goals. We have not come to the point where we need to discuss these together,' as she put it; 'each one is important'. What mattered for the deal, she added, was 'securing oil', which was a very important policy goal for Japan. But crucially she went on to qualify this by emphasizing that she would still urge the Iranians to sign the Additional Protocol and that 'Japan shares the international community's nuclear weapons concern. We are glad that the IAEA is there talking with the Iranians. We have been pressing Iran that it is very important for them to sign and implement the additional protocol.' This tone echoed Yasuo Fukuda, the Japanese government's chief spokes-man, who had shortly before also mixed altruism with national self-interest when he pointed out that 'crude oil is very important to Japan, but on the other hand the nuclear development issue has become a serious international concern'. He added that 'I don't think there will be a contract ignoring [these concerns].' [33]

By adopting such a tone, the Japanese were able to limit the diplomatic rift with the United States that the Azadegan deal had opened. In Washing-ton, the US administration proclaimed that it would 'reluctantly' acquiesce in the deal if its implementation were conditional on Iran's faithfully observ-ing its nuclear obligations, while John Bolton struck an unexpectedly upbeat note when in April 2004 he claimed to be 'very confident that the view of Japan and the US on the Iranian nuclear weapons programme is essentially the same'.

One reason why the Japanese had succeeded in placating the Americans was that they had deliberately avoided making a decision over the deal at moments of particular international tension over the Iranian nuclear programme. Had they done so, then of course a much more serious rift with Washington would have opened. Their negotiations over the issue in the summer of 2003, for example, were officially tied down over disputes about the size of the reserve and the details of the particular buyback contract, which JNOC wanted to incorporate in a 20-year term instead of the ten-year payback advocated by NIOC. The real reason for the delay, however, was that in the summer of 2003 the nuclear controversy had escalated sharply and the Japanese were working hard to find an excuse not to commit themselves until this nuclear row had been defused. At the same time, Tokyo announced that it would take heed of US pressure and consider delaying an agreement to develop Azadegan: 'suspicion about Iran's nuclear development is not an issue affecting only our country,' Yasuo Fukuda told reporters at another press conference in Tokyo, 'we can't sign the crude oil accord ignoring it.'

Tokyo certainly needed to take such measures to reassure Washington, for on 30 June the State Department had also said that it was opposing the Azadegan investment after it emerged that the Japanese consortium was in final negotiations with Iran. Although the US was opposed to investments in Iran 'at any time', as Richard Boucher argued, 'this would be a particularly unfortunate time to go forward with major new oil and gas deals, given recent revelations about Iran's nuclear programs and efforts being made through the IAEA to deal with the threat Iran poses.'[34] Washington was also deeply concerned that any such deal could also herald a rift not just with Tokyo but also with its European partners. Shell had particularly strong links with the Japanese consortium and would have had much to gain from joining it to develop Azadegan, while American diplomats also reportedly held talks with their French counterparts about Total's interest in developing the field.[35] So by delaying the signing of the deal, Tokyo was able to avoid making such a stark choice between bowing to American pressure on the one hand and reaping Iranian rewards on the other.

By the autumn of 2005 the Japanese were still delicately poised on a political tightrope as they struggled to juggle their allegiance to the United States with their investment in Azadegan. In one sense they seemed to be leaning towards Washington because at the IAEA board meeting at the end of September the Japanese had voted in favour of a resolution that condemned Iran's behaviour while Foreign Minister Nobutaka Machimura 'strongly urged Iran to seriously implement all the requirements of the relevant IAEA resolutions, including the full suspension of uranium conversion activities, and to return to the negotiations with the EU3'. This stance risked provoking Iranian retaliation. 'Those countries that have economic transactions with Iran, especially in the field of oil, have not defended Iran's rights so far,' Ali Larijani complained on 19 September, adding that the Supreme National Security Council was 'very determined' to make a balance between these two things and that 'how much they defend Iran's national right will facilitate their participation in Iran's economic field'. Asked later if this meant that countries like Japan could lose its contracts, Larijani replied that 'it is not only Japan but other countries that are concerned. We will examine their attitude.' The Azadegan contract in particular, he went on to say, 'depends on their [Japan's] conduct'. Yet Tokyo's support for the resolution was still not in any way a sign that it had firmly sided with Washington because the resolution, mentioned earlier, was watered down and any action left dependent on another IAEA meeting due to be held two months later.

But on the other hand, Tokyo's strong reluctance to surrender its economic interests was at the same time also infuriating some influential people in Washington. In mid-September US Senator Gordon Smith wrote a letter to Hiroshi Okuda, the chairman of Toyota Motor Corporation, chastising him for what he called the company's 'immoral' decision to expand its business in Iran. 'Seeking business advantages at the expense of America's security is antithetical to the values for which our country stands,' the Oregon Republican wrote to the head of Japan's largest automaker. Although Toyota's spokeswoman, Martha Voss, denied Smith's charge that the company was expanding its business in Iran, she nonetheless did acknowledge that its 70 dealerships in the country had sold 4,000 vehicles during the first nine months of this year compared with 327 during all of 2004.[36]

There is another reason why the extent to which Tokyo was being pulled in Washington's direction should not be exaggerated. For although American pressure had also prompted one member of the consortium, the Tomen Corporation, to pull out of the deal altogether, what deterred other companies from joining the consortium, or made its existing partners less certain of their commitment, was not so much American displeasure but quite a number of other factors. When in September 2004 it had also emerged that Japex was 'thinking of pulling out',[37] and when Royal Dutch Shell Group also declined an offer from the third partner, Inpex, to join the consortium, a highly respected oil consultancy argued that the main obstacle was really the viability of the particular buyback contract. 'Many international oil companies may not find the rate of return attractive enough under the revised buyback system, although Azadegan is seen to have similar terms to Darkhoin [an oil field in Iran], which is a relaxed version of the revised buyback system', ran a report on the deal by the Honolulu-based consultancy FACTS.

The row over Iran's nuclear ambitions escalated during 2006, and the Japanese interest in Azadegan was inevitably embroiled. As Iranian Foreign Minister Manouchehr Mottaki toured Japan and the Far East in February, Japanese Chief Cabinet Secretary Shinzo Abe argued that 'our country, which maintains friendly relations with Iran, will see to it that Iran, which wields influence in the field of energy, will not be isolated in the international community'. Such a moderate line alarmed John Bolton, now US ambassador to the UN, who told a Japanese news agency that 'Iran has used its oil and natural gas as a weapon, and used it very skilfully. I hope there's a way to work around the energy question, but it may be awkward for Japan.'[38] Bolton knew the strength of Tokyo's concern that any loss of its Iranian foothold would present its strategic rival, China, with an opportunity to move straight in. The following month Japanese ministers were reported to have simply ignored US requests, made informally by Deputy Secretary of State Robert Zoellick, to halt work on Azadegan while Iran was hauled before the UN: 'we hope that Iran will listen to the international community's concerns,' stated Vice Trade Minister Hideji Sugiyama, 'but at the same time it is important to have a stable supply of crude oil from Iran.'[39]

The US and North Korea

The lure of Iran's natural resources has not just compromised American influence over Japan but also over other countries. One is North Korea, whose own nuclear weapons programme has also been a source of great international concern since the end of 2002, when its government renounced an eight-year agreement and instead announced its intention to withdraw from the 1968 Non-Proliferation Treaty. Yet Washington's considerable and protracted efforts to persuade Pyongyang to end its ambitions to build a bomb have not been helped by its dispute with Tokyo over Azadegan.

This has been because the US administration has tried to maximize pressure on North Korea by presenting a united front with some of the six countries, including Japan, that since August 2003 had been involved in the negotiations to resolve the nuclear issue. Yet the Azadegan deal was struck just as the second round of talks on the issue had begun and Washington was particularly keen to step up pressure on the North Koreans. It was for this reason that US officials tried hard to downplay the importance of the new Tehran–Tokyo accord: John Bolton argued simply that 'the Azadegan arrangement has just been proceeding on a completely separate track [from the talks on North Korea] and the government of Japan has made it very clear that they remain very concerned about Iran's proliferation activities and very concerned that Iran be held strictly accountable' under the Non-Proliferation Treaty. But such words could not disguise the disunited front that the US and Japan presented in the negotiations with Pyongyang, which collapsed on 25 February – one week after Azadegan – and were not properly revived until after President Bush's re-election in November 2004.

Japan and the European Union are not the only American allies whose loyalties have been put under increasing strain by the temptation of Iran's natural resources. Another such ally is Pakistan, while Washington's alliances with some other countries, notably South Korea, Iraq and perhaps Canada, may in future also be undermined.

America, Iran and Pakistan

Since the early 1990s tension between Washington and Islamabad has been growing over plans to build a pipeline that could move huge quantities of Iranian natural gas into Pakistan. As Chapter 3 points out, this pipeline could also form part of a much wider network that would eventually help feed the massive Indian market.

Pakistan's interest in Iranian natural gas is based essentially on the simple dictates of a growing inequality between increasing demand and diminishing supply. On the one hand, the country continues to experience a very rapid increase in domestic demand, not least because of a high annual birth rate that, despite numerous government initiatives to control it, is reckoned to be somewhere around 3.5 per cent. Its own natural resources of oil and gas are expected to be wholly insufficient to meet this burgeoning demand, for despite a century-long history of commercial production and the vigorous pursuit of oil exploration and development in the 1980s and early 1990s, Pakistan remains a modest producer of oil and currently imports around 80 per cent of what it needs.

At first sight Pakistan appears to have much more promising natural resources of natural gas, estimated to be around 23.4 trillion cubic feet, and the recent discovery of important new fields has also added to its production potential. The Zamzama field in Sindh province, which was first discovered only in 1998, produced 89.9 billion cubic feet of gas and 597,347 barrels of condensate in 2004, amounting to around 15 per cent of the country's overall output. But officials in Islamabad's Petroleum Ministry who, like their Indian counterparts, plan to make gas 'the fuel of choice' for the future, still feel sure that the overall rate of extraction in domestic fields will fall far short of future demand. So in 2000, when national consumption of gas amounted to 0.7 trillion cubic feet, it was widely predicted that 'Pakistan's demand for natural gas is expected to rise substantially in the next few years, with an increase of roughly 50 per cent by 2006',[40] and by 2004 estimates varied widely but broadly painted the same alarming picture: one highly respected official estimated that 'Pakistan's shortfall by 2010 would be 0.2

billion cubic feet per day (bcfd), going up to 1.4 bcfd by 2015 and 2.7 bcfd by 2020',[41] while other projections anticipated a figure of closer to 0.6 bcfd by 2010 alone.[42]

But although everyone in Islamabad agrees that foreign sources of gas supply are badly needed, solutions have been much harder to come by and, of all the various different schemes that have been cooked up, most are not now considered to be really viable. A natural gas pipeline from Turkmenistan would not only have to be built across Afghanistan, which since the late 1970s has been volatile and lawless, but would also be fed from gas fields whose potential as long-term sources of supply is far from certain: Islamabad officials are quick to point out, for example, that the Turkmen authorities have so far been unable to certify the gas reserves potential in the key Daultabad field. Another proposal, to move gas from Qatar, would involve the construction of an underwater pipeline through deep waters that would be extremely expensive as well as technically very tricky. So this really just leaves only one viable solution, which is the construction of an overland pipeline from Iran that would stretch thousands of kilometres and cost perhaps $4 billion to build.

Besides supplying Pakistan with the natural gas it needs, such a pipeline would also bring quite a few other benefits. If it eventually reaches the Indian market, its construction would provide Pakistan with highly lucrative transit fees, although no one is quite sure just how much. During his early years in power, General Pervez Musharraf regularly claimed that an Iran–India pipeline would earn Pakistan between $500 and $600 million in transit fees, although it has been subsequently claimed by Ministry of Petroleum officials that the real figure would be much closer to a relatively meagre $70–$80 million.[43] A pipeline would also give a huge economic incentive to the Indian and Pakistani governments to strike a lasting peace, thereby allowing both countries to massively reduce their vast military budgets. It was for this reason that, after meeting Khatami in New York in September 2000, Musharraf expressed Pakistan's willingness to participate in the pipeline venture and promoted the idea as an example of 'regional cooperation'. The Pakistani leader also stated that its development could eventually be Pakistan's 'economic salvation' because it would stimulate the domestic oil and gas industry and thereby 'break an age-old dependence on cotton and textiles as Pakistan's main export earners'.[44]

It was with these considerations in mind that, after seizing power in a military coup in 1999, General Musharraf pushed the pipeline project right to the top of his agenda, especially when a new thaw in relations with India suddenly made it a more viable proposition than ever before. In December, just weeks after his coup, Musharraf visited Tehran to discuss not only bilateral relations between the two countries in general but also the pipeline project in particular. More high-level trips soon followed. In Tehran in March 2000 the Pakistani Minister of Petroleum formally agreed to the pipeline project, and the following month Iranian government officials travelled to Islamabad to sign an initial memorandum of understanding. After two years of talks, Zanganeh and the Pakistani Oil Minister, Usman Aminuddin, agreed to more detailed proposals in Islamabad on 22 February 2002 before formally commissioning a pre-feasibility study.

Not surprisingly, the prospect of a Pakistan–Iranian pipeline, which would feed the Tehran regime with foreign exchange and help cement its political ties with a government that has long been a key American ally in the region, has alarmed Washington. On 10 June 2005 the project was discussed at length by Pakistani Foreign Minister Kurshid Mehmood Kasuri and Secretary of State Rice, who pointed out that even if the US administration dropped its opposition there would still be numerous other powerful groups in Congress and the media that were capable of mounting a vigorous campaign of protest and inflicting serious damage on US–Pakistani relations. Rice particularly had in mind a vociferous number of Congressmen and women who had already demanded that the administration invoke ILSA against Pakistani companies and perhaps even cut off the $700 million of US aid that Islamabad receives every year. They had other bargaining chips, since in March the Bush administration had agreed to sell F-16 fighter jets that were much needed by the Pakistan Air Force. But because the pipeline potentially offered an indispensable supply of natural gas as well as such handsome transit fees, this threat doubtlessly did not seem nearly so strong to Pakistan as it would have otherwise done.

Islamabad has appeared unbowed by such threats, arguing that it would not be 'investing' in Iran's energy infrastructure, thereby violating US sanctions, because it would only finance those parts of the pipeline on its own territory, not Iran's. In an interview with a British newspaper on 16 May 2005, Musharraf argued that he would not be persuaded by the United States to drop plans to build a gas pipeline from Iran but would instead take a decision by the year's end that was based solely on what suited Pakistan, not Washington. 'We are short of energy. We need gas immediately. Our industry is suffering, investment coming to Pakistan is suffering, so our interest is to get gas fast. Iran is the fastest source,' he told the *Financial Times*. Other officials in Islamabad reaffirmed that the pipeline would also proceed: 'our president and prime minister have stated on a number of occasions that we will proceed with this project based on our national interests,' Pakistan's Oil Secretary Ahmed Waqar informed one news agency.[45] One of Iran's petroleum ministers, Mani Shankar Aiyar, and his Pakistani counterpart, Amanullah Khan Jadoon, have also issued statements arguing that 'the transnational pipeline projects should be given top priority as there would be substantial advantage to both countries in pursuing and realizing cooperation in these projects, to serve their energy security interests, and to create linkages and inter-dependencies for establishing an enduring relationship between the two countries'.

As the controversy over Iran's nuclear programme reached a climax, one of many, in the autumn of 2005 such strong commercial and economic ties appeared to be swaying Pakistan's loyalties towards Tehran. During a visit to Moscow to attend the meeting of the heads of the Shanghai Cooperation of Organization (SCO) as an observer, Pakistani Prime Minister Shaukat Aziz said in an interview with the Interfax news agency that 'we are convinced that Iran's nuclear problem should be settled through dialogue rather than by using force or trying to refer this issue to the UN', especially when 'any state, including Iran, has the right to a peaceful use of nuclear energy'. Adding that 'any state, including Iran, should assume obligations concerning guarantees of non-proliferation of nuclear technology', Aziz claimed that he shared the same position on the Iranian nuclear issue as Russia and many other countries. While he did not admit that his views were in any way shaped by an interest in Iran's energy, Aziz did say that the presence of the two countries in the Shanghai pact was an impetus for closer bilateral ties.[46]

Some other future disputes?

There are other countries whose growing dependency on Iran's natural resources could in future easily herald some very strong disagreements with the United States. One such country is Iraq, which in August 2004 agreed to a framework agreement on crude oil swaps with neighbouring Iran: 'we stand ready to supply our electricity and gas to Iraq and to facilitate its oil exports through our oil terminals or enter into a swap arrangement that can amount to 350,000 barrels every day,' Iran's Foreign Minister Kamal Kharrazi told the International Donors conference in 2004. A year later, on 19 July 2005, the deal was formally sealed in Tehran by the Iraqi Oil Minister, Ibrahim Bahr al-'Ulum, and his Iranian opposite number, Bijan Namdar Zanganeh.

Under the terms of this deal, three new pipelines would be built to deliver Iraqi crude oil to Iranian refineries in return for deliveries of gasoline, heating oil and kerosene to Iraq: these three links included a 40km pipeline, with a 150,000 b/d capacity, to take crude from Basra to Abadan, a products line to deliver fuel oil and kerosene from the Iranian refinery of Abadan to the southern Iraqi city of Basra, and another products line to carry imported oil from Mahshahr to Basra.

Such an agreement threatened American interests in the region essentially because any Iraqi dependency on Iranian resources easily leads to the establishment of a much wider political relationship: as Kharrazi had said, the swap offer was seen in Tehran as part of 'a comprehensive package of economic cooperation comprising development aid, investment, trade, tourism, project financing and so on'. For this reason, Washington had over the preceding months downplayed Tehran's offers to establish such an oil swap arrangement. On 27 October Richard Boucher had emphasized that 'there is no such arrangement, no such swap arrangement with Iran at present. And as you know we have a lot of concerns about Iranian behaviour that would lead us to be concerned. There would be issues that would have to be examined with regard to any such arrangement with Iran.'

The crude-for-products deal still went ahead despite American concerns, suggesting that Washington recognized the futility of further protesting at a deal that it had already tried to prevent, and when its hands were so strongly tied by the war against the Iraqi insurgents, the US administration scarcely had the time for fighting yet more battles. The State Department's Sean McCormack told reporters that 'we've always said that we encourage Iraq to have good relations with all of its neighbours, including Iran. And we have encouraged, likewise, Iraq's neighbours to play a positive role in Iran's development as it moves towards a more peaceful prosperous stable and democratic future.'

Yet Iraq's links with Iran are in future likely to stir up trouble with the Americans. A glimpse of what lies in store came in October 2005, when the Iraqi President, Jalal Talabani, played down the allegations of Iranian involvement in Iraq that had been suddenly levelled by the British government, whose forces were based in the south of the country. 'The prime minister said they [British officials] are not sure' about Iranian involvement, protested Talabani before a meeting in London on 6 October. 'They [the British government] have some evidence that the device used was made by Iranians. It doesn't mean that the Iranian government gave it to those people. It may be that the Iranian government gave it to some other organization and they gave it to Iraqis.' These words were much more moderate than those of Prime Minister Tony Blair, who had said that 'there are certain pieces of information that lead us back to Iran. ... There is no justification for Iran or any other country interfering in Iraq. Neither will we be subject to any intimidation in raising the necessary and live issues to do with the nuclear weapons obligations of Iran under the Atomic Energy Agency Treaty.' Already, it seemed, there were discernible disagreements over Iran between Baghdad and the allied powers of occupation.

South Korea is another American ally that has strong commercial ties
with Iran that might in future lead it to stray from Washington's preferred
course. These ties are partly made up of contracts to develop South Pars,
and in September 2002 the South Korean firms LG and GS E&C signed
a $1.6 billion deal to help develop Phases 9 and 10 of the massive gas field,
teaming up with a number of other firms, both Iranian and international, to
do so. Other companies have also had a strong involvement in downstream
projects or in various other spin-offs from Iran's oil and gas industry. In
2000, for example, Hyundai Engineering and Construction was awarded
a $1.2 billion contract to build an onshore gas treatment plant at Phases
4 and 5 of South Pars, and has also been particularly successful in securing contracts from the National Iranian Tanker Company (NITC), which
in June 2002 took delivery of the first of five giant tankers, each costing
$78 million, that it had ordered from the South Korean firm. Habibollah
Seidan, the NITC's commercial director, was quoted by one news agency
as saying that his company would probably buy at least ten other carriers to
make deliveries of liquefied gas to India and China, and that Hyundai was
a leading contender to build the $160 million vessels, which would have a
capacity to transport at least 130,000 tons of liquefied natural gas.

For America's allies across the world, the lure of Iran's natural resources
is clearly very powerful, one that has already created political fissures with
Washington. What, though, of America's rivals and those countries with
a much more neutral allegiance? Chapter 3 looks at the political effect on
them.

CHAPTER THREE

US Rivals and Non-Aligned States

I f Iran's energy resources are creating fissures between Washington and its international allies, how are they affecting America's relationships with its rivals, or for that matter with those countries that are usually termed 'non-aligned'? The answer is important because there are currently three such countries that are already heavily importing Iranian oil and gas, and whose commercial, political and military relationships with Tehran are certainly set to grow even more in the near future. Two of these, Russia and China, are widely considered to be 'rivals' of the United States, while another, India, has long been a member of the Non-Aligned Movement of states and one that has had often distinctly cool and sometimes even hostile relations with Washington since its formation in 1947.

There are three distinct ways in which Iran's relationships with these countries are challenging American global influence. On the one hand, its supply of oil and gas can play an important or even pivotal part in fuelling the economic growth of a country that is then in a position to pose a strategic challenge to the United States. Of the three countries this chapter concentrates on, this is only really true of China, whose long-term ascendancy as a regional or even global power is being sustained by its import of vast quantities of oil and gas, and while these imports originate from different parts of the world, Iran's supplies are currently playing a particularly important role: by early 2006 Iran was China's leading oil supplier, accounting for nearly 14 per cent of its imports and exporting 447,300 barrels there every day.

What is more, in the case of all three countries, the influence of Iran's natural resources challenges American power in the same way that it also undermines Washington's ties with its allies. So instead of bowing to American wishes or striking a compromise, countries like Russia, China and India are increasingly tempted to do the very deals with Tehran that Washington has in recent years been so keen to prevent, thereby allowing new alliances to emerge that are antagonistic or even hostile towards Washington. For with such a large stake in Iran's oil and gas, these countries simply have very different interests from those that keep the mullahs wholly at arm's length. So even if we just suppose that tomorrow's China matures into a much smaller economic power than most people widely expect, or that it adopts a much more 'neutral' stance than most Americans currently fear, it might still very easily prefer to sacrifice any ties with the United States in order to pursue a relationship with Tehran.

But this divergence can also undermine American power in another, much more subtle way if Washington goes overboard in trying to buy the loyalties of any country that is lured by the temptations of Iran's oil and gas. So when in July 2005 President Bush promised the Indian government nuclear technology that it badly needed, he found a very persuasive way of building an alliance with a country that was striking up a strong rapport with Tehran. But many independent experts also claimed that the relaxation of stringent controls on the export of nuclear technology was a dangerous step that in the longer term could easily backfire on the supplier. To sell sensitive nuclear technology and military hardware to any other country is, after all, always a potentially counter-productive policy because the recipients may at some future moment be tempted to sell them on to third parties that are hostile to the original supplier. The original supplier also sacrifices his unique right to something that would otherwise have been a bargaining chip in a future dispute. Put bluntly, any country that forfeits such valuable assets risks undermining its own power, and such risks are of course considerably greater if the recipient's loyalty is in question and the provision of such valuable supplies represents a bid to buy that loyalty. 'Give somebody one thing and they ask for two', runs an old adage that succinctly captures the emptiness of trying to buy loyalty.

These, then, are the different ways in which Iranian resources can undermine American power. In what ways, then, are they true of the one country that has in very recent years so seized the American imagination – China?

China

China has been a relative latecomer to the Iranian energy market, one that has followed the well-trodden footsteps of European countries that have continued to import Iranian oil since the 1979 revolution and of European companies, such as Total, Shell and Repsol, that have been developing its energy infrastructure since the mid- to late 1990s. Yet this late start has not stopped China from subsequently building a close alliance with Iran, one that is based almost entirely on its own growing and seemingly insatiable demand for oil and a relative abundance of Iranian supply. By 2005 the Chinese president, Hu Jintao, was openly paying ample testimony to the closeness and success of this new relationship, one that seemed to have barely reached its early stages, when he publicly expressed his keenness to 'enhance exchange and cooperation with Iran in all aspects' and 'to push the friendly cooperation ties, which was long-term stable and rich in content, to a new high'.[1] China, proclaimed the president, 'welcomed and supported' a friendship with Iran that had a 'profound basis', was based on a 'shared broad consensus' on numerous issues and now had 'great potential' for the future.[2]

This new axis between Tehran and Beijing poses a discernible threat to American influence over China in the first of the two ways mentioned above. In the first instance, Iranian oil is fuelling China's development as a rival for international power and influence: as Ali Larijani, the new head of Iran's Supreme National Security Council, has claimed, China 'can play a balancing role in today's world' at the expense of American power, and this 'balancing role' is to an important degree being created and sustained by the emerging Sino-Iranian axis. Secondly, even if we just suppose that China were not on course to pose the long-term challenge to the United States that Larijani and many others generally suppose, then its leaders would still have more reason than ever before to prioritize their association with Tehran at the expense of Washington. Furthermore, this new alliance, like every other considered in this book, also undermines American influence over the Iranian mullahs, who can count on Beijing's support in the event of any international controversy.

So what kind of long-term challenge to American power is it that China poses, and how far is this being fuelled by Iranian oil?

China's rivalry with the US

If any single gesture has recently exemplified both China's economic growth and its perceived threat to American interests, it was the $18.5 billion bid that China's National Offshore Oil Company (CNOOC) made in June 2005 to buy Unocal, the ninth largest oil company in the US. Before it was thwarted by another American firm, Chevron, the Chinese bid set Capitol Hill alight with talk that Beijing was not just preying on American commercial interests but was also muscling in on her wider strategic concerns. As an overwhelming majority in the House passed a resolution declaring that the deal would threaten national security, opponents of the proposed purchase certainly made claims in language that was powerful, emotive and sometimes even deeply alarming. The former CIA chief R. James Woolsey, for example, claimed that it was 'naive' for the proposed takeover to be seen as just a narrowly commercial matter that bore no relation to any secret Chinese strategy to dominate the world's energy markets. Rep. Duncan Hunter, the chairman of the House Armed Services Committee, wanted to introduce a bill to block the purchase because China, as a significant provider of natural gas to Southeast Asia and a primary investor in pipelines that cross Azerbaijan, Georgia and Turkey, 'would dramatically increase its leverage over these countries and therefore its leverage over US interests in those regions' as a result of the purchase. Others labelled the bid as 'disastrous' for America and 'a wake-up call' for Washington, and suggested that the president should devote all his attention to preventing it.[3] After these very powerful calls were made, the House of Representatives overwhelmingly issued a statement saying that the sale would 'threaten to impair the national security of the United States'.

In the United States there is of course nothing new about Sinophobia. The fall of the Chinese mainland to Mao's forces in 1949 had devastated the morale of a US administration that was committed to containing communism, while the invasion of Korea the following year and the subsequent insurgencies in Southeast Asia in the decades that followed appeared to vindicate the worst fears of an organized communist conspiracy to undermine the free world. Tensions between the two countries also particularly rankled over the official legal status of Taiwan, which Beijing has regarded as a 'renegade province' ever since it was torn from China after its defeat by Japan in 1895, and where the remnants of anti-communist forces had fled, out of Mao's reach, in 1949. This has meant that America's subsequent support for Taiwan's government, which it is legally bound to defend under the US–Taiwan Relations Act, has always been harshly condemned by Beijing as 'interference': Wen Jiabao has angrily argued, for example, that 'solving the Taiwan question is an entirely internal affair and brooks no interference by any outside forces', while China's top arms negotiator, Sha Zukang, has previously angrily blasted Washington by claiming in almost hysterical tones that 'Taiwan is the territory of China but some people treat it as one of their states which is most ridiculous! It is a part of China ... it is none of your business!'[4]

But by 2001, as the new Bush administration took office promising to change American policy towards China from one of 'strategic partnership' – a term used by the Clinton administration – to that of a 'strategic competitor', it was not so much Taiwan or any ideological threat from communism that made the fire of the Chinese dragon look so dangerous. By this time what lay at the root of American fears of China was its rapid and massive economic growth, growth that many people felt sure would allow Beijing to soon challenge the various types of 'hard power', outlined in Chapter 1, that Washington has exerted unchallenged since the fall of the Soviet Union in the early 1990s. For any state that possesses such massive strength can not only create a large and well-equipped military force and sustain a protracted war effort but can also offer subsidies and access to its domestic market that effectively buys the loyalty of other countries. It is this stark reality that lies behind the dark American prophecies of the 'peer competitor'[5] status that China currently looks set to acquire, which has also prompted some academic commentators to draw a comparison with imperial Germany in the run-up to the First World War and which has caused a respected Sinologist to claim that 'sooner or later, if present trends continue, war is probable in Asia'.[6]

As things stand, China looks to be well on course to present a longer-term challenge of this sort to Washington. By September 2005 China already was the fourth largest economy in the world, with foreign trade worth $851 million, and the OECD predicted that by the end of the decade it would have overtaken Britain, France and Italy to become the third largest economy in the world and that it could even push the American economy into second place sometime around the year 2050. This estimate is based on China's staggering rate of growth over the previous decade or so, which the OECD proclaimed as an 'extraordinary economic performance, ... one of the most sustained and rapid economic transformations seen in the world economy in the past 50 years'. In both 2003 and 2004, for example, the growth rate of its GDP had hovered around the 9.5 per cent mark, forcing the Beijing central bank in October 2004 to increase its core interest rates for the first time in nine years while the outside world stood back and watched with awe. This strength has appeared all the more awesome since in the course of the last few years it is Chinese growth that has bankrolled America's ballooning trade deficit, helping keep the US economy afloat.

But American fears of a 'Chinese Peril' are based not just on any supposed future economic growth in its own right but also on its strategic implications. Military analysts point out that even if the rate of Chinese economic growth proves to be much lower than the OECD estimates, then the size and power of its armed forces will nonetheless still increase considerably, presenting the United States with a challenge that it simply cannot afford to ignore. Such fears have been further heightened by the studies of the leading RAND group of defence analysts, which has estimated that by the year 2015 China's military expenditure will be six times greater than Japan's, and have been shared and expressed by US Defense Secretary Donald Rumsfeld, who said during a visit to China in October 2005 that Beijing's high level of defence expenditure 'raises some questions about whether China will make the right choices, choices that will serve ... regional peace and stability'.[7] Five months earlier, Rumsfeld had also challenged Beijing to explain why it is increasing its military expenditure even though it currently faces no major strategic threat.

If any single issue is likely to spark military confrontation with America or her regional allies, it is China's future demand for oil. One American study, prepared for the US Defense Secretary and published in January 2005 by the consulting firm Booz Allen Hamilton, has already clearly pointed to the tensions that will arise as Beijing seeks to guard its future sources of supply and starts deploying its military forces to stake out new ones. Pointing to what it termed Beijing's 'string of pearls' strategy, the report emphasized that 'China is building strategic relationships along the vital sea lanes, along which cargo is moved from the Middle East to the South China Sea, in ways that suggest defensive and offensive positioning to protect China's energy interests but also to serve broad security objectives'.[8] This particular strategy, continued the report, affected a number of countries. The Chinese were reportedly making a bid to build a container port facility at Chittagong, Burma, for example, and had built naval bases and communication facilities on islands in the Bay of Bengal and near the Straits of Malacca, through which most of China's imported oil passes. Beijing had also signed a military agreement in November 2003 with Cambodia to provide training and equipment, and was also considering helping the Thai government to fund the construction of a $20 billion canal across the Kra Isthmus that would allow ships to bypass the Straits of Malacca.

Beijing's tactic of using military force to guard its supplies of oil makes prophecies of future conflict with the United States seem not altogether far-fetched. The CIA has already drawn a portrait of a future 'energy war' between China and Japan, two neighbouring powers with a massive thirst for oil, but even if such a nightmare scenario never becomes reality, China's economic growth has caused a deep sense of alarm in Washington circles simply because it threatens America's own future supplies. For with the US expected to import 17.52 million barrels of oil every day by 2020[9] – an increase from around 12 million in 2005 – at the same time as the world's resources will almost certainly be dwindling, the Americans will face much greater competition than ever before to find secure sources of long-term supply.

China will undoubtedly prove to be a much stronger competitor than most, since its thirst for oil is growing fast. The raw statistics speak for themselves. By 2004 China's daily demand for oil was already 6.5 million barrels, and its economy, which in that year accounted for 40 per cent of total growth in world oil demand,[10] had by this time already overtaken Japan as the world's second largest oil market after the United States. And with this demand still growing annually at a rate of 15 per cent, China is also projected to import more than 75 per cent of its oil requirements by the year 2020.[11] The strength of this demand has already had an important impact on America in particular and on the wider world, since by 2005 much of the surplus oil produced by OPEC was being shipped to the Far East rather than Europe or the US, thereby putting considerable pressure on supply and helping push up prices. 'China's energy needs are going to be enormous in the future,' the State Department's Assistant Secretary for East Asia and the Pacific, Christopher Hill, told a Senate Foreign Relations Committee in June 2005, 'and the question is, are they looking to develop energy or are they looking to take it off the market?' When the cost of fuel at the high-street petrol pumps soared in the summer of 2005 and consumers suddenly heard more than ever about China, Hill's words seemed far from hollow.

This thirst for energy supplies has come about partly because of a massive rise in China's population, which drastic measures have so far been unable to restrain. Its population is officially said to be 1.3 billion but is probably far more. But the essential reason is the country's economic growth, which has generated a huge demand for oil and gas in industry, notably in the trans-portation and petrochemical sectors, as well as the much higher consumer expectations that are always raised by any increase in the standard of living. In recent years the strength of this demand has doubtless also been boosted by a dramatic increase in air travel, the existence of price controls that ignore or even encourage the uneconomic use of fuel and by a sudden surge in the number of car owners: 'China and India together are a third of humanity, and they don't want to ride bicycles anymore,' Anne Korin, the co-direc-tor of the Institute for the Analysis of Global Security in Washington, has said. 'Their transportation demand, which is to say their oil consumption, is growing at a phenomenal rate.'[12]

Why, though, can't China meet its own energy needs?

China's increasing demand for oil and gas

One hot afternoon in June 2004, a Western businessman seized a chance to look at a giant clothing factory – one of China's largest – in Ningbo, a coastal city in Zhejiang province. But as he looked inside, he was astonished to see only a small number of workers, around 50 or so, huddled together in just one isolated corner, all of them doing little more than cutting out a few patterns from some old material, while the rest of the vast factory floor was pitch black, still and eerily silent.[13] This was hardly how he or anyone else had imagined the Chinese economic miracle in action.

All 6,000 workers, it turned out, had been sent home for the simple reason that there was no electric power to keep the factory running. For during that long, hot summer, the Chinese authorities had at times placed heavy restrictions on the use of electrical power by industry, often forcing businesses throughout the country to cease work for up to four days a week and instead switch to night-time operations. 'Even now, we still suspend production on Thursdays due to power shortages,' sighed Zhang Fan, the general manager of a furniture factory run by the Xiamen Polo Metal Industrial Company, a firm in southern China which supplies Wal-Mart stores, among other American retailers, and which was hoping to boost production of such items as computer desks by 30 per cent in the course of 2005. 'We hope the local government can boost the power supply next year.'[14]

China had at one time been kept largely self-sufficient in oil through the output of the massive Daqing oil field in the northeast of the country, which had been discovered in the late 1950s and heavily exploited ever since. Even today it continues to provide a daily output of 900,000 barrels out of the country's total production of around 3.6 million. But whereas until the early 1980s China had been East Asia's largest oil exporter, by the early 1990s there were signs of a growing energy crisis, as a sharp increase in demand coincided with a slowing rate of domestic production caused by the exhaustion of some of the major oil fields, coupled with a lack of any large new discoveries. In 1993, as consumption grew by nearly 18 per cent but production increased by less than 3 per cent, China was forced to import 309,000 b/d of both crude and refined oil and by doing so became, for the first time, a net importer of oil. The Beijing authorities made considerable efforts to bridge the growing gulf between supply and demand by boosting domestic production, particularly in the deep wells of the South China Sea, and by 1996 had succeeded in orchestrating an increase of 5 per cent, which was equivalent to 150,000 b/d. But with an outdated infrastructure that is estimated to need perhaps $1.4 trillion of investment by the year 2020 if it is to allow any real increase in output, the Chinese were by this time becoming inescapably dependent on oil imports.

The Beijing regime is particularly keen to make less use of oil and more of natural gas, which they are seeking to raise from the current level of around 2.5 per cent of total demand to 8 per cent by 2010, and to this end have made substantial efforts to import much more liquefied gas than ever before. Besides seeking to use pipelines to link up with the Russian natural gas grid in Siberia, the Chinese are currently importing considerable quantities of LNG from Australia and Indonesia, which are fed into new receiving terminals based in Guangdong, Fujian and Zhejiang provinces, and are now preparing to build more of these terminals along parts of its coast where imported gas is transformed back to natural gas from its liquefied form before being supplied to local markets. In 2004, for example, CNOOC signed an agreement to build a $1.7 billion LNG-receiving terminal in East China's Zhejiang province which could handle as much as 3 million tons of LNG imports annually.

By the late 1990s, as their economy steamed ahead and their demand for crude oil grew annually by 9 per cent, the Chinese were looking with a needy eye at foreign sources of supply. Beijing had already made moves to boost the imbalance between supply and demand by cutting tariffs on oil products from 12 per cent to 3 per cent and by investing heavily in its oil refineries. But Oil Ministry officials also sought to establish close links with international suppliers, and by 2005 had signed deals to invest in oil production facilities in places as far apart as Algeria, Canada, Gabon, Russia, Ecuador and Sudan, while also looking to countries such as Australia, Brazil, Jamaica, Papua New Guinea, Peru, Zambia and Canada. Beijing has also been particularly keen to identify and fill gaps in the market that have been left wide open by the absence of American competition, and this emphasis has led them to places such as Burma, Sudan and Venezuela. Most of all, however, it has driven them into the arms of a supplier that is much nearer than any of these others, Iran, whose vast oil supplies are the driving force that also lies behind the newly emergent Beijing–Tehran axis.

The Beijing–Tehran axis

The commercial alliance between Beijing and Tehran really dates back to the mid-1990s. From this time, it is fair to say that Iran has been helping China mount a challenge to American global pre-eminence in two distinct ways, partly by helping to fuel Beijing's long-term strategic challenge to the United States but also because, even if China never becomes Washington's 'peer competitor', its existing demand for oil and gas would still give its rulers good reason to go against American policy towards Tehran and do their own thing instead.

In the mid-1990s there was a sudden leap in Chinese imports of Iranian oil from just 0.5 million barrels in 1992 to 16.87 million in 1994. Two years later the figure had jumped again, this time to 26.43 million, and by 2004 Iran had become China's second largest energy supplier by providing 14 per cent of its gross oil imports in 2003.[15] Beijing was at this time also preparing to import huge quantities of liquid natural gas, and in April 2004 a Chinese firm clinched a deal, due to start in 2008, to export more than $20 billion worth of Iranian LNG into its home market.[16] 'Japan is our number one energy importer for historical reasons,' Iranian Oil Minister Bijan Zanganeh told *China Business Weekly* in November 2004, 'but we would like to give preference to exports to China.'

Chinese oil companies have also won numerous other deals to develop Iran's oil sector: as Ali Akbar Salehi, Iran's former representative to the IAEA, has said, 'we [Iran and China] complement each other. The Chinese have the industry and the Iranians have the energy resources.' In 2000 two subsidiaries of the Chinese National Petroleum Corporation (CNPC) were awarded a major contract to work with two Iranian organizations to develop the Tabnak field, where by the end of 2003 they had constructed five deep production wells. In September 2004 CNPC also took over the operation of the Masjid-i-Suleiman field by buying out the existing contractor, the Cyprus-based subsidiary of Canada's Sheer Energy, which two years previously had been awarded an $88 million redevelopment contract aimed at raising the field's output by an extra 20,000 b/d. The state-owned China Petrochemical Corporation, usually known simply as Sinopec, has also scored other successes in Iran, not only having won a massive contract to develop Iran's vast Yadavaran oil field[17] near the Iraqi border but also by drilling a new high-yield oil–gas well during venture prospecting in the country's Kashan oil field in December 2004. The International Oil Prospecting and Exploitation Corporation within Sinopec has not only taken part in the bidding for the exploitation rights of 16 new fields but at the end of 2004 was invited to bid for a part of the Azadegan project.

The Iranians have also given a strong welcome to China's new presence in its natural gas sectors. 'All Chinese companies are welcome to market Iranian LNG,' a vice-president in the Tehran regime, Mohammed Sattarifar, announced on 12 April 2004; 'both China and Iran see each other as long-term partners. Iran takes China as an energy market while China can take Iran as a long-term energy supplier. We hope to strengthen our cooperation in exploring and developing oil and natural gas fields and oil refinery too.' The Iranians are particularly keen that China will be the biggest single buyer of its liquefied natural gas and hope to begin supplying them in the course of 2007: 'we are hoping and expecting China to be the number one buyer of Iran's gas in LNG form as well,' Mohammad Souri, chairman of the National Iranian Tanker Company, has said, 'and we hope China will consider buying up to 10 million tonnes of LNG from Iran.' Moreover, besides striking agreements to explore, develop and produce Iranian oil and gas, the Chinese have also secured important downstream deals. In January 2001, for example, NIOC awarded a $150 million contract to Sinopec for the upgrading of its northern refineries at Tehran and Tabriz and for the construction of an oil terminal at the Caspian Sea port of Neka. Other deals in the 'wider' Iranian energy market have included orders to build large-capacity oil tankers that can carry 300,000 DWT (deadweight tons) of crude oil.

China's stake in Iranian energy resources has been part and parcel of a much wider political relationship that has been growing equally fast. In June 2000 President Mohammad Khatami's six-day trip to China broke diplomatic ice, while in August the following year China's People's Daily reported that Iran's ambassador to China, Mohammad Hossein Malaek, had held a reception in Beijing to mark 'the 30th anniversary of the establishment of diplomatic relations between Iran and China'. In March 2002 a member of China's State Council, Wu Yi, made a visit to Iran to meet President Khatami with a view to improving trade and economic ties, and in April was followed by the Chinese President Jiang Zemin, whose visit to Tehran was only the second such trip by a Chinese head of state since the Islamic revolution in 1979. Hailed by some commentators as 'a turning point' in Sino-Iranian ties because it came less than three months after President Bush had made a landmark speech accusing Iran of being part of an 'axis of evil', it also gave the leaders of both countries an opportunity to further develop relations. Jiang and Khatami signed six agreements on economic, scientific and cultural cooperation as they started a new round of talks on bilateral ties as well as on regional developments, while Iran's head of the Chamber of Commerce, Ali Naqi Khamushi, signed another deal with his Chinese counterpart on the establishment of a joint council on commerce between the two countries. Such ties followed in a long tradition, or so both parties claimed: 'our forefathers began friendly exchanges through the world-famous Silk Road more than 2,000 years ago,' the conservative *Tehran Times* quoted Jiang as saying in April 2002.

By the time that Foreign Minister Kamal Kharrazi travelled to Beijing in August 2003 for more talks on 'transportation, the construction of dams, power plants, petrochemical industry along with gas and oil projects', bilateral trade between the two countries had increased fast, with the volume of trade by this time reaching some $3.3 billion, several times higher than a decade before. In November 2005 the Chinese ambassador to Tehran, Lio G Tan, said that this trade volume was expected to reach $10 billion by the end of the year, which was a very considerable increase over the previous year, with the trade balance being strongly in Iran's favour. But although recent official trade statistics have put China in sixth place behind Germany and several other Western European countries among importers into Iran, the real figure is probably considerably higher and in 2004 was estimated to stand much closer to $7 billion. The Chinese have invested particularly heavily in Iran's fish canneries, sugar refineries, paper mills and mining sector while also becoming a major exporter of manufactured goods, including computer systems, household appliances and cars, into the Iranian market.

Although it is oil that lies at the heart of this newly emerging axis between the two countries, other commonalities have helped to reinforce it. China and Iran appear to have remarkably similar views on a number of foreign policy issues, such as the situation in the Middle East, Afghanistan and Central Asia, and both advocate the need for a 'multi-polar' international community that would challenge the strength of American global

influence. These shared concerns emerged clearly enough in talks that were
held in April 2002, when Jiang Zemin stressed that China is pursuing policies to create 'a peaceful global environment' and voiced Beijing's opposition to any country's expansionist tendencies. Describing Iran's efforts to
reinforce peace and stability in the war-shattered Afghanistan as 'positive',
and stressing that all of Afghanistan's neighbours welcomed peace, stability
and sustained development in that country, he also argued that 'China has
always supported the just demands of Arab nations, including Palestine, for
sovereignty, territorial integrity' and made a pledge to try and broker peace
through international diplomatic channels. Such sentiments have also been
echoed by other Beijing officials, such as the Chinese ambassador to Iran,
Sun Bi Gan, who has told state-run Tehran television that 'China supports
a multi-polar world, is critical of Israeli killings and believes peace in the
Middle East will not be achieved without the materialization of the rights
of Palestinians, including withdrawal of Israeli troops from occupied territo-
ries', adding that such shared concerns would help Iran and China to 'revive
their golden Silk Road ties'.[18]

But although there are some other shared interests and perspectives, none
of them play a role as decisive as Iranian oil, the lure of which really stands
behind the new Beijing–Tehran axis, and is now powering the Chinese challenge to American global power and influence. But what happens if we just
suppose that Beijing poses no such long-term threat and it is instead a strictly
non-aligned state which has nothing but the most peaceful and neutralist
intentions?

In this situation Iran's oil still presents a different type of challenge to
America because China's economy, even if we just imagine it growing at a
very steady rate, would still have great need for Iran's natural resources, and
its businesses would still be as keen as ever to exploit the considerable market
opportunities that Iran offers. This alone gives the Chinese less reason than
ever before to strike deals with Washington. But has there hitherto been
any conspicuous sign that the lure of Iranian natural resources has already
undermined America's influence on Beijing?

China and US power

The emergence of this new alliance between China and Iran has occasionally prompted some loud but futile noises of protest from an anguished Bush
administration. As Sinopec continued its negotiations with Tehran on the
Yadavaran deal in early 2004, for example, officials at the US embassy in
Beijing reportedly contacted the company's local officials and demanded that
Sinopec withdraw its bid, thereby prompting the Chinese press to report and
retort that 'Sinopec is paying no attention to the US request and will do

its utmost to carry on its bidding for an exploitation project in an Iranian oil field'.[19] And a year later, on 18 March 2005, the Iranian ambassador to China, Fereydoun Verdinejad, pointed out that with the Chinese involved in more than 100 major projects in Iran and with the value of economic transactions between the two countries hitting the $7 billion mark, Washington's protests would only fall on deaf Chinese ears: 'despite some countries' pressures on both Iran and China,' he announced with an unmistakable swipe at Washington, such protests 'could not affect bilateral ties'.

Much more important than any effort to cancel individual deals, however, have been American moves to line the Chinese government up against Tehran over particularly important matters, most notably the Iranian nuclear dispute. But as the issue gathered pace in the autumn of 2005, China's president, Hu Jintao, declined to back any US–EU move to refer Iran straight to the UN Security Council or, if it was referred, threatened to use its veto as a permanent member of the Council to stop any subsequent resolution in its tracks. Jintao is reported to have made such views clear to President Bush during a meeting earlier in the month, while Chinese Foreign Minister Li Zhaoxing told European diplomats at the United Nations that it would be 'counter-productive' and 'not constructive' to refer Iran to the UN because such a move would instead merely 'encourage Iran to take extreme measures'.[20] Instead Vice-President Zeng Qinghong, speaking in Beijing during a two-day visit to the Chinese capital by Iranian Foreign Minister Manouchehr Mottaki in mid-October, simply reaffirmed that 'China hopes that Iran, the EU and other relevant sides maintain patience, show flexibility and take concrete and practical steps to break the stalemate and promptly resume dialogue, consultation and negotiations'.

By the end of November, US and EU diplomats were admitting defeat in their struggle to secure Chinese, and Russian, support of an IAEA resolution that would refer Iran to the UN: 'there will be no resolution for sure. The Russians and Chinese oppose this,' an EU diplomat told Reuters on 21 November. This was one reason why Washington appeared to bow to pressure and suddenly back a Russian proposal to allow Iran the right to enrich uranium but carry out some of the more sensitive parts of the process on Russian territory.

Over the months that followed, Washington's fears proved well founded. Although Beijing proved cooperative in trying to rein in Tehran's nuclear ambitions, supporting the IAEA's referral on 4 February and endorsing a UN 'presidential statement' of 28 March that expressed 'serious concern' about Iran's nuclear violations, the Chinese refrained from taking the serious action that the US wanted. But Li Zhaoxing, the Chinese Foreign Minister, who was also busy concluding the Yadavaran deal that had been originally struck in October 2004 and which was now being finalized, repeatedly appealed for 'more time for diplomacy' and distanced himself from the veiled threats his Western counterparts were voicing. 'I think, as a matter of principle, China never supports sanctions as a way of exercising pressure because it is always the people that would be hurt,' Wang Guangya, China's ambassador to the UN, put it. His approach exasperated his Western counterparts who wanted some commitment to economic sanctions if all else failed, and forced Condoleezza Rice to admit that US diplomacy had to 'walk a fine line' between respecting Chinese economic interests on the one hand, and the need to build a united international front against Tehran on the other.

In Washington it is often said that by protecting Iran against the imposition of sanctions, China is putting a concern for its own oil supplies ahead of the considerations that really matter. Beijing is being enticed by 'the short-term attractions of currying favour with a potential ally, one increasingly important in terms of China's growing need for oil,' Henry Hyde, the chairman of the US House International Relations Committee, said in December 2004. Of course such claims are hotly contested in Beijing: 'this criticism is invalid,' retorted Liu Jianchao, a spokesman for the Chinese Foreign Ministry; 'we object to this characterization and find it insulting', adding that his government was adamantly opposed to the proliferation of weapons of mass destruction. But such simple denials cannot fail to sound hollow when they are weighed against the raw statistics of China's oil dependency on Iran. And in June 2004 Chris Hill, the Assistant Secretary of State for East Asian and Pacific affairs, told a subcommittee of the House of Representatives that a major task for the US and its Asian allies was 'to ensure that in its search for resources and commodities to gird its economic machinery, China does not underwrite the continuation of regimes that pursue policies seeking to undermine rather than sustain the security and stability of the international community'.

Of course the role of Iranian oil in explaining the gulf between Beijing and Washington should be seen in perspective. This is not just for the obvious reason that there had of course been mistrust and sometimes hostility between them long before any real ties were established between China and Iran, but also because there are other very important issues over which the Chinese authorities are prepared to openly challenge Washington's preferred course of action. One contemporaneous example is the way in which Beijing threatened to block a strong UN resolution, put forward in September 2004, that condemned the genocide in Sudan. Such a resolution could have imposed economic sanctions on the Sudanese government and therefore threaten China's $3 billion investment in the energy infrastructure of a country that supplies 7 per cent of Chinese oil imports. Another such issue is North Korea, for in the spring of 2003 American moves to secure a UN resolution and the imposition of economic sanctions against Pyongyang in retaliation for its renunciation of the 1968 Non-Proliferation Treaty were vetoed by China. Yet so vital will Iranian oil be to China in the years ahead that Sino-American disputes over how to deal with Tehran are nonetheless set to become particularly important.

Another reason why the influence of Iran, for the moment at least, should not be exaggerated is that China's trade with the United States far outweighs its commerce with Iran. In the last ten years, China's exports to the US have risen from a relatively meagre $35 billion to $200 billion, and, put in such stark terms, Beijing cannot afford to sacrifice its American ties at the altar of doing business with Tehran. But over the coming years its increasing dependency on imported oil will be one of the factors that erodes the weight of such crude, raw statistics.

But while it is possible to exaggerate the degree to which Iran's resources have created or sustained the strategic gulf between Beijing and Washington, America's influence over Iran has undoubtedly been undermined by China's support for the Tehran regime.

Undermining US power over Iran

When on 17 September 2005 President Ahmadinejad stood up before the United Nations General Assembly and advocated his country's nuclear cause, his strident and aggressive tone took the watching world wholly by surprise. Rather than making any real effort to move the negotiations on the nuclear issue forward, he instead aired grievances relating to events that had taken place more than half a century before, discussed his personal conspiracy theory about the terrorist attacks of 11 September 2001 and openly accused the United States of creating and supporting the Al Qaeda terrorist network. The new president also called for a Middle East free of nuclear weapons, pointing a highly accusatory finger at Israel in doing so, while blasting the state of 'nuclear apartheid' that he claimed had come about. Ahmadinejad also asserted with unhesitating verve an Iranian right and ambition to develop its own nuclear-fuel cycle, offering to strike up a 'serious partnership' with other countries that were willing to help him do so.

So what lay behind this new audacity, which contrasted with the relatively tranquil and conciliatory tone adopted by Iranian negotiators in October 2003 or November 2004? Partly it was because Ahmadinejad and the mullahs knew that the Americans were tied down more than ever before by the fast-growing Iraqi insurgency, which by this time was no longer seen by many people as just a fight with 'terrorists' but rather as an all-out civil war with clear parallels to the Vietnam War. With its armed forces so severely overstretched, it certainly seemed difficult to imagine the Americans taking any military action against Iran, particularly when any assault on Iran would have incited reprisals – whether spontaneous attacks or those incited by Tehran – against American targets inside Iraq and elsewhere.

There were other reasons too. In October 2003 the Iranians had been deeply worried about the discovery by IAEA inspectors of traces of enriched uranium at Kalaye and Natanz, but two years on were feeling much more confident: 'they had convinced themselves that the inspectors had not found any more damaging facts and would therefore not find any grounds for "non-compliance",' a senior European diplomat told me in November 2005, adding that 'they also made the mistake of thinking that the IAEA's rules are much more black and white than they really are, whereas in fact board members have much more freedom than that to interpret them as they think fit'.

Another reason for such strong Iranian defiance was the dramatic rise in the price of oil over the preceding two years or so, with the price of a barrel of crude leaping from under $25 in September 2003 to the record price of just over $70 that the markets briefly touched on 11 August 2005. As the US administration took emergency measures and met with Saudi leaders to discuss levels of output, any threats of economic sanctions must have sounded hollow to the mullahs as they tuned their sensitive antennae into the fast-changing wavelengths of world political opinion.

But perhaps the most important single reason was that the Iranians had been emboldened by their newly founded relationship with China, whose support of Iran in the event of any dispute with Washington would be hugely important. At a diplomatic level Beijing could most obviously use its veto as a permanent member of the UN Security Council to torpedo any attempt to impose economic sanctions, and Chinese diplomats have certainly signalled unmistakably that they will not support any such moves. During a visit to Tehran in November 2004, Foreign Minister Li Zhaoxing had made clear that because he did not regard the Iranian nuclear programme as a matter for the UN he therefore saw 'no reason' not to keep it within the remit of the IAEA.

But even if we suppose that such economic sanctions were ever imposed on Tehran, with or without UN sanction, then Chinese demand for oil could conceivably still allow the Iranian economy to survive. Although in 2004 the Iranians exported 370,000 barrels to China every day, out of its daily total 2.5 million, the Chinese could easily increase their intake by a considerable amount. Moreover the Iranians could also foster relationships with some of China's other regional economic allies in the Shanghai Cooperation Organization (SCO), which was formally created in 2001 to promote the mutual interests of its member states. Originally dubbed the 'Shanghai Five', the group now includes China, Russia, Tajikistan, Kazakhstan, Kyrgyzstan and Uzbekistan, which all share the same wish to increase cooperation on political, diplomatic, economic and commercial issues. Iran was formally appointed as an observer of the SCO in July 2005. The potential threat to American regional dominance posed by the SCO briefly emerged on 15 June 2006, when President Ahmadinejad addressed its members during a week-long meeting and called for 'cooperation' against the 'threats' posed by 'domineering powers'. The speech heightened concern in Washington that the SCO is emerging as an anti-US bloc.

Besides finding such strong diplomatic and economic support, China is also in a position to offer Iran the up-to-date military support that would help deter any possible American or Israeli military attack on its nuclear infrastructure. In the past Beijing has certainly proved willing to provide Iran with some of the raw materials it needs to build a nuclear bomb, having helped its development of a 300–330 Mw reactor and having sold hundreds of tons of the anhydrous hydrogen fluoride that is used to enrich uranium. Of more immediate use to the Iranians, however, is China's strong support in supplying the aerospace and satellite technology that could be used in Iran's long-range missile programme, support that has also been a cause of particular concern to Washington. In April 2004, as the CIA reported to Congress that China was 'helping Iran move towards its goal of becoming self-sufficient in the production of ballistic missiles', the Bush administration invoked the Iran Non-Proliferation Act of 2000 to impose new sanctions against some of those companies – notably China North Industries and China Precision Machinery Import/Export Corporation – that were thought to be responsible. According to the sanctions announcement, the penalties were imposed because of 'the transfer to Iran of equipment and technology controlled under multilateral export control lists … or otherwise having the potential to make a material contribution to the development of weapons of mass destruction (WMD) or cruise or ballistic missile systems'. The sanctions were invoked after reports were published by a leading journal, *Aviation Week and Space Technology*, that Iran was developing a new, long-range cruise missile that was very clearly based on the Chinese Silkworm airframe.

But American pressure has not deterred either country from making moves to cement their growing military relationship. In August 2005, for example, Iran hosted a Chinese military delegation whose task was to help pave the way for much wider cooperation in the defence field. Citing Brigadier General Nasser Mohammadi-Far, the commander of the Iranian army's ground forces, a state-run news agency in Tehran announced that the dele-

gation had arrived for talks on 'developing military relations, deepening
bilateral ties and paving the way for military cooperation' and to 'upgrade
defence and military technology' in order to deter 'mutual enemies [who]
possess advanced military technology, and [who] would undoubtedly rely on
this technology in any possible future wars'.[21] The head of the Chinese delegation, Lieutenant General Zoa Nekoen, expressed his gratitude for being
given the opportunity to meet Iranian military officials: 'Iran and China
have always had close bonds in various arenas and maintained this prox-
imity throughout history and the two countries also have common goals,'
he said on 17 August, while Mohammadi-Far returned the compliment by
claiming that 'the excellent discipline in the Chinese Army is one of the
most illustrious characteristics of the country'.

In the longer term it is also possible that the new Tehran–Beijing axis
could herald the emergence of an even larger military coalition in which
Russia could join Iran and China in a bid to thwart any future American
expansion in the region. In 2005 there had certainly been some signs that
a Sino-Russian alliance was emerging, when in August the two countries
carried out a week-long joint military exercise on China's Shandong peninsula. This 'Peace Mission 2005' operation, which was described by the
participants only as an 'anti-terrorism exercise', attracted little attention in
the American media, coinciding as it did with Hurricane Katrina's devastation of Louisiana and New Orleans, but was considered by the experts who
monitored it to be hugely important. 'The scale of the operation suggests
something more than anti-terrorism, as was claimed,' argued Stephen Blank,
a professor at the Strategic Studies Institute of the US Army War College,
who pointed out that the number of soldiers involved – nearly 10,000 troops
– and the nature of the exercises they undertook, which involved amphibi-
ous landings on a theoretically hostile coast and mass drops of more than
1,000 paratroops, were more akin to a dress rehearsal for a possible future
Chinese invasion of Taiwan.[22]

Viewed in these terms, it seems that, more than a decade and a half
after the end of the Cold War, Russia is still antithetic towards American
global influence, even if not a longer-term rival to seize Washington's crown.
But although this antithesis also has much deeper causes, in the same way
that is true of China's relations with Washington, Iran's energy also helps to
explain it.

Russia

Being endowed with vast quantities of both oil and natural gas that it exports
into many international markets, Russia's strong interest in Iran's energy
sector clearly does not reflect, unlike that of many other countries, any

dependency on the import of its resources. Instead the Russian government has long suffered from a desperate need for the foreign exchange and taxable revenues that its business can earn from lucrative contracts to develop Iran's energy infrastructure and from the wider market opportunities in Iran that are created, to an important degree, by the proceeds of the sale of oil. Yet these pressing economic demands have in recent years led to some serious disputes with Washington in a way that has further undermined America's political grip over both Moscow and Tehran.

The strength of Russian interest in developing its ties with Iran became particularly clear in July 2002, when premier Mikhail Kasyanov approved a draft programme aimed at heightening mutual cooperation on commercial, economic, industrial, scientific and technical matters over the coming decade. These plans also included increasing productivity from existing oil wells as part of a project that was to be implemented by both the Russian oil company Slavneft and the National Iranian Drilling Corporation (NIDC), while Russian firms would also help to design, finance and construct the proposed Iran–India pipeline (see below). Furthermore Kasyanov was reported in the press to be considering 'other plans including conducting an examination into the Nurabad–Khasani oil pipeline as well as development of a project to carry Russian oil to Iran', while the two countries were also said to be planning to jointly build an underground gas storage facility as well as arrange the construction of some gas storage facilities near the cities of Tehran and Tabriz. Finally the programme included 'cooperation in oil refining [and] to improve technological processes at heavy oil refineries in Iran, build refining modules with a capacity of 25,000 b/d as well as create facilities for primary refining'.

This is the central political framework within which Russian companies have subsequently sought to secure some key contracts. Some of these have been mentioned earlier, most notably the joint venture to develop South Pars that was set up in 1997 between Total, Malaysia's Petronas and Russia's giant state-owned oil monopoly Gazprom. Another company with a particularly strong representation in Iran is Tatneft, which in January 2002 was awarded a lucrative contract for the supply and deployment of specialized equipment in the Kupal oil field and which has subsequently also struck separate deals to reconstruct wells on behalf of the Iranian Southern Petroleum Company and to survey both the high-density Zagdeh oil deposit in southern Iran and parts of the Ahwaz and Ramshir fields. In February 2005 Tatneft board chairman Rustam Minnikhanov and the director of an Iranian organization, the Mostazafan and Janbazan Foundation, Mohammad Foruzande, also formed a joint venture that would represent any future dealings in Iran by Russian companies. Overall, these various deals have brought both the companies and the Moscow tax collectors some handsome profits: Tatneft's contracts to survey Ahwaz and Ramshir were worth $808,000, and another deal to work with the Research Institute of Iran's Petroleum Industry was worth $740,000.

Of the numerous contracts on Iran's commercial horizon that Russian companies are currently making determined bids to win, first and foremost among them is the construction of the Iran–India pipeline. 'We are keen on participating in the Iran–India pipeline project,' the Russian Minister of Industry and Energy, Viktor Borisovich Khristenko, announced during negotiations with his Indian counterparts in early October 2005. Gazprom representatives have also previously held extensive talks with authorities in both Iran and India in order to win some involvement alongside the Indian Oil Corporation and Gail (India) Ltd in the international consortium that will lay sections of the link, and on 6 October a ten-member company delegation, led by Gazprom's chairman, Alexei Miller, visited Pakistan to begin discussions about joining this international venture. This was the first visit to Pakistan by the company's chief executive; five years earlier another visit had been cancelled at the eleventh hour owing to strong opposition from India, where President Vladimir Putin had at the time been paying an official visit. These October 2005 talks resumed an earlier dialogue that had been held the previous year between Alexei Miller and Pakistan's ambassador to Russia, Iftikhar Murshed, who also went on to sign a memorandum of understanding about the possibility of collaboration in the exploration and development of Pakistan's oil and natural gas fields and infrastructure.

There is also a much less direct way in which Iran's energy sector has aroused Russia's commercial interest. For as Chapter 4 points out, the sale of oil and gas has generated huge quantities of foreign exchange that have allowed the Tehran authorities to pursue an extremely expensive programme for nuclear energy, and this has in turn created some highly lucrative contracts that the Russians have been most anxious to win. In January 1995 Russian Atomic Energy Minister Viktor Mikhailov and the head of Iran's nuclear programme, Reza Amrollahi, signed an $800 million deal that gave Russia the right to complete one unit (1000 Mw) of the Bushehr energy reactor. Other huge deals also followed. On 25 December 2002, for example, the two countries signed a $1 billion agreement to speed up Bushehr's completion, which the Russians had initially undertaken to finish by the end of 2003 but which had fallen far behind schedule, and in February 2005 Moscow also struck a further $800 million deal to supply Bushehr with nuclear fuel, reassuring the outside world that the fuel would be returned to Russia straight after use and could not therefore be diverted to any other, more sinister use. Moscow has also benefited from plans to build more reactors, and during a summit between Vladimir Putin and Mohammad Khatami in March 2001, the Iranian premier confirmed plans to build a second civilian energy reactor, costing another $1 billion, that the Russians would help construct.

But when in July 2002 Moscow confirmed its willingness to complete four reactors at Bushehr by 2012 as well as two new 1 Gw nuclear units at Ahvaz, its announcement infuriated Washington. These deals, which were collectively worth around $3.2 billion, provoked a particularly angry American response because they flatly contradicted an earlier assurance by Atomic Energy Minister Alexander Rumyantsev, made less than a fortnight before, that Russia would limit its nuclear cooperation with Iran only to existing projects and saw 'no other future work with Iran besides this agreement'. On 30 July, as Moscow backtracked dramatically, State Department deputy spokesman Philip T. Reeker told reporters in Washington that 'we find it disturbing that Russia is considering assisting in the construction of additional reactors in Iran. We have talked about our concerns on this for some time and we have consistently urged Russia to cease all nuclear cooperation with Iran, including assistance on the reactor at Bushehr.'

Yet despite provoking harsh condemnation, Moscow has displayed scant regard for American wishes. Russian officials showed nothing but contempt and indignation when in August 2001 President Bush renewed ILSA's original five-year term. Citing Russian Foreign Ministry sources, Moscow's Interfax news agency argued on 4 August that the renewal was 'a mistake which may bring more difficulties to the life of the international community and to Russo-US relations in particular. The United States is once again trying to impose its internal laws upon the outside world and put pressure on other countries under an invented pretext. Moscow has cooperated and will continue cooperating with Tripoli and Tehran. Russia has its own economic interests in those states and pursuing them cannot damage any third party.'

American efforts to pressurize Moscow over Iran's nuclear programme have also met with particularly bloody-minded defiance from Russian Foreign Minister Sergei Lavrov, who on 16 October 2005 openly declared that no country will ever force Russia to abandon its nuclear commitment to Tehran. This uncompromising statement came one day after Condoleezza Rice failed to win Russian support for hauling Iran before the UN Security Council for possible sanctions. Lavrov instead argued that Iran had the same right as other countries to develop what he called 'peaceful nuclear energy' and reaffirmed Moscow's intention to continue helping Iran build a nuclear reactor near Bushehr. 'No one,' Lavrov added, 'including the United States, will challenge our right to continue building the atomic electricity station in Bushehr.'

Pipelines

There are a number of other ways in which Iranian oil and gas have altered Tehran's geopolitical relationship with Moscow. In particular, the Russian government regards Iran as an important transit point for crude oil that needs to be moved across the landlocked Caspian Sea, and this has led the two countries to arrange a series of 'swap' arrangements whereby Caspian oil is moved into Iran and then sent to northern Iraqi refineries while equivalent amounts are then exported from terminals on Iran's Persian Gulf coast. In March 2003, for example, Lukoil confirmed plans to sign a long-term contract with NIOC for the annual supply of 1 million tonnes of crude oil. Under this arrangement, oil produced by Lukoil's subsidiary, Nizhnevolzh-skneft, would be shipped from ports in Astrakhan and Volgograd to the Iranian Caspian port of Neka and fed to the markets 'in Iran's northern regions' through the Neka–Sari pipeline. Lukoil had already shipped a first consignment of 30,000 tonnes of oil and by the end of 2003 was supplying Iran with about 100,000 tonnes per month.

Besides seeking to export their own oil and gas through Iran, the Russian authorities also want to prevent some other countries from receiving Iran's own supplies, and Moscow is particularly concerned by the prospect of a new pipeline that could potentially carry as much as 706 billion cubic feet of Iranian gas to the Ukraine each year and perhaps eventually reach European markets. The Russian government has such strong objections to this proposal that its support for Iran over issues such as the nuclear dispute is probably intended to be a bargaining chip designed to dissuade Tehran from proceeding with the project.

The proposed new pipeline certainly has much to offer both Iran and the Ukraine. It would allow the Iranians to access the European market while bypassing Turkey, whose government has repeatedly obstructed the operation of the new Tabriz–Ankara natural gas pipeline that was first opened in 2002. The pipeline also offers the Ukraine an alternative source of gas supply that would elbow aside Gazprom, which directly supplies around 30 per cent of its demand and also controls the wider pipeline network across Turkmenistan along which another 45 per cent of Ukrainian gas imports have to move in order to reach their market. Overall this means that at least 75 per cent of the Ukraine's gas supplies are to some degree dependent on Gazprom, making the republic highly reliant on the goodwill of not just this gas company in particular but also of the Russian government that owns it. Since the 'Orange Revolution' in October 2004 brought a more pro-Western government to power, the Ukraine has attempted to loosen the energy supply noose that Russia has tied around its neck, and the challenge of lessening Gazprom's grip over all its energy supplies has become a matter of national security and sovereignty under President Viktor Yushchenko, who is seeking to wean his country from its dependence on Russia by diversifying its source of supplies.

The pipeline would damage Russian interests for more or less the same reasons as it would benefit the Ukraine. Gazprom has no interest either in allowing Iran to access a market that is traditionally in Russia's sphere of interest, or in letting it compete for a share in the massive and lucrative European market, and although it is keen to force the Ukraine into a more market-orientated, business-like trading relationship, replacing their current transit-for-supplies agreement with separate deals, it is not willing to do this at the expense of losing any business. For the Moscow authorities, the implications are just as alarming, because it would lose not just very large quantities of foreign exchange and taxable revenues but also the political leverage over the Ukraine exerted by its virtual monopoly of energy supply.

At present some tentative steps have been taken towards making the pipeline dream a reality. In July 2005, for example, officials from Nafto-gaz Ukrainy, the state-owned Ukrainian oil and gas holding, travelled to the Iranian capital and signed a memorandum of understanding with their Iranian counterparts. But opposition from both Turkey and Russia, along with the expected multi-billion-dollar cost of such a pipeline, estimated to be at least $5 billion, is likely to keep the idea on the shelf for the foreseeable future.

Undermining US leverage over Iran

Harbouring such strong economic interests in Iran, Moscow has been most reluctant to toe the Washington line by condemning Tehran's nuclear activities with a threat of sanctions, and this means that Iranian natural resources are undermining American power not just over Russia but also over the mullahs' regime.

This became clear during September 2005, when the US administration united with its European counterparts to demand an IAEA resolution that would refer, or threaten to refer, Iran to the UN Security Council. As Moscow insisted that it could never support any Iranian nuclear weapons programme and was only prepared to assist a peaceful programme of nuclear energy that it claimed posed no risk to the outside world, serious tension began to mount with the United States. Well before the key board meeting began, Foreign Minister Sergei Lavrov denounced such moves, arguing that 'while Iran is cooperating with the IAEA, while it is not enriching uranium and observing a moratorium, and while IAEA inspectors are working in the country, it would be counter-productive to report this question to the UN Security Council'. And in a speech at Stanford University on 22 September, he also claimed that 'it will lead to an unnecessary politicizing of the situation. Iran is not violating its obligations and its actions do not threaten the non-proliferation regime.' Iran's compliance, he continued, was instead an issue only for the IAEA's perusal and any UN referral would in all likelihood lead to 'unpredictable sentiments' and spark 'the radicalization of sentiment in Iran'.

During talks in Washington two weeks before the IAEA meeting, the two presidents, Vladimir Putin and George W. Bush, continued with their efforts to present a united front following their talks at the White House. But although both reiterated their commitment to preventing the mullahs from developing nuclear weaponry, their underlying differences quickly came to the surface. Proclaiming his confidence that 'the world will see to it that Iran goes to the UN Security Council if it does not live up to its agreements', President Bush clearly struck a very different note from his Russian counterpart, who said that Moscow would continue to cooperate in dealing with North Korea as well as supporting Iran's nuclear ambitions and claimed that diplomacy with both countries was far from being at an end: 'the potential of diplomatic solutions to all these questions is far from being exhausted and we will undertake all of the steps necessary to settle all of these problems and issues, not to aggravate them. We do not want our careless actions to lead to the development of events along the North Korean variant.' [23]

It was quite predictable that as the nuclear watchdog's meeting got under way, Russian delegates were immediately deadlocked in their talks with EU and US counterparts and were quite unable to agree on how to deal with the Iranian conundrum. Bowing to Russian and Chinese pressure, France, Britain and Germany were now forced to drop their initial demand to report Iran to the UN Security Council and instead drafted a new text, now much more diluted, declaring that Iran had only been in 'non-compliance' with the Non-Proliferation Treaty. But the Russians also rejected this second version, saying that Moscow would refuse to allow the issue to go before the Security Council at all: 'the Russians don't like it. They say it's a move in the right direction but not far enough,' one EU diplomat told Reuters on the sidelines of the IAEA board meeting, and Russia's subsequent statement to the IAEA board certainly made this position clear, claiming as it did that Moscow was 'decisively opposed to an artificial exacerbation of the situation, including the transfer of this question to the UN Security Council'. Moscow was in fact willing only to accept the revised draft if it removed any language that would oblige the 35-member IAEA board to report Iran to the Security Council, even though this was a 'non-negotiable' demand for the Europeans, who wanted the board to put on record that Iran had a long record of non-compliance with its treaty obligations.

Still disagreements persisted, as the Russians advocated giving the Iranians more scope to 'enrich' uranium than the Europeans wanted. Under the new plan, put forward by Moscow in late October 2005, Iran could conduct low-grade uranium processing work at its Isfahan uranium conversion plant, provided it agreed to fully suspend all other activities in line with the Paris Accords. Tehran would be granted the right to manufacture the uranium tetrafluorife (UF4) which would then be shipped to Russia for conversion into the more enriched uranium hexafluoride (UF6). This proposal found some support from some of the non-aligned countries on the IAEA board.

Although on 4 February 2006, Russia, along with China, had voted to support Iran's referral by the IAEA to the UN on condition that the resolution did not contain any immediate threat of sanctions, Russia's obstinacy remained as the nuclear issue reached New York. On 5 March a serious rift emerged when Moscow floated a last-minute proposal to allow Iran to make small quantities of nuclear fuel, threatening to undermine US attempts to rush Iran's case before the Security Council.[24] And although Russia, along with China, signed the 29 March UN 'presidential statement' that condemned Iranian behaviour, it made clear in unmistakable terms its very strong objections to economic sanctions. When Washington sought to obtain a resolution under Chapter 7 of the UN Charter – which makes any demands mandatory and paves the way for sanctions or force – some particularly angry exchanges took place between Condoleezza Rice and Russian Foreign Minister Sergei Lavrov, who attacked US policy and condemned a tough speech directed at Moscow by Dick Cheney.

India, Iran and the US

Like China and Pakistan, India's newly founded relationship with Iran is largely a product of its domestic energy crisis. Having experienced rapid economic growth throughout the past decade, with a staggering GDP growth of 8.2 per cent in 2003 and more than 6 per cent in each of the two years that followed, and with a dramatically increasing population, India's industrial and consumer demand for oil and gas is growing fast and shows no sign of slowing. It is widely reckoned to be the world's sixth largest consumer of oil, currently using up 2.4 million barrels every day, and its daily consumption of oil is expected to reach 2.8 million barrels by 2010. This contrasts sharply with its relatively meagre daily intake of just 474,000 barrels in 1973.

This increase in demand is not, however, likely to be met by any corresponding increase in production from its own fields. India does have some very substantial oil reserves of its own, amounting to a total of perhaps 5.8 billion barrels, although the real figure may perhaps be much higher. The offshore Mumbai High field is easily the country's largest producing field, whose average daily output of around 260,000 barrels comprises a large proportion of India's average national total of 819,000, and there are also some other large deposits in the Upper Assam, Cambay, Krishna-Godavari and Cauvery basins. Yet this overall output is unlikely to increase significantly over the coming decades and will certainly fall far short of the demands of a country that in 2003 had to import more than 1.4 million barrels of oil every day and which was by this time the world's ninth largest net importer of oil. In the future its dependency on imported oil is likely to dramatically increase, and some estimates have even projected a threefold increase by the year 2020.

Nor will India's own resources of natural gas suffice to meet its future needs. The country certainly has some very considerable indigenous reserves that are estimated to total around 25 trillion cf with perhaps many more large deposits still waiting to be unearthed. A major new discovery was made as recently as December 2002, when an Indian firm detected a new reserve in the Krishna-Godavari Basin that was estimated to contain around 7 trillion cf. But although both gas production and utilization have grown markedly since the early 1970s, its domestic consumption has since risen faster than that of any other fuel: from just 0.6 trillion cf in 1995, demand for natural gas reached 0.9 trillion cf in 2002 and is projected to continue growing at around 4.8 per cent each year before eventually reaching 1.6 trillion cf by 2015.[25]

Although India currently has 15 nuclear power stations and has another seven under construction, these meet only 2.7 per cent (3,300 Mw) of its overall energy needs. One of the main reasons for the slow growth of India's nuclear power programme is that, after its inception in the mid-1950s, it succeeded in attracting considerable animosity from the outside world, resulting in a highly effective international ban on the transfer of technology and assistance. Such restrictions have been made all the more effective because India has only a very limited supply of the high-quality nuclear fuel that every reactor is wholly dependent on in order to produce civilian energy.

With the domestic production of both oil and gas expected to satisfy only a small proportion of national demand, the Indian authorities have made their importation something of a priority, so much so that Prime Minister Manmohan Singh has publicly proclaimed that 'energy security is second only in our scheme of things to food security'. By 2005 Indian oil firms had, like their Chinese rivals, already been participating in projects very far from home – including Vietnam, Sudan, Russia, Iraq, Libya, Syria, Australia, the Ivory Coast, Qatar and Egypt – and were investigating opportunities in Venezuela, Kazakhstan, Kuwait, Yemen and numerous other countries. New Delhi has even tried to create a new energy forum – an 'Asian Oil Community' – and on 6 January 2005 invited representatives from a number of oil-producing countries, including Saudi Arabia, Kuwait, the Emirates, Oman and Qatar, to a Community conference in New Delhi to talk oil issues with officials from China, Japan and South Korea, the prime Asian consumers.

But although India has historically depended largely on imported crude oil, its officials are now putting much more emphasis than ever before on natural gas, which is regarded as less susceptible than oil to sudden price shocks as well as being a more environment-friendly, cost-effective and efficient fuel. This has prompted them to consider shipping LNG from places as far afield as Indonesia, or building overland pipelines with neighbouring or regional countries which have an abundant supply, notably Burma and Turkmenistan. But because the resources of these other countries have an unproven capacity, or because the construction of a pipeline would be fraught with risk – any link with Turkmenistan would have to cross a volatile and lawless Afghanistan – New Delhi has come to regard Iran as one of the most promising providers of its future energy requirements. For despite the distance between the two countries, vast quantities of Iranian oil and gas can still reach the Indian subcontinent either by tanker or by pipeline.

Growing Iran–India ties

The best-known and most contentious scheme to transport Iranian resources into the Indian market is the construction of a 2600km pipeline, costing $4.16 billion, that by 2010 could allow the Indians to import around 2 billion cubic feet of Iranian natural gas every day. By the end of 2005 the Indian authorities appeared ready to defy strong American pressure and start building the link in the course of the following year: 'there is simply no other way in which any other interested party could help us meet our energy needs,' Indian Oil Minister Mani Shankar Aiyar declared, 'and we are desperately foraging for energy wherever we can get it.'[26] Nor did American pressure deter Aiyar from issuing a joint statement on 7 June 2005 along with his Pakistani counterpart, Amanullah Khan Jadoon, arguing that 'the transnational pipeline projects should be given top priority as there would be substantial advantage to both countries in pursuing and realizing cooperation in these projects, to serve their energy security interests, and to create linkages and inter-dependencies for establishing an enduring relationship between the two countries'.

The story of the proposed Iran–India pipeline goes back to 1989, when the first serious proposal to export Iranian gas to the Indian subcontinent by land pipeline was presented to the Asian Energy Institute in New Delhi. But although several other international companies, such as Broken Hill Petroleum, soon picked up the idea and put forward their own proposals, all stumbled over the same political obstacle: such a link would have to cross Pakistani territory and therefore make India dependent on the goodwill of a country with which it had long had relations that were always tense, often difficult and, having fought three major wars since partition in 1947, sometimes violent. Yet without an overland link across Pakistan, the project was wholly unrealistic. Another proposal to construct a pipeline that ran offshore, far from Pakistani waters, was dismissed as technically far too difficult and financially far too demanding. Laying a pipeline more than 3,000 metres underwater on a mountainous seabed was and still remains an unprecedented venture, and a proposed $10 billion deep-sea gas pipeline was cancelled in 1996 after a three-year study, which had cost more than $20 million, concluded that it was simply too hard a task. Even an underwater pipeline running much closer to Pakistan's coast was considered to be too practically demanding, especially in the deep, volatile stretch where the Indus River pours into the Arabian Sea.

But the thaw in relations between New Delhi and Islamabad that first set in during 2000 made the pipeline project seem less of a dream. In November 2000, as Iranian Deputy Foreign Minister Mohammed Hossein Adeli visited the second conference of the Iran–India Oil and Gas Committee in New Delhi and an Indian business delegation travelled to Tehran to discuss the assistance that India's private sector was willing to offer, both governments declared their support for the project. By March the following year, as Islamabad accepted in principle the idea of building a pipeline through its territory to India and even started to encourage the proposal, further feasibility studies were commissioned and more detailed plans drawn up.

The new gas pipeline now formed just part of a much wider picture of growing Indian–Iranian ties. The supply of Iranian liquefied natural gas to India by tanker, for example, had already been the subject of several deals. During a visit to the Indian capital on 27 January 2003 President Khatami had stood in front of large crowds as the chief guest at India's Republic Day parade before signing the 'New Delhi Declaration' that promised to expand trade between the two countries. In January 2005 a much more detailed agreement on this issue, under which the Iranians had promised to deliver up to 7.5 million tonnes of LPG to India annually over the next 25 years, was struck, and this deal, worth $40 billion, was then revised over the months that followed before a new agreement was formally signed in the Indian capital on 13 June that obliged Iran to export 5 million tonnes of LNG over the same term as before. The $22 billion agreement, which was signed by representatives of NIGEC, the Indian Oil Company and two other Indian businesses, Gail and Baharat India, was due to come into effect in 2009.

New Delhi has also sought to use such deals to drive a bigger stake in Iranian oil and gas resources. The Indian Oil and Natural Gas Company (ONGC) Videsh, for example, has had a strong presence in Iran since October 2002, when it was earmarked for a major contract, worth $30 million over four years, to develop the offshore Farsi exploration field and it formed a new consortium, alongside the Indian Oil Company and Oil India Ltd, in order to pursue this. The following January, Khatami also agreed in principle not only to arrange the delivery of Iranian gas but also to help encourage public and private sector companies in India to increase their cooperation with NIOC.

At the same time there was heightened Indian interest in winning the pending contracts to develop the massive Yadavaran field. On 28 June 2004 an Iranian delegation, led by the Deputy Minister of Petroleum, Hadi Nejad Hosseinian, had met with Mani Shankar Aiyar in New Delhi before opening talks covering the exploration and development of the Yadavaran complex. ONGC Videsh and Petronet were then also invited to bid for the oil field development before the Iranians formally offered India a 20 per cent stake in developing the field, a slice that was equivalent to 60,000 barrels per day of oil, in return for New Delhi's annual purchase of 5 million tonnes of LNG at an agreed cost. However, India did not initially agree to this fixed price and it was not until after several further rounds of negotiations between Energy Minister Bijan Zanganeh and Aiyar that a deal was finally clinched. The two subsequent agreements, made in early 2005, formally assigned ONGC both this 20 per cent stake in Yadavaran's development, one half of which would also be taken over by China's Sinopec, as well as a separate contract to develop the Jufeyr field. In return India committed itself to importing Iranian natural gas over the next 25 years, buying it at a price that would be linked to Brent crude oil: India would pay $1.2 plus 0.065 of the Brent crude average, with an upper ceiling of $31 per barrel. Iran would also ship 5 million tonnes of LNG to India annually, with a provision to increase the quantity to 7.5 million tonnes.

On 1 November 2004 the Indian Oil Corporation also clinched its biggest ever foreign investment deal when it signed a $3 billion contract to develop one of South Pars' gas blocks and to sell the liquefied natural gas it produced, partnering Iran's Petropars to undertake this operation. The IOC–Petropars consortium was also contracted to build a liquefaction plant in South Iran which was designed to produce more than 9 million tonnes per annum of LNG that could then be exported to India and other countries. The IOC was given a 40 per cent stake in the development of South Pars with the remainder designated to Petropars, while in the liquefaction plant the Indians would have a 60 per cent share and the marketing rights to sell the entire 9 million tonnes of the LNG wherever it wanted. This deal cemented a relationship that had been growing over the preceding few years, since another key Indian energy company, Reliance, also took a 25 per cent interest in a $10m feasibility study of South Pars in which NIOC also held 50 per cent, and had subsequently also formed Iran LNG, a joint venture with Britain's BP and NIOC that was expected to eventually market natural gas to India and other foreign markets.

The growing strength of the relationship between the two countries partly reflects India's ability to help satisfy an Iranian need not just for foreign currency, like any other potential purchaser, but also its appetite for refined oil (gasoline). In recent years Iran has consistently had to import lead-free gasoline in very large quantities and in 2002, as NIOC was forced to put its nine refineries out of service while it upgraded them, the Iranians imported between 100,00 and 150,000 tonnes of mostly 95-octane gasoline each month.[27] Yet this has played into New Delhi's hands because in the 1990s Reliance had brought some new refineries into service that currently process 660,000 barrels every day and export 7 million tonnes of refined products, even though India was once Asia's largest buyer of diesel. In the course of 2005, Reliance was supplying Iran with about 25 per cent of its gasoline imports.

By the summer of 2005 India's energy requirements had pushed the two countries closer together, and Washington was particularly concerned that such trade links could easily lead to the formation of a formal Indo-Iranian military alliance. The task of safeguarding its supply of oil and gas, securing a possible overland route into the markets of Central Asia and Europe, and checking any future Pakistani or perhaps even American aggression in the region gives India good reason to consider building a strategic alliance with Tehran. Although there had been a limited degree of cooperation between the two countries during the 1990s, when they had both sent supplies to the militia organizations in Afghanistan that had fought the Taliban movement, signs of a more formal relationship began to appear only later. In March 2003, just weeks after signing the New Delhi Declaration and not long after the Indian Chief of Naval Staff, Admiral Madhvendra Singh, had also visited Iran as part of a programme of exchanges of high-level defence personnel, the two countries conducted a joint naval exercise.[28] Iran has also reportedly been seeking India's help to service its naval and air force equipment, since both countries use Russian military equipment that Indian personnel are reputed to be highly adept at maintaining and repairing.[29]

The choice for New Delhi

By 2005 the Indian government was still confronted with a very difficult choice that was steadily becoming more pressing. Did it continue its drive to secure future sources of energy from Iran? Or should it bow to American pressure and look elsewhere instead?

Washington officials certainly made little secret of their displeasure over the proposed Iran–India pipeline and their preference instead for the Trans-Afghan Pipeline (TAP) from Turkmenistan. Members of the powerful House International Relations Committee repeatedly warned India that it would 'imperil' its relationship with the United States if it went ahead with a gas pipeline deal with Iran, while high-level officials reiterated their warnings. Assistant Secretary of State for Economic and Business Affairs, E. Anthony Wayne, for example, objected to the proposed Iran–Pakistan–India gas pipeline, saying that such negotiations could undermine US energy policies. 'A troubling aspect of the recent surge in overseas energy deals by China and India,' Wayne told the Senate Foreign Relations Committee, 'is their willingness to invest in countries that are pursuing policies that are harmful to global stability and energy security for all.' Numerous other influential voices echoed these calls: Tom Lantos urged the Indian government to remember that it 'will pay a very heavy price for their total disregard of US concerns vis-à-vis Iran, the single most important international threat we face', while Nicholas Burns sought to reassure those critics who argued that the Bush administration wasn't turning up enough diplomatic heat on New Delhi, emphasizing simply that 'we have raised our concerns with the Indian government'.

But meeting the irresistible American force was the immoveable object of India's energy requirement, and many high-ranking Indian officials were dismissive of American pressure. Hamid Ansari, a member of the Policy Advisory Group to Foreign Minister Singh, said simply that 'we have done our sums with regard to Iran – it isn't an area where we will be pushed to resolve our position', while Aiyar also reportedly shrugged off US pressure on New Delhi to abandon the pipeline plan altogether. The strength of Indian determination to proceed with the project sometimes reflected a much more general suspicion of the United States, or even outright hostility, and traits of such a mindset were perhaps discernible in the attitude of Subir Raha, the government-appointed head of India's biggest oil company, the Oil and Natural Gas Corporation, who openly made much more general criticisms of the United States: Washington would be 'stupid' to attack Iran and risk imposing record oil prices on the global economy, he declared, because 'you launch one more attack and you can't even guess where the speculation will go. With the stalemate in Afghanistan, stalemate in Iraq and elsewhere, you already have a price of $55 a barrel.' Raha, who had worked for state-run oil companies for the past 35 years, saw 'no reason why India's priorities should be subservient to US priorities. The US is chasing oil and gas as badly as China or India or anybody else.'[30]

US–India deal

To tilt the political balance in its favour, Washington sought to win Indian favour by offering New Delhi a landmark deal that effectively ran counter to the administration's own declared national security policies. Under the terms of this agreement, which was announced as Prime Minister Singh visited the American capital on 18 July 2005, the United States would provide India with access to sensitive technology to help its civilian nuclear programme and also supply highly sophisticated nuclear-capable weapons systems. It was planned to come into effect as soon as it received Congressional approval.

This agreement was by any standards a radical step. The Indians had previously been forbidden from receiving any such closely guarded know-how under both American legislation, such as the Non-Proliferation Act 2000, and wider international agreements. The 1968 Non-Proliferation Treaty, for example, which has been signed and ratified by the United States, calls on existing nuclear powers not to transfer their nuclear knowledge to countries, such as India, that are not signatories, while the rules of the 44-nation Nuclear Suppliers Group also oblige their members to forgo nuclear trade with any country that does not subject itself to the International Atomic Energy Agency Safeguards regime.

By relaxing rules on the export of nuclear technology that were in its own interest to maintain, Washington was in the longer term inadvertently undermining its own power. The purpose of such a tight body of legislation is clearly to protect the security of every signatory state, nuclear or not, while also allowing members of the elite 'nuclear club' – the handful of countries that do have a nuclear arsenal – to maintain the political influence and prestige these weapons bestow. It was with these considerations in mind that President Bush had in 2004 made a number of proposals to strengthen the anti-proliferation regime, advocated expanding his Proliferation Security Initiative (PSI) to outlaw illicit transfers of nuclear technology by 'proliferation networks' and urged the adoption of a UN Security Council resolution that proposed criminalizing such transfers. The president had also specifically urged the Nuclear Suppliers Group to close a loophole in the 1968 Treaty by limiting the transfer of enrichment and reprocessing technology by NSG members to those states that already possessed them. Yet in a bid to win Indian support, Bush was now ready to sacrifice these higher ends. A report published in August by the Congressional Research Service – the public policy research arm of the US Congress – made the important point that the new Washington–New Delhi agreement would not only contravene the NSG's control guidelines but would also open the floodgates to nuclear proliferation and allow rogue countries outside the Non-Proliferation Treaty to build nuclear weapons with imported civilian nuclear technology.

Washington's willingness to compromise its own longer-term national security for the immediate end of winning Indian support was a reflection of several geopolitical calculations. The US administration undoubtedly sought to build an alliance that could counter the growing power of China. As a former US ambassador to India, Robert Blackwill, pointed out, 'on the rise of Chinese power, there are, in my opinion, no two [other] countries which share equally the challenge of trying to shape the rise of Chinese power. ... Both the US and India will be enormously affected by what kind of China emerges over the next decade.'[31] Yet it is nonetheless questionable that the Chinese factor was really the most important. Why, after all, had such a deal been struck at that particular moment?

What was imminent, however, was the construction of the Iran–India pipeline, and because the Bush–Singh agreement gives India crucial access to both the fuel and the cutting-edge technology that it desperately needs if it is to fulfil its ambition of generating 20,000 Mw of nuclear power over the next two decades, the deal appeared to be a way of keeping New Delhi away from exactly the new sources of gas supply that were now in the pipeline. The connection between the proposed India–Iran link and the new deal with Washington seemed even closer still when on 27 July, just days after Singh's visit to the American capital, spokesmen for the US administration expressed 'serious concerns' over New Delhi's earlier efforts to buy natural gas from Iran. As the Congressman Tom Lantos argued, 'this pattern of dealing with us will not be productive for India and they have to be told in plain English that this great new opening which we support is predicated on reciprocity. ... If they persist in this, this great dream of a new relationship will go down the tubes.'

But just how successful, then, has Washington's nuclear deal really been in winning political influence over New Delhi?

India, Iran and the IAEA

In one important respect, the July deal made little difference to Indian foreign policy towards Iran. During a visit to Afghanistan on 28 August, Prime Minister Singh made it clear that he had no intention of renouncing his plans to build the new gas pipeline, which he emphasized would play an essential role in meeting India's future energy needs. Asked at a joint news conference in Kabul with the Afghan President, Hamid Karzai, about the

proposed trans-Afghan link to Turkmenistan, Singh answered simply that
'it is not a question of preferring one [pipeline] over the other [because] we
need both pipelines [and] India's needs for commercial energy are increasing
at an explosive rate'.

But while continuing to draw up plans for the India–Iran pipeline, New
Delhi seemed to be following the Washington line over other issues, notably
Iran's nuclear programme. For at the crucial board meeting of the IAEA in
September 2005, Indian representatives took the watching world by surprise
and voted in favour of a resolution that condemned Iran's behaviour and
raised the possibility of a referral to the UN Security Council.[32]

Such an outcome had initially looked to be far less likely than an absten-
tion. On 2 September, during a two-day visit to Tehran, Indian Foreign
Minister Natwar Singh reportedly informed the Iranian premier that New
Delhi would not be in favour of a UN referral and pointed out that 'India's
relations with Iran are not predicated on positions and views attributed to
some governments'. On 19 September, as they met to forge a common position, 12 of the 14 IAEA board members from the Non-Aligned Movement to
which India belonged believed that Iran's case should be solved only within
the confines of the IAEA, not the UN, with only Peru and Singapore ready
to back a referral. 'Everybody would like to avoid a contentious debate in the
Security Council,' Natwar Singh told the Indian NDTV network in New
York, adding later that 'the IAEA should be given a chance to win with a
consensus'.

But behind the scenes US diplomats were working furiously hard to win
India's backing, knowing that its support for Washington's preferred IAEA
resolution would send an unmistakable signal to Tehran that it could not use
its energy resources to curry international favour. In Washington, moreover,
pressure on India was also mounting heavily. Criticizing the remarks that
Natwar Singh had made in Tehran, Tom Lantos said that while he strongly
supported closer ties with India, its government 'will pay a very hefty price
for its total disregard of US concerns vis-à-vis Iran, the single most important international threat we face'. And at a Congressional hearing to discuss
new developments in US–India relations, he warned further that 'if we are
turning ourselves into a pretzel to accommodate India, I want to be damn
sure that India is mindful of US policies in critical areas such as US policy
towards Iran. India must decide where it will stand – with the ayatollahs of
terror in Tehran or with the United States.' Instead Lantos expected 'India
to recognize that there is reciprocity involved in this new relationship, and
without reciprocity India will get very little help from the Congress.' Other
well-established critics of Iran also joined the chorus: Congressman Gary
L. Ackerman, a New York Democrat and a former chairman of the India

Caucus on Capitol Hill, said that New Delhi must not go down the road with Iran on issues that are contrary to US policy. 'Friends,' he went on, 'do not let friends play with fire.'

When on 25 September the Indian representative on the IAEA board voted to support the US-EU resolution, it looked as though Washington's July deal had finally succeeded in winning New Delhi over. Key left-wing allies of the government accused it of buckling under US pressure, and such claims were also made by respected independent experts: 'it's difficult to think that the vote was not influenced in some measure by India's deal with the US,' Lawrence Scheinman of the Centre for Non-Proliferation Studies in Washington put it. Officially, of course, the government denied such accusations: 'there is no question of India having ranged itself on one side or the other – nothing could be further from the truth,' a Foreign Ministry spokesman said. In the same spirit Indian officials also declared that they had done nothing to provoke Iranian retaliation: 'we see no reason why there should be any apprehension in this regard,' one official statement said. 'India has played a constructive role in the IAEA and helped safeguard Iran's legitimate interests.'

The strength of American influence over India on the nuclear issue also became clear a few weeks later, when at an emergency meeting of the IAEA held on 2–4 February 2006, New Delhi's representative once again backed the US, this time by voting to refer Iran to the Security Council. The India-US nuclear deal had undoubtedly been paramount in helping to secure this diplomatic cooperation, as well as India's appointment of a new oil minister, Murali Deora, who was known to be more pro-Washington than his predecessor. US ambassador David Mulford had told his Indian counterparts that the deal would 'die in Congress' if New Delhi supported Tehran in the IAEA, and, making the first explicit link between the nuclear deal and Indian backing for America over Iran, Mulford stated simply that 'I think that Congress will simply stop considering the matter' if India failed to give its backing.

Yet despite enlisting India's support over Iran's nuclear programme, Washington was still unable to secure any promise to renounce plans to cancel the pipeline, and India's decision to join the Iran–Pakistan project seemed finely balanced. But the Bush administration's determination to stop the deal was just as strong as ever, despite some presidential remarks – 'our beef with Iran is not the pipeline; our beef with Iran is the fact that they want to develop a nuclear weapon' – that seemed to suggest a shift in policy. Soon afterwards, National Security Council spokesman Frederick Jones restated the earlier position, asserting that 'as we stated before, the US government does not support the Iran–Pakistan pipeline', and that while the US recognized regional energy needs, 'we have repeatedly expressed concerns about international participation in energy projects with Iran'. Richard Boucher, Assistant Secretary of State for South and Central Asia, also added that Washington was considering other ways to deter New Delhi from taking part. In May 2006, testifying before a Congressional panel on the India–US nuclear deal, he said the US offer of assistance to India included various options for obtaining energy. 'Not only the civil nuclear cooperation', as he put it, but 'other agreements the president [Bush] has signed during his trip [to India] including clean coal technology, expanding efficiency of power transmission, solar, wind, all of these things.'[33]

There are other non-aligned states that have deviated from Washington's preferred line towards Iran, although they have played a much less important role on the international stage than India. One is South Africa, which has adopted a more moderate approach towards the nuclear issue.

South Africa

During the international negotiations over the Iranian nuclear programme that were held in the course of 2005, the South African government put forward proposals that found some support from fellow members of the IAEA, even though they were dismissed out of hand by the United States. One such plan, supported by some other non-aligned states, was put forward in July by South African President Thabo Mbeki who had met with Hassan Rowhani, then Tehran's chief negotiator, to discuss another proposal: this would involve shipping South African uranium oxide concentrate ('yellow-cake') to Iran for conversion at Isfahan into uranium hexafluoride that would then be shipped back to South Africa for further enrichment into nuclear fuel. The proposal, which was formally put before other IAEA states two weeks later, was intended to allay fears that Iran could use its facilities to develop nuclear weapons and was viewed by Pretoria and Tehran as an interim measure to help Iran in the negotiating process and gain the trust of the outside world: 'for further confidence-building we are ready to sell the output to a third country in cooperation with the EU and under the IAEA supervision,' Ali Aghamohammadi, a spokesman for the Supreme National Security Council, told one newspaper.[34] But the proposal had little chance of finding European support, let alone American, and was quietly dropped: 'countries like South Africa, Brazil, India and Venezuela don't want to let the Iranians have their own complete fuel cycle,' one diplomat who had been heavily involved in these negotiations told me in November 2005, 'but neither do they really see why the Europeans and the Americans attach so much weight to a complete suspension of uranium enrichment.'

How much did the temptations of Iran's oil explain Pretoria's willingness to stray from Washington's preferred course? It is no coincidence that South Africa is heavily dependent on imported oil and, despite recent efforts to diversify its sources, is particularly reliant on Saudi Arabia and Iran. Iranian oil currently makes up about 40 per cent of its overall supply, and in both 2004 and 2005 constituted nearly all of the 7 billion rands' worth of goods that Iran exported into the South African market.

South Africa has had this dependency on Iranian oil ever since 1994, when after a 15-year break the Iranian Ministry of Foreign Affairs made moves to re-establish the strong ties that had been completely ruptured by the 1979 revolution. Limited economic relations between the two countries now resumed, although gradually and discreetly: the National Iranian Oil Company, for example, quietly took a 17.5 per cent share in the Sasolburg refinery of the South African National Petroleum Refiners, even when wider relations between the two countries were still suspended. But in the course of 1995 and 1996 South Africa pressed for closer ties with Iran both to acquire oil imports on favourable terms and to demonstrate Pretoria's willingness and ability to defy American pressure to shun the mullahs' regime. Iran's post-1979 oil embargo on South Africa was now brought to an end and full diplomatic and commercial relations were at this point formally restored.

Besides this national dependency on oil imports, South African companies also have some large-scale investments in the Iranian energy infrastructure and a strong commercial interest in acquiring a bigger stake. Chief among them is probably the giant petrochemical company Sasol, which has sought to use Iran as the location for its third main overseas gas-to-liquids (GTL) plant, similar to those its engineers have already built in Qatar and Nigeria. Negotiations with Tehran began in September 2002 about a possible joint venture to establish the $1 billion GTL plant that would utilize gas produced in the South Pars field, and a feasibility study was commissioned the following year. But although a preliminary agreement on the price of gas needed for this and other projects had been struck by November 2004, the finalization of these deals was held up by the election of Mahmoud Ahmadinejad as president in the summer of 2005, a development that deeply alarmed Sasol's chairman, Pat Davies, and prompted him to announce that any final decision on the company's Iranian ventures was unlikely to be made 'in the next year or so'.[35]

Numerous other South African companies have also acquired a stake in Iran's oil and gas markets, notably PetroSA, which has struck deals to construct two plants that convert natural gas to environmentally friendly sulphur-free fuels, as well as Mossgas, MINTEK, Bateman Engineering,

Standard Bank, Klein Karoo Livestock Exports, Al Jabber Grinaker, Intel-
con and Global Railway Engineering. Many of these companies have been
represented on some of the official South African delegations that have made
commercial treks to Tehran. These official visits have not only sought to
augment economic ties between the two countries but also reaffirmed their
shared hostility towards Washington's view of the outside world. During the
sixth session of the South African–Iran joint commission that was held in
Tehran in February 2002, for example, both countries issued a statement that
delivered an unmistakable rebuke to George W. Bush's 'axis of evil' speech
made just days before: while expressing its 'regret' for 'the negative statements uttered against Iran, Iraq and North Korea in the context of international terrorism', the communiqué instead demanded 'dialogue rather than
confrontation amongst civilizations and [the] fostering [of] understanding
between nations of the world and creating a peaceful and stable international environment'. The statement's call for the international 'recognition
of the legitimate right to self-determination of the Palestinian People, return
of all Palestinian and Arab Occupied Territory and the establishment of
a Palestinian State' as a 'prerequisite for a comprehensive, lasting and just
peace in the region' also emphasized the delegation's distance from, if not
outright hostility towards, the policies of the US administration.

There are perhaps some other similarities between the two countries.
South African Foreign Minister Nkosazana Dlamini Zuma has said, for
example, that both Iran and South Africa wanted to forget about their
unfortunate pasts. 'We have both had to make certain sacrifices and certain
adjustments to get to the point we are at today. Bilateral relations are excellent, with more than 40 agreements, memorandums of understanding and
joint statements signed in the decade since diplomatic relations were rekin-
dled,' she claimed on 22 July 2003.

So if Iran's natural resources are undermining America's influence over
other countries, what effect are they having on the Tehran regime itself? As
Chapter 4 shows, there are many respects in which the proceeds of the sale
of its oil are also reinforcing the mullahs' grip on power and allowing their
regime to pose an even greater challenge to Washington.

CHAPTER FOUR

Supporting the Iranian Regime

To the foreign traveller who observes an alien national mindset, even insignificant incidents can sometimes prove to be unexpectedly revealing. During a trip to Iran in 2003, I saw a dispute between two drivers suddenly erupt into ugly violence, as each lashed out at the other, their fists flying with fury, while some passers-by ran towards them and tried to restrain them. In Western newspapers of course we all read reports of 'road rage' and random violence, but this was the first time I had personally ever seen an exchange like the one that was now taking place in front of me in Tehran.

It was difficult not to be reminded of some of the occasions when violence on a very large scale had suddenly flared up in Iran. While Britain may have been fortunate in knowing no really major disturbances since the 'Peterloo Massacre' of 1819, the Iranians have long shown a tendency to suddenly break into furious, almost uncontrollable orgies of violence that nearly always lead to serious bloodshed. It happened in the heady days after the Second World War when protestors seized control of parts of Iranian Azerbaijan and Kurdistan before declaring the formation of autonomous republics, and it also happened, most obviously, in the months that preceded the shah's downfall in 1979. The same volatility of temperament was also noted by a number of Western travellers of an earlier age as they made their way through nineteenth-century Persia and noted the susceptibility of local governors to mass street protests that could suddenly erupt if unpopular policies were ever implemented.[1]

Nor has the present regime been spared from such outbursts. The most serious protests took place in Tehran in the summers of 1999 and 2003, when thousands of mainly young people took to the streets, usually around the campus of one of the capital's universities, setting them alight and attacking riot police over several days until law and order was eventually restored. These particular protests were largely political in nature and were accompanied by vociferous demands for more social freedoms, but some other serious outbreaks have been sparked by the imposition of 'unfair' taxes, such as the riots in Ahwaz in December 2002, or by economic hardships, such as those that shook Isfahan in October 2001, when as many as 10,000 textile workers protested in the streets against a parliamentary bill to close down their state-run factory. The city of Ahwaz, where there is a very large Arab population, was also the scene of some very serious rioting in April 2005 in which several people were reportedly shot dead and perhaps hundreds arrested.

Iran's rulers are also no doubt painfully aware of a story about early Islam that is well known among Muslims. According to the Shiite version of what happened, Uthman 'the third Rightly-Guided Caliph', one of the earliest leaders of Muslims who ruled in the seventh century, had tried to implement a series of financial reforms but succeeded mainly in provoking the wrath of his subjects, some of whom stormed his palace in protest and demanded what they believed to be their rightful share of the public purse. Uthman was attacked and cut to pieces by the crowd, and his grisly fate almost exemplifies the worst fears of those who lead the present political order. Differing significantly from the Sunni view of events, this particular version of the story exemplifies the spirit of corruption and nepotism that all Shiite Muslims particularly abhor.

Not surprisingly the present regime is desperate to stave off protests, knowing that demonstrations even on the smallest scale can sometimes quickly escalate beyond control. So far they have succeeded in doing this partly by effectively buying off dissent, using large-scale financial subsidies to alleviate painful economic pressures and to compensate for a lack of social freedom, as well as by expanding their security services to crush any dissent well before it becomes a threat. The basic reason why they have proved so successful at doing this is simply that they have the spare cash to do so, and nearly all of this spare cash comes from the proceeds of the sale of just one commodity – oil.

Put in more general terms, Iran's energy resources play a critical role in not only sustaining the present regime's grip on power but also in creating a more proactive threat to America's regional strategic interests. This is not just because the sale of oil has generated vast proceeds that have allowed the mullahs to keep Iran's stricken economy afloat and repress their potential enemies, but also because they have also been able to sharply accelerate a nuclear programme that, although ostensibly only for the production of civilian energy, is widely feared to hide a covert programme to develop a warhead.

There are also some other, less obvious, ways in which Iran's reserves of oil and gas also buttress the regime. So by using these reserves to build alliances with countries like India and China, the mullahs have been able to take away the stigma of international isolation that has been highly unpopular with many ordinary Iranians, while these resources have also allowed Tehran to cement relations with another state that is also castigated by the Americans – Syria. What is more, in an age in which material considerations rule supreme, there is another asset of undervalued importance that Iran's possession of such resources greatly enhances, and that is its sense of self-importance, or 'prestige'.

When viewed in this way, Iran stands alongside several other countries whose prestige has been considerably heightened by their possession of large quantities of oil and gas. So in the summer of 2005, for example, the chairman of the Senate Foreign Relations Committee, Richard Lugar, pointed out that 'oil is the new currency of foreign policy', as countries such as Iran, Russia and Venezuela have become 'not only less cooperative but almost gleeful that they are able to make trouble for us'. Pointing out that in 2005 Moscow expected to earn nearly $110 billion from oil exports during that year, an increase of more than 22 per cent over the previous 12 months, Lugar emphasized how this new money was undercutting US and European leverage over them.

The first section of this chapter looks at the Iranians' earnings from their sale of oil to international markets, and the way in which the proceeds it generates have then allowed them to tighten their grip on power at home and also to sharply accelerate their nuclear and military programmes in a way that has caused such deep consternation in Washington and elsewhere.

Foreign exchange earnings from oil

Many Western travellers on their first trip to Iran are taken aback by the reality of north Tehran. In my own case, I had already witnessed the poverty in which many ordinary Iranians live but now also saw a very different side to a country that in recent years has become very visibly polarized between rich and poor. In stark contrast to the relatively humble and pious simplicity in which their fellow nationals live in other districts of the capital and elsewhere in the country, in these northern suburbs the signs of an affluent and fast-growing middle class are unmistakable. Large, flashy and expensive Landcruisers glide up and down the highway, while along the streets walk well-dressed young people who use their sophisticated and up-to-date mobile phones to send texts and chat with friends and family. This was certainly not how I had imagined the capital of the Islamic Republic of Iran to be.

The new affluence of the capital's fashionable districts is one unmistakable sign of the vast earnings that Iran has made from the sale of oil. Although these proceeds initially fall only into governmental hands, they can easily be circulated more widely in Iranian society when they are spent on or allocated to particular projects by government ministers. But whereas the prosperity that is born of free commerce benefits many more people in any society, the concentration of oil revenue in governmental hands has meant that only those who are closely linked to the current regime, and enjoy a high degree of its patronage, have really benefited from this state-owned income. It is mainly the members of this small political elite that are so visible in north Tehran.

Despite considerable efforts over at least the past decade to diversify exports and make the country less vulnerable to any sudden fall in the price of a barrel, the vast majority of Iran's foreign exchange earnings – about 80 per cent – are derived from the sale of oil. The sheer enormity of this income was made clear by Oil Minister Zanganeh in April 2005: in the course of the Iranian year that ended in March 2005, as NIOC exported a daily average of 2.52 million barrels, the country earned $31.5 billion from the sale of oil and expected to increase this amount by another $4.5 billion over the next year if a barrel's market value averaged $35. Put another way, every time the price of crude oil rises by just $1 a barrel, Iran gains annually about $900 million in export revenues, and as this price increased suddenly in the latter half of 2005 it looked as though Zanganeh's original prediction had considerably underestimated these earnings. By the end of March 2006 Iran had earned $45 billion in oil revenue over the preceding year, almost 50 per cent more than the year before.

The Iranians have not always been in quite such a fortunate position. In the 1980s, for example, Iran's output of oil had been hit very hard by the long and protracted war with Saddam Hussein, whose warplanes made repeated and sometimes successful efforts to bomb its heavily defended oil installations. Although during the conflict the Iranians still managed to produce a daily average of about 2 million barrels, they lost the confidence of many important international consumers, whose concerns about Iraqi and, in the latter stages of the war, American attacks on both Iranian oil rigs and their own tankers prompted them to turn instead to other Middle Eastern producers, most notably Saudi Arabia and Kuwait. In their desperate bid to boost exports, Iran was forced to lower its oil prices, offer special insurance to compensate for any Iraqi threats to tanker traffic in the Gulf, extend credit facilities and shuttle oil by tanker from the main terminal on Kharg Island to other destinations from which buyers could move it more safely. Yet these drastic measures could not stop Iran's earnings from oil exports from falling dramatically, and in 1988 the shrinkage of national income forced Ayatollah Khomeini to strike a ceasefire with Iraq.

After the end of the eight-year war, both oil production and its export increased, and as annual revenues from its sale averaged more than $19 billion in the period 1990–96, Iran experienced a period of relative prosperity. But by 1997 things were changing, and independent analysts were openly warning that the price of a barrel could fall to just $15. This was not so much because there was any diminution of international demand – far from it, there was a moderate increase – but because supply was still rising at an even faster rate as an increasing number of new producers from outside OPEC turned on the tap properly for the first time. By June the following year market prices had hit a new ten-year low, and at one point Iranian crude was traded at just $9.50 per barrel. During this time, Iran's foreign sales of oil were generating only between $10 and $12 billion, threatening a serious economic crisis.

It was not until the late 1990s that the years of stagnant and declining oil prices came to an abrupt end and Iran's fortunes, like those of every other oil-producing state, decisively changed. Prices jumped to $17.98 in 1999 and then again to $28.24 in the course of the following year. The causes of such a dramatic transformation were complex. One report by the Petroleum Industry Research Foundation in June 2000[2] argued that the low stocks built up by consumers over the preceding years, coupled with more stringent environmental regulations and other technical hitches, had all played a part in contributing to the sudden upward pressure on oil prices. Others pointed to an unexpected surge in demand, due in part to some unusually cold winters in Europe and to a more rapid rate of global economic growth than anyone had anticipated. The problem may have also been aggravated by a drop in American refining capacity over the preceding 20 years, from 18.6 million barrels per day to 16.5 million barrels, and by an even sharper fall in the number of refineries, from 315 to 155, which made the United States much more vulnerable to interruptions if a small number of refineries should stop production, however briefly. As President Bush has put it, 'a single accident, a single shutdown, can send the price of gasoline and heating oil spiralling all over the country. The major reason for the dramatic increase in oil prices is lack of refining capacity.'[3]

After such a dramatic surge, some market correction was perhaps inevitable, and oil prices headed somewhat downward in the course of the following year, with the average price of a barrel of Gulf crude dropping 14 per cent, from $26.24 in 2000 to $22.80 in 2001. This happened despite an atmosphere of political uncertainty over the Middle East that had been created by the attacks on the World Trade Center, in which 15 Saudis had been involved, and despite widespread market concern over the negative reactions throughout the Arab world to US military operations in Afghanistan. Yet even though such uncertainties would ordinarily have driven them upwards, oil prices dropped further in early 2002 before reversing course once again and ending the year sharply higher. The price of a barrel of 'OPEC basket' crude – that is, the blended average of several countries' oil, which OPEC uses as its benchmark – rose from a low of $18.51 in early February 2002 to a new high of $30.50 in late December.

This time, the causes lying behind the latest upsurge in oil prices were once again the usual ones. There was political turmoil in some of the more unstable oil-producing countries, notably Venezuela and Iraq, which were two of the seven largest oil-exporting nations. Venezuelan output suffered at the hands of industrial disputes within the state-owned oil company, and on 2 December a general strike began which cut oil production from the 2.85 million barrels per day of early 2002 to an estimated 450,000 barrels per day. At the same time, oil traders and consumers had many good reasons to feel concerned about Iraq's supply of oil. If the Americans attacked Iraq, as most people expected by the summer of 2002, then Saddam could easily retaliate by setting Iraq's oil wells on fire with the same ruthlessness with which he had so effectively destroyed Kuwaiti wells in 1991, putting them completely out of action for years. There was also concern that a US invasion of Iraq could provoke unrest or terrorism in other Muslim countries. As if these concerns were not enough to make oil consumers and traders nervous already, Iraq then dramatically announced a temporary suspension of its oil exports after 8 April 2002, in solidarity with the Palestinians whose territory was then under attack by the Israeli armed forces.

Oil and state expenditure

There are several ways in which earnings from the sale of oil help to sustain the regime's grip on power. One is that they are spent on specific projects that stop a badly flawed economy from crashing down in the way that many people have for a long time wrongly predicted would happen in Iran.

How, first of all, do these proceeds reach the wider Iranian economy? Some of the earnings are earmarked for long-term investment, while the rest are allocated to more pressing concerns. This is because after 1997 the Khatami administration developed a 'Stabilization Fund' that allows the government's budget to benefit from its own predetermined oil price that in practice may differ significantly from the market price. The difference between this pre-determined value and the actual market price, which is usually considerably higher at any given moment, is put into the Fund in order to shield the country from any sharp future fluctuations in world oil prices similar to those that had hit the Iranian economy and other oil exporters so hard in 1998. If the high oil price is taken into account then the Iranian budget would in the last few years have always shown a big surplus, but because of the price cap it has typically shown a small deficit of around $150 million that can be financed out of the sale of participation certificates, which are specially issued bonds yielding an approximate 20 per cent rate of interest over their five-year span.

Whereas the money allocated to the Fund benefits the economy in the longer term, the rest helps keep it immediately afloat even though, as things stand, the government is still trying to rely more than ever before on direct taxation rather than oil revenues. In December 2003, for example, as he put forward the forthcoming 2004-5 budget to parliament, President Khatami said that his spending plans were relying on oil revenues for about 48 per cent of their income and stressed his determination to make state reserves much more independent from oil revenues. And in January 2005 he once again tried to play down the role of these petro-earnings, announcing that 'current government expenditure should come from tax revenues' while 'oil revenues should be used for productive investment'. The strength of his determination was barely surprising, given that in the late 1990s Iran's vulnerability to low oil prices had meant that it had at times faced budget deficits up to 22 trillion rials ($3.4 billion), only a small portion of which could be financed through participation certificates: in June 2000, for example, national debt had stood at 62 trillion rials, which was owed to its Central Bank, and another 7 trillion rials to governmental commercial banks.

Yet despite such efforts to diversify, Iran's economy is inescapably dependent on oil. This was not immediately apparent from the 2005-6 budget, which planned to increase government expenditure to 1,546 trillion rials ($175.6 billion), significantly more than the previous year's total of 1,070 trillion rials, and based this figure on an increase in taxation to $14.3 billion, a rise of more than 40 per cent over what was expected from the previous year, while oil revenues were expected to fall to $14.1 billion from $16 billion in the year to March 2005. Yet even if Khatami's hopes of raising new taxes are eventually successfully realized by the Ahmadinejad administration, there is no escape from the fact that this $14 billion is still indispensable in keeping the economy afloat and lots of people in employment, 'both in the longer term or, despite an official injunction, as short-term expedients'.

The state bureaucracy

One way in which these oil revenues have helped the regime maintain its political power is by funding a high level of government expenditure that is partly intended to stave off a crisis of unemployment. Of course the idea that it is the role of the state, rather than the individual, to create employment opportunities is today very alien to many people in Britain, America and other countries where the state sector has been significantly curbed back in the past two decades or so, or where there is no comparable history of state economic activism. In Iran, however, the state has played a central role in the economy over the last half-century, and after 1979 the new post-revolutionary constitution placed some major economic activities under the ownership of a state sector whose long reach has subsequently been only modestly pushed back. This state activism is also complemented by popular expectations, a 'statism-populism', that it is up to the state to 'create' economic growth and employment opportunities, and that to reduce the government's heavy involvement in the economy would be as disastrous as Rafsanjani's economic experiments, aimed at market liberalization, of the mid-1990s.

The very strong political pressure on the government to increase public expenditure in order to 'create' employment opportunities has also been accentuated by a population growth that far outstrips the rate at which even the most dynamic economy, let alone one as beset with problems as Iran's, is ever likely to grow. This population growth manifests the 'Islamic baby boom' of the mid-late 1970s, which is to some extent explained by the efforts of the newly founded revolutionary order, anxious to beef up the future Islamic Republic, to encourage high birth rates. For in the decade that followed the mid- to late 1970s, the annual rate of population growth reached 3.2–3.9 per cent before suddenly tailing off to a relatively meagre 1.6 per cent from the early 1990s. This spectacular increase accounts for the expansion of the population by nearly 50 per cent in the decade after 1976 and also means that today around 65 per cent of the population is under the age of 30, and perhaps half under 20. The reality of raw statistics like these becomes highly apparent to any visitor to Tehran, the size of which has grown from just 2 million in 1970 to at least 10 million today, and where it is young people who predominate in the street.

Put another way, this means that there is a demand for an extra 800,000 or so jobs each year to absorb all those who leave full-time education, even though a great many – well into six figures each year – emigrate and head, in particular, for Canada, the United States and Western Europe. Yet although the economy would need to grow at an annual rate of at least 8 per cent in real terms to absorb this number of new job seekers and by 9.5 per cent to reduce unemployment below 10 per cent, Iran's GDP grew only at about 5.4 per cent during each year between 2000 and 2004, and by around 5.8 per cent in 2004. Nor is it expected to increase by much more than 4.5 per cent in the course of 2005 and 2006.

The result is a staggering rate of unemployment, or at least underemployment, in modern-day Iran. No one knows the real figures but what is certain is that the 'official' figures are the most contested and some of the least reliable in the country, containing a margin of error that is perhaps huge.

Lacking any objective basis, the figures quoted by governmental and official sources vary considerably, and the vice-president, the minister of economy and finance and the head of the Labour Ministry each gave a different rate of unemployment for the first quarter of the Iranian year 2004-5, figures that range from 10.4 per cent to as much as 11.8 per cent. By the Iranian Statistics Centre account, unemployment is no more than 2.5 million while other sources put the figure at more than 3 million and private estimates as high as 4–4.5 million.

Yet the huge oil revenues that the Tehran regime has at its disposal have allowed it to employ far more people than it really needs. One of the most important single forms of government expenditure is the vast, bloated state bureaucracy that employs hundreds of thousands of civil servants. Whereas Iran had a total of 560,000 people on the government payroll in 1977, this figure grew enormously in the post-revolutionary years, increasing by 23 per cent between 1986 and 1996 to reach 3.2 million, and by 2005, according to official figures released by the Management and Planning Organization in Tehran, had stabilized at 2.3 million.

By employing so many workers in the state sector, the regime secures its power not just by providing job opportunities for its young population but also by making this employment conditional on showing allegiance to the political order: do as you are told, the regime sometimes almost says to its workers, or you lose your job. Every year, on the last Friday of the Ramadan month of fasting, hundreds of thousands of protestors march through the streets of Tehran to mark the 'Qods (Jerusalem) Day' that is held to show solidarity with the Palestinians, and when in November 2003 I watched this rally myself, I had a chance to talk to some of those who took part. It became quickly clear that many of them were not participating because they wanted to but simply because they worked in conservative-sponsored state bodies and had been told to attend. Yet the participation of so many people in this and other protests helps to reinforce the regime's grip on power by giving ordinary Iranians, and outsiders, the impression that it has much more support than it really does.

Besides funding such a large bureaucracy, the state sector also deploys its oil revenues on a wide range of other projects that in some cases employ a very large number of people. In recent years it has spent billions of rials on new construction projects, particularly in the capital, in order to alleviate a chronic housing shortage that has allowed the price of property to spiral way beyond the means of most young people. The booming state of the construction industry is certainly very visible to anyone who visits the capital, particularly its northern suburbs, and sees a large number of cranes along the horizon. This is not a particularly recent phenomenon but has been in

evidence over the past 20 years, during which time the domestic construction industry has expanded to meet the increasing demands made both by
industry, which is booming in particular areas, as well as the demands of the
'baby boom' generation of the 1970s and after. Every year there are around
an extra 800,000 new families that each need their own private housing,
and although this demand is expected to continue growing at the same rate
until around 2010, the government currently has the capacity to build only
an extra 450,000 new homes each year and constantly struggles to avert a
social crisis.

Some of the funding that is needed to meet this demand comes from
private investors, and the Tehran authorities have also said that they are
willing to look overseas, to international capital, in order to finance such an
enormous project. Yet most of the money still comes from the state, which
in 2004 provided much of the $3.6 billion that was invested in the housing
sector, funding more than 170,000 new construction projects and employing
hundreds of thousands of workers by doing so. The Central Bank of Iran
said that in 2004 private investment in the housing sector in urban areas
throughout the country has in recent years increased by an annual average
of 11 per cent, even though during the first half of 2002 the construction
of 98,000 housing units in the urban areas started by the private sector was
5 per cent less than those that were built during the same period the year
before.

Government subsidies

Besides subsidizing an excess of bureaucrats and state employees, there are
some other ways in which the proceeds of Iran's oil have also allowed the
regime to reinforce its grip on power. In particular, government ministers
have sometimes ended a great many serious industrial disputes, and thereby
averted brewing political controversy, by awarding pay increases that would
simply be unaffordable if the price of oil fell significantly. In the summer
of 2003, for example, a strike by high-school teachers, who in the course of
the preceding few months had on occasion closed around half the capital's
schools for several days at a time, was eventually solved when the government suddenly gave in and met their wage demands.

The Tehran authorities also make sure that the price of essential foodstuffs
is heavily subsidized, and in February 2001 a report noted that in the course
of the preceding year the government had paid out twice as much in subsidy
as it had in 1996. Some 70 per cent of these subsidies, which total around
$6.5 billion, were spent specifically on reducing the price of wheat and flour,
according to a senior Commerce Ministry official, Hassan Youness-Sinaki,
who also warned in January 2005 that any change in the bread subsidy

mechanism would have some highly adverse social and economic effects. 'If the government decides to pay direct subsidies to the people for wheat and flour, bread prices would jump to unacceptable levels which would not go with the prevailing social and economic conditions,' he claimed, adding that bread is the most widely used consumer item for the low-income strata of Iranian society. It is just such fears that prompted many parliamentarians to resist the efforts made by former president Khatami to significantly reduce the level of subsidy, even though such moves enjoyed much support from high-level economists: the governor of the Central Bank of Iran (CBI), Ebrahim Sheibani, warned in April 2005 that the 'avalanche of subsidies' was posing a threat to the government's economic growth programmes.

Unlikely though it may seem, the proceeds of the sale of Iranian oil also allow the regime to subsidize the cost of petrol at its own pumps. For by a curious paradox, Iran is not only a major exporter of oil but also a country in dire need of the refined oil – the 'gasoline' of American slang or 'petrol' of the British – that can be used by both industry and the ordinary consumer, and this dependency on importing refined oil also renders its economy highly vulnerable to oil price increases.

The reason that Iran is so short of gasoline is that it has hitherto lacked the spare cash to upgrade the technically complex infrastructure needed to refine crude oil. In January 2005 it had nine such refineries, all fairly antique, with a combined capacity to produce 1.47 million barrels of gasoline every day. But it has been a long time since their output could keep pace with demand, and Iran has had to heavily import refined products since 1982, and although in June 2004 Tehran officials struck a deal with Japan's JGC corporation to massively expand the output of some of these installations, it will be some time before there is any discernible difference. In any case, Iranian consumption is rising at a much faster rate – more than 10 per cent each year – than output is expected to grow even in a best-case scenario, and in 2004 daily demand reached 390,000 barrels, 82,000 of which was consumed in the capital.

But if Iran's supply of gasoline was in any way disrupted, leading to a sudden increase in domestic prices, then its leaders know that there could be very severe consequences for the economy and, by extension, for political stability. Evidence that their fears are not exaggerated emerged clearly enough during the winter of 2003–4, when a national fuel shortage led to sporadic unrest and violence, and the mullahs can hardly have been reassured by similar events elsewhere in the world, notably in Nigeria, where in 1993 a political crisis that soon led to a military coup was suddenly and unexpectedly sparked by an increase in the price of petrol. This is why the regime has gone to such immense lengths to heavily subsidize gasoline, and in January 2005 froze prices at 2003 levels which, at less than 40 cents per gallon, were much lower than the market price. Even after implementing a 23 per cent price hike in the course of the 2004–5 financial year, pump prices were still close to two-and-a-half times less than the real cost, with the difference being made up by subsidies totalling $3.5 billion a year.

The government's dependency on the huge proceeds of the sale of its own crude oil to finance these prices has become particularly clear in recent years, with the cost of imported oil rising sharply. So by the summer of 2004, barely five months into the new financial year, the government had spent nearly all of the $1.5 billion budgeted to import refined oil and was forced to ask parliament for a further $1.1 billion to cover the unexpected extra costs. The head of the state-owned National Iranian Oil Company's international affairs department, Hojatollah Ghanimifard, told the official IRNA news agency that rising international oil prices were to blame, pointing out that a tonne of petrol costing some $210 in January 2003 had shot up to $460 18 months later. On 21 September the Majlis approved this extra allocation, one that was expected to allow the purchase of an extra billion gallons of gas in the second half of the year.

Iran's president, Mahmoud Ahmadinejad, also looks likely to reap some popularity during his tenure of power by making large hand-outs of Iran's oil wealth to those whose political support he is keen to enjoy. After winning the elections in June 2005 with vague pledges to redistribute these earnings more fairly than before and 'put the oil manna on everyone's *sofreh* [dinner table]', the new president soon began his task and within weeks of taking up office, in August, set about wooing Iran's young people with a number of measures. First came the 'Reza Love Fund', named after a Shiite Imam whose shrine is located in eastern Iran, which the new government wants to use to give young couples a financial helping hand. A frequent complaint among young Iranians is that the high costs of living have made it prohibitively expensive to get married, since the traditional ceremony demands dowries, feasts, dresses and other heavy costs that even prosperous families struggle to meet. 'I can't afford to get married and I think one should try to marry by twenty-four,' as Mehdi, a 22-year-old shopkeeper, told one Western newspaper reporter,[4] adding that 'these plans sound really good but I'll wait and seen if they are carried out.' The new fund would be distributed at a provincial level by local boards of trustees who decide how much money should be allocated to hopeful young couples and how such funds should be made available. Previous administrations tried to distribute funds through low-interest loans, and the Love Fund was likely to go the same way. However these plans are eventually implemented, it remains to be seen if they will compensate for the lack of social freedoms that many young Iranians bemoan.

Similar moves to popularize the regime were made soon after, when in November the state-owned Keshavarzi agriculture bank reduced its lending rate to 9 per cent, well below the rate of inflation. The reduction, from 13.5 per cent, came days after the managing directors of seven state-owned banks, including Keshavarzi, were replaced by the new government of Ahmadinejad and signalled that the new premier was pressing ahead with his populist agenda of 'social justice'. Sadeq Khalilian, a deputy agriculture minister, told the official Iranian news agency that the ministry would 'mix' part of its own resources with the bank's assets to boost lending to farming five to tenfold.

Security

The large amounts of cash made spare from the sale of oil have not only allowed the Islamic regime to employ an army of bureaucrats, keep the economy afloat and subsidize the price of vital items. They have also enabled its security chiefs to expand the size of their forces, helping them to keep a tight grip on dissent and to prepare for any large-scale disturbances that could challenge the stability of the regime.

One example is the Basij Resistance Force, a paramilitary organization connected with the Islamic Revolution Guards Corps, which has appeared to be undergoing something of a revival under the administration of Ahmadinejad. Iranian dissidents are among those claiming that both the number of Basiji and the equipment and training they receive have suddenly increased thanks to the patronage of the new president, who seems to have allocated more funds to their cause. General Mirahmadi, the first deputy commander of the Basij, announced in Tehran on 25 September 2005 that an extra 2,000 special battalions within the Basij were soon to be created.

The reason why the Basiji in particular have benefited from this patronage could be connected with the organization's alleged role during the presidential campaign in securing votes for Ahmadinejad, who in mid-August also appointed Hojatoleslam Heidar Moslehi, the Supreme Leader's representative to the militia, as an adviser. But the main reason is probably that such an expansion simply helps secure the regime's grip on power, since the particular type of forces that are being expanded – the 'Ashura' units – are given the particular responsibility of quelling riots and urban unrest. This became particularly clear when, in late September 2005, its members staged a series of urban defence exercises in eight cities across the country. 'The objective of the current phase of the military exercise is to confront [urban] unrest,' the leader of Friday prayers in Ahwaz, Ayatollah Mohammad Ali Musavi-Jazayeri, was reported by the Iranian press as saying, while a Guards Corps commander, identified only as Rastegar, added that there will be 'operations to confront internal unrest and agitation as well as relief and rescue operations'.[5]

Of course exactly how much these and other security forces are now being expanded is a matter of secrecy, even by the standards of a regime that has always been highly opaque. Basij commander General Mohammad Hejazi told the Fars news agency on 14 September that his militia movement could already claim to have more than 11 million members across the country, adding that 'among the most important tasks of the Basij are boosting everlasting security, strengthening development infrastructures, equipping resistance bases, [and] increasing employment', and describing the prohibition of vice and the promotion of virtue in society as the 'divine policy' of the Basij. But the precise size of the Basij is very much an open question. Iranian officials frequently cite a figure of 20 million, but this is just a hollow boast based on revolutionary leader Ayatollah Khomeini's decree in November 1979 that 'a country with 20 million youths must have 20 million riflemen or a military with 20 million soldiers; such a country will never be destroyed'. A somewhat more plausible figure was put forward in a 2005 study by the Center for Strategic and International Studies in Washington, which says there are about 90,000 active-duty Basij members who are full-time uniformed personnel, backed up by 300,000 reservists. The study further adds that the Basij can altogether mobilize up to 1 million men, since its membership also comprises mainly boys, old men and those who have recently finished their military service. The real figure might be greater still, however, if members of the university Basij and former tribal levies incorporated into its ranks are also taken into account.

Overall there are several different ways in which any wealthy political order can use its spare cash to reinforce its grip on power, and Iran's petrodollars have allowed the present regime to stave off economic collapse, employ a very large number of people in a bloated public sector and expand the security services. But if this has allowed a regime inimical to the United States to stay afloat, how does wealth affect Iran's external challenge to Washington? Once again, the vast earnings from the sale of oil have also played a key role here too, having financed Iran's nuclear and conventional armaments programmes.

Military

Iran's petro-earnings are currently being used to update its ageing military forces, much of which continue to be armed with former Soviet equipment that is not just outdated but increasingly difficult to keep in good working order.

It is no coincidence that the Iranian leadership initiated a major drive to expand and update its military forces soon after there had been an upswing in the price of oil. Defence expenditure increased significantly in the mid-

1990s, and this allowed the size of the army to expand from 300,000 in 1993 to 345,000 in 2004.[6] Tehran also looked abroad with an increasingly acquisitive eye. From the end of the 1990s the regime began to actively lobby Moscow for the sale of a defence shield that could protect its key industrial military installations from enemy attack, and in December 2000, in the wake of a sharp oil price increase, Russia and Iran agreed to launch a new long-term programme of political and military cooperation. At the end of a three-day visit to Tehran Russia's Defence Minister, Igor Sergeyev, heralded the opening of 'a new chapter in our relations, marked by the reopening of military cooperation between Moscow and Tehran', while the Iranian Defence Minister, Ali Shamkhani, championed the advent of a 'historic day'. Three months later, in mid-March, President Mohammad Khatami made a landmark four-day visit to Moscow and signed an arms purchase 'framework agreement' that was valued by Russian military experts at an estimated $7 billion.

Relations between Iran and Russia continued to warm, and on 1 October 2001 Shamkhani arrived in Moscow to negotiate other weapons deals that were believed to be worth a further $300 million a year. Before he left, Shamkhani told a press conference in Tehran that during his visit he would be discussing bilateral military issues that included the signing of arms deals, developments in the Caspian Sea as well as the looming US military strikes against the Taliban regime in Afghanistan. 'We will sign deals to revive the military contracts that had previously been suspended [since] our defence cooperation with Russia is within the framework of international conventions,' he told reporters. One of his opposite numbers, the head of the Duma's Commission for Defence Affairs, Andrey Nikolayev, also echoed these sentiments, claiming that 'Russia provides Iran with any defensive weapons it needs to protect its security. Russia would implement all contracts it has signed with Iran.' He added that 'Iran and Russia are two regional powers which play a key role in guaranteeing the peace and security in the region.' By this time, independent observers were reckoning that Iran had become the world's largest purchaser of Russian military equipment after India and China, having already bought an estimated $4 billion of its military hardware, technology and services since 1989.

It is also significant that Iran's own space programme took off, in every sense, when the spare cash for such an expensive project had been made available by oil sales. The product of joint Iranian–Russian cooperation, the $15 million Sina-1 research satellite was launched for the first time in October 2005 and is currently being used to take pictures of Iran, to monitor natural disasters and to obtain information about the state of the country's agriculture and natural resources. Yet it was significant that the Director General of Iran Electronic Industries, Ebrahim Mahmoudzadeh, said that although the project had been unveiled in 1998, the satellite's actual construction had not begun until 2002, when oil revenues were starting to really pour into the government's coffers. Nor did he seem to think that future funding would be hard to get, since he stressed that the satellite represents only the first step in Iran's space programme and emphasized that 'considering that the satellite weights 170kg and is carrying a camera, it is an initial model as far as technical know-how and experience are concerned'. When in January 2005 the Russians signed a contract with Tehran to build the 'Zohreh' communications satellite, due to be launched in mid-2007, it also looked increasingly likely that the Iranian satellite programme was also destined to have some military purpose.

Oil can in a different way also help Tehran secure the military equipment it so badly needs if, instead of paying with the hard currency oil sales have helped to generate, it merely offers to deliver supplies instead. Since the early 1990s, for example, the Iranians have secured arms deals from the Ukraine in return for the supply of oil, and the Ukrainian government is recently believed to have offered to supply Tehran with large deliveries of T72 tanks and the highly sophisticated S-300 air defence system with deals that only strong American pressure has so far persuaded them to put on hold.

In November 2005 the German magazine *Der Spiegel* cited unidentified Western intelligence sources and reported that Iran offered North Korea oil and natural gas as payment for help in developing nuclear missiles. A senior Iranian official had travelled to Pyongyang during the second week of the previous October to make the offer, the magazine quoted the sources as saying, although North Korea's response was unclear.[7]

Another country that has swapped arms for oil is China, and in June 2004 a new report from the US Congress accused China of passing nuclear technology to Iran in exchange for oil supplies. In its annual report, the US–China Economic and Security Review Commission said that Chinese experts had supervised the installation of equipment to enrich uranium in Iran and claimed further that such actions were putting American security in serious jeopardy. 'China's continued failure to adequately curb its proliferation practices poses significant national security concerns to the United States,' the report emphasized, adding that 'China's assistance to weapons of mass destruction-related programmes in countries of concern continues, despite repeated promises to end such activities and the repeated imposition of US sanctions.' The report continued by saying that 'one potential explanation for China's history of proliferation to countries such as Iran, Iraq, and Libya, countries that have been on the State Department's list of terrorist sponsors, is China's growing dependence on Middle East oil.' Citing newspaper articles that Iranian front companies were procuring materials from China and elsewhere for secret nuclear weapons facilities, the report also said that about 50 Chinese experts had been observed working at a uranium mine at Saghand, which could produce the raw materials from which a nuclear bomb can eventually be made.

Just how much military support Beijing has given Iran is of course impossible to judge, but most experts believe that it has provided the F8 'Finback' fighter and a considerable amount of technical support for Iran's long-range missile programme, which is said by highly respected independent sources to have experienced 'dramatic growth' in the last few years. With Chinese as well as Russian and North Korean assistance backing up its efforts, Iran is said to have been 'moderately successful' in generating the low-level technology and expertise it needs for providing less sophisticated, standard weapons systems of its own.[8] Western defence experts also believe that Iran will acquire further technical expertise on ballistic missile systems from the cooperation it is receiving from Russia on its satellite programme.

The degree to which the present regime's purchasing power of arms is dependent on the price of oil is of course nothing new, since the shah had also used Iran's vastly expanded oil revenues after the late 1960s to finance both a massive military build-up as well as an unrealistically ambitious industrial and construction programme. After the shah had begun a campaign to boost Iranian oil revenues and the world became short of supply, the country had become the second largest oil producer in the Persian Gulf region, and between 1971 and 1972 its oil revenues nearly doubled from $885 million to $1.6 billion, while by 1978 its rate of production had hit a staggering 5.9 million barrels a day. In 1972 this enabled the imperial regime to buy the brand-new F14 fighter from Washington, as well as a vast range of other highly valued and up-to-date items from the American arsenal, while also expanding the size of its armed forces from 255,000 men in 1971 to a colossal 385,000 by 1975.

Foreign exchange and the nuclear programme

The other military interest that the shah's vast oil wealth allowed him to pursue was a nuclear programme, and there is evidence that by the mid-1970s his scientists were trying to develop a warhead, even if these ambitions were officially denied by Akbar Etemad, then head of the Atomic Energy Organization of Iran. In particular the shah's government is known to have discussed plans with Tel Aviv to modify Israel's surface-to-surface Jericho missiles to carry a possible Iranian warhead, while at the Tehran Nuclear Research Centre scientists studied not only missile blueprints but also ways of obtaining the weapons-grade plutonium from which the fissile material of a bomb can be made. Yet even conducting this initial research was extremely expensive, and it is highly questionable that the imperial nuclear warhead programme would have reached even these embryonic stages without the proceeds of the sale of oil, which peaked shortly before the programme got under way.

The shah's interest in pursuing a peaceful programme of nuclear energy dated back much further and stemmed from the time when the construction of a reactor had first become affordable. In 1963 Iran's proceeds from the sale of oil stood at $372 million but by 1969 the figure had increased to $791 million, and it was at this time that Mohammed Reza Shah commissioned a number of studies to examine the feasibility of building a series of nuclear power plants that, when completed, would allow Iran to become less dependent on imported refined oil. Similarly, work on the Bushehr nuclear power facility had first begun in 1974, when oil prices were at a peak, and by the time work was suspended, on the eve of the 1979 Islamic revolution, billions of dollars had already been spent on the project. Some progress on the plant resumed following the end of the Iran–Iraq War, during which time Bushehr was bombed six times and seriously damaged, and in 1995 Russia signed an $800 million contract for the completion of a 1,000 Mw pressurized light-water reactor, as well as for the possible supply of two modern VVER-440 units. Yet throughout these years, the Iranian government was simply too cash-strapped to allow much work on Bushehr, and only very slow progress was made. It was not until after 2000, as it once again earned large quantities of foreign exchange, that work speeded up dramatically, and in early March 2003 Tehran indicated that around 70 per cent of Bushehr had been completed and that the reactor was expected to come online as early as March 2004. The completion date for Bushehr was subsequently pushed back a year, supposedly because of technical difficulties, and it is now scheduled to begin operating in 2007, although that date, like every other, is also likely to be deferred. But whenever it does eventually come into use, a vast quantity of petro-earnings will undoubtedly have been lavished on it.

Both the rhythm of Bushehr's construction as well as the Tehran regime's nuclear programme as a whole have danced to the tune of the oil price. In particular, the rise in the price of oil during and after 1999 meant that this programme could move not with a slow, gentle step but instead in sudden, almost dramatic gyrations that would have otherwise been much more difficult, if not impossible, for the Iranians to perform.

One example is the massive Natanz complex for the enrichment of uranium. Some indication of the sheer cost of this project comes from the length of time it took to build. Officially designated as a project aimed at the eradication of an arid desert region, the building of this facility was said to have begun in 2000 by the Jahad-e Towse'eh and Towese'eh–Sakhteman construction companies, and by the time that the existence of the site was publicized by a dissident organization in August 2002 it was still a year or so from completion. Even then it was far from complete, since a great deal of additional technical facilities still remained to be built. In financial terms such a vast project was obviously hugely demanding. Most experts accept the figure, quoted by dissident forces, that the project had cost somewhere around $300 million, but others reckon that $1 billion is a much more realistic estimate.

In their briefing to the world's press in Washington, the dissident organization in question, the National Council of Resistance of Iran (NCRI), gave their 'inside story' of how this plant was financed, a version that has been accepted by independent commentators as quite plausible. Much of the $300 million funding for the project, claimed the NCRI, had been specially provided by the Supreme Security Council, whose members carefully set it outside the supervisory overview of the Budget and Planning Organization. They did this, it was further claimed, by using a front company that had specifically been created for the project, the Kalaye Electric Company, whose headquarters in Tehran were also the scene of a stand-off between IAEA inspectors and Iranian officials that took place later, in the summer of 2003.[9] Run under the watchful eye of a very senior regime official, Davood Aqajani, who is also the managing director of another Iranian nuclear project involved in the construction of a heavy water reactor at Arak, and by the head of the Atomic Energy Agency of Iran, Gholamreza Aghazadeh, who reportedly pays visits to the site every month in order to oversee progress, the building project was well organized and well funded.

It is a measure of the prohibitive costs of a nuclear weapons programme that even when the Natanz complex is in full working order, the overall cost of producing nuclear fuel, which is made in several other stages in addition to those undertaken at Natanz, is much higher still. Some Russian nuclear scientists, for example, are of the opinion that because Iran's uranium ore is not particularly well suited for the production of nuclear fuel, its own indigenous efforts to produce enriched uranium will cost three to five times more than an average figure. So Stanislav Golovinsky, the vice-president of the Russian company TVEL, which produces nuclear fuel for electric power plants, has been quoted as saying that Iran's reserves of uranium are 'insignificant', adding that the 'extraction cost' would be too high to make such a project financially viable. The uranium extraction cost falls into three categories of quality, this leading Russian nuclear engineer argues, and Iran's uranium is, in his judgement, undoubtedly the lowest of them.[10]

Iran's oil is not only bolstering the mullahs' regime in all these different ways but is also having repercussions on other countries that Washington deems to be its regional enemies. So by funding such an arms programme, the Iranians have also attracted the interest of other governments in the Middle East that also have good reason to feel suspicious of American motives. The vast earnings from Iran's sale of oil have in this way prompted other rivals of Washington to gravitate towards Tehran. One such country is Syria, and there are two quite distinct ways in which Iran's oil is able to undermine American threats against the Damascus regime.

Military alliances

By building up its own military strength, using the proceeds of the sale of oil to do so, Tehran has tempted Damascus to strike up a defensive alliance aimed at deterring any possible American military action. Just such an 'alliance' was tentatively formed on 16 February 2005, when the Iranian and Syrian governments directly confronted the Bush administration by declaring they had formed a mutual self-defence pact to confront the common 'threats' that both felt they were then facing. The move, which took many observers by surprise, was announced after a meeting in Tehran between Iranian Vice-President Mohammed Reza Aref and Syrian Prime Minister Naji al-Otari. 'At this sensitive point, the two countries require a united front due to numerous challenges,' Otari claimed at the end of the talks, adding that 'this meeting, which takes place at this sensitive time, is important, especially because Syria and Iran face several challenges and it is necessary to build a common front.' Similar sentiments were voiced by Aref, who added that 'we are ready to help Syria on all grounds to confront threats'.

If in the future Tehran succeeds in developing a nuclear warhead, this will almost certainly strongly tempt Damascus to establish much stronger ties with Iran and seek shelter under the protection of its nuclear umbrella. Most obviously such a development would clearly have serious military implications for the Americans, not least by making the US military much more reluctant to make incursions into Syria if the need ever arises, just as there have been several occasions in recent years when the Israelis have launched or appeared close to launching large-scale incursions into Syria in retaliation for Damascus' alleged sponsorship of anti-Israeli violence.[11] Such possible consequences have scarcely gone unnoticed by American commentators such as Thomas Donnelly, an analyst at the 'neo-conservative' American Enterprise Institute, who wrote that by going nuclear 'Iran will extend its deterrence, either directly or de facto, to a variety of states and other actors throughout the region. This would be an ironic echo of the extended deterrence thought to apply to US allies during the Cold War.'[12]

It is from this perspective that the heightened American interest in 'regime change' in Syria should be seen. Since the toppling of Saddam Hussein, some political factions in Washington have demanded the taking of a much tougher foreign policy line against the Syrian government, which is regarded by Congress as a key regional supporter of terrorism. In mid-October 2003 Congress passed the Syria Accountability and Lebanese Sovereignty Act, which called on Damascus to 'halt Syrian support for terrorism, end its occupation of Lebanon, stop its development of weapons of mass destruction, cease its illegal importation of Iraqi oil and illegal shipments of weapons and other military items to Iraq'. The Act also alleged that Syria would 'be held responsible for attacks committed by Hezbollah and other terrorist groups with offices or other facilities in Syria', while also prohibiting the sale of dual-use items – goods that could be used in both civilian programmes as well as to develop weapons of mass destruction – to Damascus.

It is possible that undermining the rule of President Asad was viewed in Washington as an indirect response to Iran's nuclear programme, whose newly discovered sophistication was now causing a sense of alarm but which even US administration hawks were recognizing could not easily be dealt with by military force alone.[13] Such American interest in Syrian 'regime change' may have instead reflected a concern to prevent the emergence of a new anti-American and anti-Israeli axis that could be realized in the worst-case but increasingly likely scenario that the Iranians did succeed in developing a nuclear warhead.

The proceeds of the sale of oil are therefore allowing Tehran to build up conventional armed forces and to develop a nuclear warhead that would prompt other regional rivals of American power in the Middle East to take its side and strike up new alliances. But there are also other respects in which Iran's oil can help to bolster the Syrian regime in particular.

Syria and Iranian oil

Tehran's willingness to defy American pressure on the Asad regime became clear in the autumn of 2003. While Washington was condemning Damascus loudly, the Iranians signalled their defiance of American pressure and in November promised to assist Syria against the impact of any proposed US sanctions. 'Iran is ready to extend assistance to Syria in all fields, especially the oil sector,' proclaimed Mohsen Mirdamadi of the Majlis' National Security and Foreign Policy Commission in a clear rebuke to American policy. His words were not empty ones because there are several ways in which Iran could offer the Syrians meaningful assistance that would pose a clear challenge to American influence in the Middle East.

The Iranians could assist Syria if Washington sought to dissuade other countries from either investing in the Syrian oil industry or from importing its crude oil. In such a scenario, Tehran would be able to offer Damascus its own technical expertise in developing Syria's dwindling oil reserves. Syria's vulnerability to such pressure is not in doubt, since in the last few years its government has made great efforts to boost oil production but has always been dependent on foreign investment to do so. But while government efforts to attract international oil companies have reaped some rewards, attracting several leading companies including Shell, Canada's Tanganyika and Petro-Canada, America's Gulfsands Petroleum and China's CNPC for the development of the Kebibe field, these successes, though small in size, have been overshadowed by the withdrawal of other companies that have either been unable to find gas and oil in large quantities or else are simply too daunted by political pressure from Washington to proceed. Some of the businesses that have withdrawn from the Syrian market include ExxonMobil, ConocoPhillips and Devon Energy, while there are also reports that Petro-Canada is planning to sell its stake in Syria's leading national oil enterprise, the Al Furat Petroleum Company.

Yet despite their dependence on Western technology to develop their own fields, the Iranians would also be in a position to help assist Syria's oil industry if the Damascus regime is ever confronted by a mass exodus of foreign investment, just as Tehran has also helped some other regimes across the world that are also inimical to the United States. In November 2005, for example, a senior official at the South Pars field, Asghar Ebrahimi-Asl, announced that Iran's Petropars was ready to participate in the development of an oil field in the Gulf of Venezuela once the contract in question had been finalized. This agreement to work on this particular section of the giant oil field, which covered 540 square kilometres and contained up to 18 billion barrels of heavy oil, was ready to be signed when the Iranian Minister of Industries and Mines visited Venezuela. Earlier on in the year, in March, Petropars and Petroleos de Venezuela had already signed an initial contract on the oil project in the Gulf of Venezuela as well as on the development of the offshore Mariscal gas field and of another oil field with four blocks in the region.

If Washington imposes economic sanctions on Damascus that prompt international oil companies to take flight, then the Iranians could not only offer the Syrians some limited support to step in and take their place but also, in the longer term, supply their own oil to bridge a looming gap between Syrian supply and demand. In the last few years, the fall in Syrian oil output has been accompanied by a surge in consumption at home, and whereas in the mid-1980s domestic consumption of oil products had averaged around

190,000 barrels every day, in 2003 this had increased to 279,000 barrels. This rapid rate of growth in demand has reduced Syria's potential to export oil, to the extent that nowadays Syria exports only around 200,000 barrels per day. Furthermore, since the country's proven oil reserves are around 2.5 billion barrels, most experts, including the main foreign operator in the country, Shell, expect that Syria will become a net oil importer within the next decade. This is why officials in Damascus make such an issue of domestic production. For instance, the Oil and Mineral Resources Minister, Ibrahim Haddad, has said that the cabinet 'underlined the need to pay strong attention to the production of oil and mineral resources so as to dispel worries in the last few years over the decrease in oil production'.

While it is much more difficult to say whether Tehran would be willing to break a UN-imposed sanctions regime, a Washington-led embargo would be a much more tempting target for an Iranian regime that fears and resents American influence in the Middle East. Yet such sanctions look increasingly likely in the future. In November 2005 President Bush called both Iran and Syria 'outlaw regimes' and decreed that any countries that support terrorism are just as guilty of murder as those who carry out the violence. 'We're determined to deny radical groups the support and sanctuary of outlaw regimes. State sponsors like Syria and Iran have a long history of collaboration with terrorists and they deserve no patience from the victims of terror,' Bush said. The United States has not only accused Syria of allowing foreign fighters to cross its border into Iraq to fuel the insurgency against Coalition forces in Iraq, but has also sided with UN investigators in blaming Syrian and Lebanese security officials for the murder of former Lebanese Prime Minister Rafik Hariri on 14 February 2005. By the following October the United States and France were openly threatening Syria with economic sanctions if it did not cooperate fully with the official UN inquiry into Hariri's assassination. 'The United States makes no distinction between those who commit acts of terror and those who support and harbour them because they are equally guilty of murder,' Bush said, adding that 'we're determined to deny the militants control of any nation which they will use as a home base and a launching pad for terror.'

Of course no regime or government is ever bolstered just by the narrowly material support of the sort that this chapter has looked at so far. A government also draws strength from much more abstract sources, such as the 'prestige' or 'esteem' in which it is held, or from the sense of 'acceptance' that it finds on the international stage, and in each case Iran's possession of such massive oil and gas reserves also buttresses the regime's power and influence in a way that can only alarm Washington.

Some other forms of support

Iran's sense of isolation

Over the past decade, the outside world's increasing dependency on Iran's natural resources has probably ended, or at least limited, the sense of international stigma and isolation that had hung over the country ever since the 1979 revolution. This is perhaps because when high-profile visits are made to the country by foreign ministers and commercial delegations, and when foreign businesses have an unmistakable presence that is frequently filmed by the national media, ordinary Iranians can more easily convince themselves that their own country is no longer the pariah that it had been in the decade or so that followed the revolutionary upheaval. Perhaps a comparison might almost be drawn with Anwar Sadat's visit to Jerusalem in November 1977, which was cheered by large crowds of jubilant Israelis because it represented a certain 'acceptance' from the Arab world that they desperately craved. But perhaps it is not just about any visit or the presence of any foreign delegation but also about what ordinary Iranians sense about their own country: perhaps just by word of mouth, not just by the news they hear and the information they digest, many Iranians can intuit the state their own country is in, just as most nationals elsewhere in the world also share similar intuitions about the state of their own.

Quite why this should help to bolster the present political order – or at least make it less unpopular among ordinary Iranians – is hard to explain. On the one hand most ordinary Iranians are strongly suspicious of foreign interference, which in the light of their history is hardly surprising, since Iran has been trampled over by the feet of foreign invaders for more than 2,000 years. The ancient Greeks invaded and brought the vast monumental palace at Persepolis and the vast Persian empire, one that had ruled vast swathes of the wider world for more than 300 years, crashing down with unforgiving violence. Then came the Arab invaders, as wild tribes rallied to the inspiration of the Prophet Mohammed and conquered Persia, bringing Islam and the Arabic script with them in their wake. Then there were other foreign armies that followed, including the Mongol hordes, that swept away westwards from their Chinese homelands in the Middle Ages and plundered much of what lay before them, the Ottoman janissaries who attacked in the sixteenth and seventeenth centuries, and the vast land armies and navy of tsarist Russia. Thus Great Britain's later involvement in Persia, which really began at the end of the nineteenth century, followed in a very long tradition: 'it all started with that Greek Alexander,' Mohammed Mossadeq sighed during the crisis with Britain over his decision to nationalize the Anglo-Iranian Oil Company.

Yet paradoxical though it may seem, most Iranians also strongly dislike the sense of isolation that they feel afflicted their country after 1979. This comes across to a foreign traveller, who is often greeted by total strangers with an overwhelming hospitality and generosity, and who is likely to quickly get the impression, when talking among them, that nearly all would much prefer to see stronger and closer relations with the outside world, particularly with the United States after more than a quarter century of diplomatic isolation. Perhaps the clearest single demonstration of this personal warmth towards outsiders came during the international relief operation that followed the massive earthquake that shook the ancient city of Bam in southern Iran on 26 December 2003: the American rescue workers who played an important part in this effort were taken aback by the displays of hospitality and friendliness that they experienced.

The Iranian clamouring for international acceptance also emerged clearly in the autumn of 2002, when a ground-breaking opinion poll caused a political storm. According to the survey conducted on 22 September by three separate institutes, 74.8 per cent of the 1,500 Iranians interviewed favoured some form of dialogue with the United States and nearly half said that Washington's policy on Iran was 'to some extent correct'. The poll's findings sent shockwaves through the political establishment, and the judiciary immediately hauled the polling institutes' directors into court and charged them with 'publishing lies to excite public opinion'. These findings also caused even more of a crisis when the Majlis, at that time a reformist body that had originally commissioned the study, defended the directors' decision to publish and called for the prosecutions to be dropped immediately.

If Iranians crave this 'international acceptance', why hasn't the Tehran regime sought to patch things up with Washington? One possible reason is that because the castigation of the 'Great Satan' has been an article of faith for the regime ever since 1979, the mullahs fear that any rapprochement with the United States will dissolve the values of their political order to such a degree that the entire framework will soon come crashing down. But it is unlikely to be the main reason, since Washington had declined to take up several Iranian offers of dialogue, notably in 1996 when Rafsanjani had offered a US oil firm, Conoco, a big opening in the Iranian oil industry that would have almost certainly have led to wider relations between the two countries.[14] Again, in May 2006, the White House did not reply to an 18-page letter from the Iranian president which requested direct talks between the two countries over the nuclear issue, despite calls from influential figures such as Henry Kissinger to explore the offer. Perhaps more important is Iran's insistence on adopting a hostile rhetorical tone towards Israel, and the obstructive behaviour of hardliners in both countries whose

vested interests have prompted them to stifle any moves towards reconcilia-
tion.

Strong international interest in Iran's natural resources can only have
helped to limit the sense of isolation from the outside world that ordinary
Iranians would otherwise have felt even more keenly, and in a way that
would have inevitably posed a clear challenge to the regime: the Iranian
media, for example, speaks voluminously about the exploration and development of the national oil and gas reserves, and of the strength of interest
shown by foreign businesses and governments in securing the contracts to
get involved. But however such ideas travel – whether by mass communications, by word of mouth or at a deeper 'intuitive' level – the attention
attracted by Iran's highly seductive oil and gas reserves can only help remove
the sense of international stigma and isolation.

This touches on another point because, looked at from another angle,
the strength of this international interest not only limits Iran's isolation but
also impacts on something else – its national prestige.

Status and prestige

If a nation's prestige, like an individual's, rests on its perception of its own
standing among its peers, then there are two essential reasons why Iran is
more likely than most to be particularly conscious of where it stands. Both
are in different ways born of Iran's unique historical condition.

On the one hand it is possible that this consciousness has something to
do with the greatness of ancient Persia, which until the invasion of Alexander the Great in 334 BC was the world's largest and most advanced empire,
one that stretched from the Aegean to the Hindu Kush and from the Black
Sea to the Nile. Its people certainly saw themselves in very grandiose terms:
'they look upon themselves as very greatly superior in all respects to the
rest of mankind,' the Greek historian Herodotus recorded, 'regarding others
as approaching to excellence in proportion as they dwell nearer to them.'[15]
Visions of such an esteemed past are often said to lurk somewhere in the
back of the minds of contemporary Iranians, and when any particular individuals or nations view themselves as the heirs of such a great inheritance,
then they can only be deeply conscious of their status in the contemporary
world. Such comparisons certainly seemed to weigh on the mind of President
Ahmadinejad as he spoke in New York in September 2005 and pointed out
that Iran was being denied its rights even though it is 'a nation with several
thousand years' history of civilization. The world owes us many moral and
humanitarian values. Now we still have the potential capability to lead the
world to those good values. The only thing we need to accomplish this goal
is not to underestimate ourselves, but believe in our own selves.'

It is probably easy to exaggerate the importance of this particular argument, not because ancient Persia reached its zenith nearly 2,000 years ago but because it did so before the dawn of Islam. For in the eyes of very devout Muslims, the pre-Islamic age is typically regarded as pagan and therefore unworthy of respect, just as contemporary Egyptians do not identify with their own extraordinarily sophisticated ancestors who built some of the great wonders of the world. Yet visions of ancient Persia probably have some place somewhere in the contemporary Iranian national consciousness, making issues like 'prestige' and 'status' particularly important. Many Iranians, for example, regard it as a fact of indisputable importance that they, as a nation, invented the first postal system, polo, human rights, calendars, wine, sewing thread, ships and perfume, and would be astonished if anyone questioned it. This becomes clear in all sorts of everyday situations. When a giant outdoor TV screen was recently installed in a square in Tehran and various officials went to inaugurate it, complaints were made by people who asked why there was so much fuss about a mere Japanese television set when Iran had given the world so many things that were so much more valuable. In the same tradition, Iranians today also claim to produce the best carpets, caviar, pistachios, pomegranates, miniature paintings and, of course, one other commodity – oil.

Perhaps a more important reason why Iranians are particularly conscious of their status and standing is that, as mentioned earlier, Persia had suffered to an unusual degree from foreign invasion, subjugation and exploitation, and any nation that suffers so badly is unlikely to be anything except conscious of its status. Of course this does not necessarily follow, because a nation or individual can simply become used to being in such an unfortunate situation, or else end up becoming wholly indifferent to what others think of them. North Korea, for example, which over the centuries has also suffered from repeated attack, has now become one of the most insular regimes in the world and arguably cares nothing for its prestige but everything for its self-defence. In Iran's case, however, these later historical events, rather than those that took place in ancient times, are probably more important in explaining the strength of its concern with where, as a nation, it thinks it stands alongside others.

Iran's consciousness of its own prestige and status has become clear from the terminology and vocabulary employed by its leadership. Throughout his tenure of office, Mahmoud Ahmadinejad's rhetoric has been saturated with references to 'equality' and 'inequality' of stature, and he has claimed that to prevent Iran from enriching uranium would be a state of 'nuclear apartheid' enforced by 'some powerful states [that] practise a discriminatory approach'. Instead, he has gone on to say, there should be 'equal rights of peoples and nations in international relations' and this means that 'access [to the peaceful technology to produce nuclear fuel] cannot be restricted to a few [that by] depriving most nations and by establishing economic monopolies, use them as an instrument to expand their domination'.

In a way, such rhetoric echoes that of another Iranian leader who, more than a century before, had also stood before the United Nations Assembly in New York in order to plead Iran's case over a different issue. In a speech that was somewhat better received than Ahmadinejad's 'rant' in September 2005, Mohammed Mossadeq had argued that the nationalization of the Anglo-Iranian Oil Company was justified because British ownership of the company imposed a form of 'economic servitude' on an 'oppressed nation' that was 'suffering in conditions of absolute misery without even the barest necessities of life'. And for the same reason, ordinary Iranians in the street are quick to point to double standards about Iran's nuclear programme that amount to an infringement of their country's dignity. 'It's a double-standard,' the reformist editor of one English-language daily in Tehran told an American reporter. 'If a signatory of the Non-Proliferation Treaty is subscribing to the so-called community of civilized nations, then why has Israel not been sanctioned?'[16] As one young Iranian student simply asked another Western correspondent, 'why should the US, Britain and Israel all have nuclear weapons and not us?'[17]

It is likely that considerations of 'prestige' play a much more important part in formulating high-level policy decisions in Tehran than is widely realized in the West. It is, for example, arguably the most important reason why Iran wants nuclear weapons, just as the 'bomb' was ultimately a symbol of national status for at least two members of the elite 'nuclear club', Britain and France, which sought nuclear compensation to make up for the loss of their empires in the post-war years. The Iranians could, after all, arguably address any concern for their national security by building closer political ties with Russia or China that would spare them both the vast costs and the international controversy that their efforts have imposed.

An example of how this consideration is underestimated or even sometimes wholly overlooked in the West is the tendency to dismiss Tehran's claim that it is seeking to build a civilian nuclear energy programme in order to make more of its own oil available for export. Such an argument does not make sense, say the Americans in particular, because the massive costs of setting up a nuclear energy programme are far greater than any effort to simply increase the rate of domestic oil production. As the former White House spokesman Ari Fleischer contested in 2003, 'our assessment when we look at Iran is that there is no economic gain for a country rich in oil and gas like Iran to build costly indigenous nuclear fuel cycle facilities. Iran flares ['burns'] off more gas every year than the equivalent power that it hopes to produce with these reactors.' Yet this narrow arithmetic does not factor in the prestige that a civilian nuclear energy programme bestows on its holders and which an oil-rich country like Iran is prepared to pay considerable extra sums to acquire. Similarly, other countries nearly always also regard their own nuclear installations in the same way, with Pakistani officials, for example, pointing out that their own nuclear research programme, at Kahuta, is a 'symbol of sovereignty'.[18] Correspondingly, 'prestige' explains why Tehran has pursued some other programmes that are of clear symbolic value but whose practicality is open to question. Thus when in the autumn of 2005 Iran launched its first satellite into space from Plesetsk in northern Russia, it immediately joined a select club of countries that already had their own space programmes even though spokesmen seemed unsure about the actual benefits that its $15 million cost was supposed to bring.

Oil and 'prestige'

There are different ways in which Iran's natural resources are important in the context of this 'prestige'. On the one hand every nationalist always plays up what is unique and special about the nation to which he or she belongs, and for the same reason Iran's possession of such vast reserves of oil and gas can only elevate its national sense of importance and status, even if this can of course only be less pronounced when the oil price is low. During the crisis over the nationalization of the Anglo-Iranian Oil Company, for example, Mossadeq made an interesting remark about the importance of these reserves, claiming that 'the oil reserves of Iran, like its soil, its rivers and mountains, are the property of the people of Iran'. Significantly, such imagery almost invokes the landscapes portrayed by nationalist artists of the nineteenth century, whose portraits and poems sought to make their fellow nationals feel 'special' about their country's divinely given natural beauty and gifts.[19]

If the Iranians are well aware of the prestige bestowed by their resources, then so too are the enemies of the mullahs' regime, and it is probably not just hard currency that these enemies want to deny Tehran by imposing their own embargo on Iran and by persuading other countries to do likewise. Although such a message is much less easy to put forward to their mass electorates than any material considerations, the US and Israeli administrations are probably deeply conscious of the extra 'status' that the Tehran regime acquires every time an international consortium signs a deal to develop an oil or gas field. This is equally true of the nuclear programme, which some Israeli leaders, such as Yuval Steinitz, the chairman of Israel's parliamentary Foreign Affairs and Defence Committee, have complained is an unmistakable sign that 'Iran is seeking to become a world power'.

This is one of the reasons why Washington has been so alarmed by proposals, put forward after 1991, to move oil from the CIS republics of the former Soviet Union by a pipeline that would cross Iranian territory and terminate at the main oil terminals in the Persian Gulf, situated at Kharg Island, Lavan Island, Sirri Island and Ras Bahregan, while allowing refined products to be sent to terminals at Abadan and Bandar Manshahr. Yet although this is by far the most direct route, successive US administrations have lobbied extremely hard on behalf of an alternative route that bypasses both Iran and Russia, another long-term adversary of American influence in the region, and which would instead go through the Caspian Sea to Baku in Azerbaijan, Tbilisi in Georgia and Ceyhan in Turkey. This 'BTC' pipeline, which was more or less finished by the summer of 2005, circumvents Iranian soil and therefore denies the Tehran regime both the prestige and the international acceptance, as well as the transit fees and political leverage, that the alternative route through Iran would have granted.

But although the status of both Iran as a nation and the present political order in particular have been elevated by the possession and commercialization of its natural resources, there is also another, more indirect way in which these reserves can heighten this sense of international prestige. For if the sale of oil and natural gas generate sufficient spare cash, then the seller is in a position to play a much larger role on the international stage than it otherwise would, and by doing so it raises popular expectations of its future place in the world.

It was just such a role that Iran temporarily assumed in the 1970s and which now helps explain why some contemporary Iranians have high expectations of acquiring prestige, or rather re-acquiring what they think they have lost. As he watched the price of oil soar and petrodollars flood into the country, Shah Mohammed Reza Pahlavi dreamt of acquiring a new role for his country, and instead of continuing to take an insular, defensive course that would enable it to withstand foreign pressure and fend off would-be invaders, he now wanted Iran to be recognized as a key player in the entire Middle East region. In 1973 he sent a detachment of troops to Oman to help defeat the communist guerrillas who were trying to topple the pro-Western rulers, and soon afterwards supplied arms and training to the Somalian government, which was then battling a Soviet-backed Ethiopian militia that threatened to overrun much of the country. Other troop detachments turned up in places even further afield, such as Vietnam and sub-Saharan Africa, while the Iranian navy aggressively patrolled the Gulf Straits, and in 1971 captured two small islands, Abu Musa and Tunbs, that were claimed by the new government of the United Arab Emirates. But such posturing was

actively encouraged by the Nixon administration, which was busy fighting
the Soviets on numerous fronts and therefore encouraged the emergence of
a regional ally in the Middle East that would help relieve the pressure it felt
it was under.

With so much spare cash put into his hands by the big oil buyers, the
shah could afford to spend lavishly in other ways that also created an exaggerated Iranian sense of self-importance, and which also help explain why
an issue like 'prestige' is of such importance to the country's contemporary
leaders. Perhaps the best-known single episode was the shah's famous, or
rather infamous, five-day extravaganza that was held in the ruins of Persepolis in 1971 to celebrate what was claimed to be the 2,500th anniversary of
the foundation of the Iranian monarchy. Spending more than $100 million
on this spectacle, the shah arranged for food to be flown in every day from
top Parisian restaurants that provided luxuries such as quail eggs filled with
caviar and roasted peacock stuffed with *foie gras*, infuriating those who
angrily pointed to the shocking poverty in his own country but at the same
time doubtlessly also making many Iranians even more conscious of their
national status.

It is clear, then, that there are lots of different ways in which oil stands
at the heart of Iran's relationship with the outside world in general and of
its challenge to American global power in particular. How, then, should the
United States respond to this challenge, and try to mitigate or even end the
destructive political influence of Iran's energy resources? This question is
considered in the concluding chapter that follows.

Conclusion

Confronted by all these different pressures from its allies, its rivals and the non-aligned, the United States might at first sight seem to be in something of an impossible situation. If it starts to trade with Iran, or allows its allies to do so without making any effort to stop them, then it is clearly open to allegations of funding a hostile nuclear weapons programme and of financing terror. Yet if the current impasse continues, then it is clearly at risk of undermining its own global power, accentuating its own decline and, it is no exaggeration to say, even writing several paragraphs of its own obituary. How, then, should it proceed? And is there any way of reconciling these conflicting interests even if, in a worst-case scenario, Tehran persists in trying to develop the bomb?

If the controversy over Iran's nuclear ambitions is ever resolved to Washington's satisfaction, then of course the way forward should not be too difficult to find. The scope of existing primary economic sanctions against Tehran should be immediately reviewed and gradually rolled back, depending on the scale of Congressional opposition, while ILSA should be completely revoked. Such an economic relationship would in all likelihood quickly lead to a much wider political rapprochement that would open a new chapter in the story of the Middle East.

In Washington, however, even a resolution of the nuclear dispute might not ensure the normalization of relations because Tehran is still considered to be a leading sponsor of 'terror', one that is said to have been highly obstructive of peace in the Arab–Israeli dispute. In the wake of the *Karine A* incident[1] and Ahmadinejad's open boasts about annihilating Israel, is this not a strong objection?

There are several reasons why Iran's association with 'terror' in the Middle East should not obstruct any rapprochement with the United States. Above all, it should be recognized that the Iranian *government's* role in giving material support to militant Arab groups like Hamas and Islamic Jihad, if it has ever really assumed such a role at all, is of highly peripheral importance to the Arab–Israeli dispute. There would, after all, still be the same level of Palestinian unrest, which has its own inner dynamic, and the same number of suicide bombings without this supposed Iranian support. And again, if we assume that Tehran really has supplied these groups with the material support it has long been said to have done, then it is far from clear exactly who inside the Iranian establishment has been implicated. Is it businessmen or corrupt officials seeking handsome profits? Or are ideologically driven military or clerical elites really to blame? If so, why should a whole regime be penalized because of the activities of a mere few? During the Bosnian civil war, America's own ideologically driven elites within the Pentagon are reliably said to have conducted their own personal foreign policies and delivered arms to the Muslim forces, joining forces with the Iranians to do so.[2] So does that mean that the whole American administration had to be judged in the same terms?

It should be emphasized in this context that all the threatening Iranian references against Israel made by Ahmadinejad and many clerics are not propounded as meaningful statements of policy but deployed as rhetorical devices designed to please mass audiences. In all likelihood the Iranian mullahs would, like most Arabs, ideally like to witness the annihilation of Israel but, in the real world, would in fact be quick to strike a deal with Tel Aviv if it were in their interests to do so. To prevent Iraqi dominance during the 1980–88 war, for example, the Israelis secretly channelled military equipment and support to Iran that the Tehran regime gratefully accepted. Instead this gulf between 'statements' and 'policy' simply reflects the immense political differences between Western democracies and Middle Eastern states, differences that allow each to wholly misunderstand the statements and gestures of the other. In the Middle East it has always been commonplace for political leaders to speak in two quite distinct voices that, to the Western world where such a marked duality is unknown, appear to be wholly inconsistent: on the one hand there is the quieter tone with which policy is rationally debated and expounded in the 'high' world of politicians and diplomats, while on the other hand is the much louder, more strident pitch that just the same individuals can adopt, in person or on the airwaves, before the large crowds upon whose strong support their personal standing may in part depend. But to an outside world perhaps unacquainted with such marked cultural differences, the boasts and threats made to great rhetorical effect before large crowds are easily conflated with statements made in the realm of high politics.

Such an erroneous conflation of 'rhetoric' with 'policy' is not without precedent. British and French fears for their security at the time of the nationalization of the Suez Canal Company in July 1956 were much heightened by the fiery rhetoric of Egyptian President Gamal Abdul Nasser before huge Arab crowds. Promising to 'work so that the Arab homeland may extend from the Atlantic Ocean to the Persian Gulf', Nasser had on 28 July declared that the company was the property 'of the Egyptian people' and that its employees, many of them Western expatriates, 'must continue their work and are forbidden to leave'. But this strident message was easily misunderstood. The Egyptian Foreign Ministry quickly stated that foreign staff could leave at will, while many Western politicians also took Nasser's hollow boasts of pan-Arab nationalism far more seriously than they deserved. French premier Guy Mollet, for example, was convinced that such sentiments unmistakably revealed an ambition to undermine French colonial rule in North Africa, even though the Egyptian leader really had no such policy.[3] The catastrophic military venture that followed showed unmistakably enough the dangers that eventuate when someone who is ordinarily rational, level-headed and cautious loses his judgement in the same way that Eden lost his to the sound of Nasser's empty rhetoric.

So if a solution to the Iranian nuclear conundrum is found to Washington's satisfaction, then there should be no reason why serious moves cannot be made to open up trade between the two countries and also to repeal secondary sanctions. Much more difficult, however, would be formulating a response if the nuclear issue remains unsolved and continues to cause increasing international alarm as the Iranians move closer towards the nuclear threshold and succeed in developing a warhead. How should Washington respond in this scenario if it is to avoid the very pressures with the outside world that have been outlined in this book?

A starting point would be the recognition that America's own embargo on Iran, and its efforts to stop its allies from investing in Iran's oil sector, will in any event have no real impact on Tehran's purchasing power. While Washington claims that such restrictions will deprive the Iranians of the hard currency the regime needs for its nuclear programme and support of terrorism, it is plain that the absence of one country's investment in such a valuable market merely creates a void into which others will step. The American embargo on Iranian oil in 1995, for example, only prompted Tehran to switch to alternative buyers and therefore barely dented its foreign exchange earnings, while the imposition of commercial sanctions has lost American businesses billions of dollars in trade which have instead only gone straight into the pockets of their foreign rivals. So the central premise on which these sanctions are based is, therefore, fundamentally flawed.

There are also at least two ways in which large-scale trade, far from merely subsidizing the Tehran regime in the short term, might also help to change its character in a way that proves to be distinctly advantageous to the United

States. The construction of the India–Iran pipeline, for example, which Washington has lobbied so hard to prevent, offers a way of not only binding India and Pakistan together but also of giving Iran a much greater stake in the stability of the region as a whole. For by integrating the Iranian regime into the wider regional economy, the pipeline could arguably help to moderate the 'aggressive' and 'reckless' foreign policy that its enemies in Washington say it has hitherto shown an unmistakable inclination to conduct. In the same way, some of the most aggressive states have also been economically isolated from those towards which they have shown such aggression – some examples being North Korea towards its southern neighbour in the 1990s, or South Africa and Rhodesia towards the surrounding states in the 1970s. Nor did Israel and the Arab states conduct bilateral trade at the height of their mutual antagonism until Sadat's formal recognition of the state of Israel in 1981. The same argument also supports the case for strong commercial relations, including more 'oil-swap' arrangements, between Iraq and Iran, which in such a situation would clearly have a vested interest in maintaining law and stability in the post-Saddam order rather than undermining it in the way that the British and American governments have frequently contested.

According to one theory, which has become fashionable in the last decade or so even though it originates in the work of the eighteenth-century thinker Immanuel Kant, democracies do not fight each other. Yet this is contradicted by the experience of the First World War, waged with strong popular support by democratic Britain and Germany, and by subsequent conflicts or war scares between India, which is properly a 'democracy', and Pakistan, which is an emergent one. There are instead stronger grounds to believe that the stronger the economic ties between two states, the less likely military conflict becomes. America and North Vietnam, Western Europe and Serbia, India and Pakistan, Iran and Iraq, Britain and Argentina – these countries have all waged war in the post-war years and had little to lose in mutual commerce when they did so.

There is another reason why the central premise on which the American argument for trade sanctions against Tehran is flawed. When the large amounts of foreign exchange earned from such trade are circulated widely throughout any society, then of course standards of living rise and attitudes change. In other words, there could be no better way for the enemies of the Tehran regime to erode its values from within than by encouraging the outside world to increase its volume of trade with Iran. A new middle class would inevitably emerge in the country in the same way it has already emerged in India and China, where its appearance would have important political repercussions that are at present unclear. In Iran this new class would undoubtedly have more materialistic and Westernized tastes that are wholly incompatible with the values of the Islamic theocracy that has ruled since 1979, and the regime would have no choice but to watch these changes unfold with the same sense of powerlessness with which their Western counterparts have watched their own societies change as they have become increasingly affluent. 'Prosperity ripened the principle of decay,' as the great Whig historian Edward Gibbon wrote of ancient Rome.[4]

One possible parallel is with South Africa in the 1980s, when the strongest opponents of the apartheid regime argued that only the imposition of full economic sanctions on Pretoria would bring freedom for the millions of oppressed black Africans. Yet this was just as emotive a response as the argument that only US primary and secondary economic sanctions can stop Tehran from bankrolling terror and building the bomb, and sanctions instead caused great hardship for both white and black. A much more constructive and thoughtful way forward would instead have been to encourage more overseas trade with South Africa, thereby allowing a black middle class to emerge whose appearance would have allowed a gradual extension of the franchise and so spontaneously undermined the racial divisions of the apartheid regime.

So how can these conflicting interests best be reconciled? Is it possible to avoid charges that American trade is subsidizing a regime that has long declared the United States to be 'the Great Satan', while at the same time helping to economically integrate Iran with its neighbours and making its people wealthier? It would not be politically unrealistic for Washington to return to the situation it was in until 1995, when the overseas subsidiaries of American firms were able to openly trade with Iran and compete with any overseas rivals that were then unthreatened by the imposition of the Iran–Libya Sanctions Act, which was not passed until the following year. In this hypothetical situation, Washington could still officially maintain its full economic prohibition on trade by its own companies, while making clear to the Iranians that this embargo could be lifted, and their businesses offered full access to the American market, if they renounced their nuclear ambitions and quietened their harsh rhetorical tone against the United States and Israel.

On paper this looks like a position that is very moderate and one that would be wholly realistic for any US administration, whether Republican or Democrat, to take. But ask anyone who is familiar with the workings of American politics and it is immediately dismissed as an almost unthinkable policy option. This means that to sketch such a hypothetical course of action does not quite get to the root of what America's dilemma with Tehran really is.

Some commentators might reply that the really fundamental problem is the strong grip that small, unrepresentative interest groups exert on the American political process. Some foreign affairs analysts, for example, have claimed that the influence of the Israeli lobby in Washington is comparable to that of the pro-Serb faction in St Petersburg on the eve of the First World War, a faction that was determined to drag the tsar into open confrontation with the Austrians over the future of the Balkans no matter what the cost to the Russian national interest. But this, surely, is not the full answer, because opening up trade with Iran is considered to be unthinkable even by those who are not known to have any links at all with the pro-Israeli lobby in Washington.

At the root of the issue really lies the degree to which Iran has become demonized in the United States. Policy towards the country has at times been couched in highly emotive terms that obscure more rational consideration of the issues involved. The regime in Tehran is of course in many ways objectionable, but that is not a reason to make some policy proposals wholly unthinkable. Yet highly emotive terms such as 'terrorism', 'nuclear terrorism', 'aggression' and 'human rights' saturate the debate on Iran in both the United States and, to a lesser degree, elsewhere in the world, and the result is that free discussion is being stifled because it is clearly very difficult to take sides with anyone or anything that is so immediately castigated in such strong terms. Comparisons with British foreign policy towards Hitler in the late 1930s are also frequently invoked by commentators who talk about 'Islamofascism' and 'appeasement' in the same emotive, manipulative and wholly inappropriate way that preceded other foreign policy disasters – Suez in 1956, Kosovo in 1999 and Iraq in 2003. So it is very difficult for anyone in the US Congress to call for relaxed trade sanctions against such a regime when the debate is restrained so tightly.

This irrationality of mindset is seriously distorting foreign policy discussion in the United States, demonizing Iran and sidelining any suggestion that relations be normalized, just as in the 1950s and 1960s sceptics like George Ball 'marvelled at the way ingenious men can, when they wish, turn logic upside down' as they tried to make the facts fit their preconceptions.[5]

An example of how such emotive terms cloud rational judgement comes from a book on Iran that was written by the American commentator on Middle East issues, Kenneth Pollack, in 2005. In his text, Pollack made numerous contradictory or inconsistent statements that strongly suggested that his views on Iran as a foreign policy issue were really highly emotive rather than rational. He rightly points out, for example, that 'all of the reporting indicates that [the Iranians] want nuclear weapons to deter an American attack',[6] but six pages earlier argues that 'this regime has demonstrated that it is aggressive, anti-status-quo and anti-American'. And the opening chapters convincingly emphasize that historically 'a weak Iranian state became prey to powerful external actors' whose 'relentless foreign intervention and humiliation had a traumatic impact ... that has reverberated to this day'. But would not this make Iran much more 'defensive' rather than 'aggressive', as the rest of his book claims? Pollack also points out how the US list of terrorist organizations and their state sponsors can be based on 'cynical reasoning'[7] and on standards not always 'punctilious', and admits that on this issue the Iranians have had 'some ground to call the United States hypocritical'.[8] But if the term is unreliable, why are phrases such as 'Iranian involvement in international terrorism' constantly invoked throughout the text? He also admits at one point that peace in the Middle East will be determined by 'factors internal to itself, not by Iranian actions'.[9] Why, then, does his book so emphasize the 'crucial role' of Tehran's 'violent opposition' to Arab–Israeli peace?

Such inconsistencies in Pollack's text would seem to illustrate how distorted even the most rational judgement can become when such emotive words are overplayed. Put in more general terms, it seems that America is now at risk of being hypnotized by these words in the same way, for example, that less secular societies were once gripped by fears of 'heresy' and 'popery' and, in the twentieth century, by fear of communism. One such parallel might be with the run-up to the Vietnam War, when Washington policymakers were deluded by their own rhetoric about communist 'aggression' – a term that, significantly, also saturates the writings and speeches of the time.[10] From the moment of the signing of the 1954 Geneva Accords, which partitioned post-colonial Vietnam between governments of north and south, American leaders made constant references to the 'aggression' of the communist regime in Hanoi. The United States had been 'asked for help against communist aggression' in Vietnam, Lyndon B. Johnson announced in typical vein in his State of the Union address on 4 January 1965, 'and to ignore aggression now would only increase the danger of a much larger war'. There would only be regional peace, he continued, 'when aggressors leave their neighbours in peace'. To take a more recent parallel, it is hard not to be reminded of Saddam's WMD and of Pentagon hawks 'skewering' intelligence reports, looking away from inconvenient facts and instead only finding what they wanted to find. Now it is Iran, not communism or Saddam, that has become demonized and, as Pollack himself points out, there are some Americans who are 'predisposed to see the Iranian bugbear behind every problem'.[11] As other phenomena such as stock market bubbles unmistakably show, modern-day democracies, with a relatively educated electorate, are just as prone to the same irrationality and hysteria of mind as any other society that has preceded them.

So how can this be challenged? As Pollack's book shows, the foreign policy debate on Iran is also being distorted to a lesser extent by the deployment of the label 'aggression'. While this is a less emotive word than 'terrorism', it is nonetheless still pejorative and imprecise. It is unfairly pejorative because it implies the use of *wanton* force, even though there are in international affairs few circumstances when any actions can unreservedly be called unjustified: a massive retaliatory response to minor acts of provocation, for example, is easily labelled 'aggressive' but might well be justifiable. The term is also imprecise because it could perhaps refer to an expansionist or proactive agenda, to recklessness of intent or to ruthlessness of method. But such language easily misleads because many of the cited instances of Iranian 'aggression' deserve to be carefully clarified. The deployment of the Revolutionary Guard to Lebanon in 1982 was a response to the invasion of the country by an Israeli government that harboured an expansionist agenda,[12] while Iran's complicity in both Hezbollah's 1982 bombing of an American marine base in Beirut and in the 1996 attack on Khobar Towers in Saudi Arabia remains unproven. Although it is true that in 1982, during the Iran–Iraq War, Tehran needlessly continued the fighting, it was still Saddam Hussein, not Ayatollah Khomeini, who initiated the conflict in 1980 and only in retrospect does the futility of Khomeini's decision become apparent.

At the heart of America's Iranian dilemma is its inability to challenge the terms in which Iran is typically viewed and defined. Other, more helpful terms should be used to describe the Tehran regime instead of the 'terrorist' label that has been fixed on it firmly in recent years. This is always a very misleading label because it falsely implies that 'terror' is an objective term in the same way that is true of 'war' or 'violence', whereas of course in the world of international affairs there are really only the particular interests of individual states and individuals. Much more accurate, and much less manipulative of debate, would instead be terms like 'national enemies', 'insurgents' and 'militias'. But not 'terrorists'.

Another label that has been firmly pinned on Iran but which needs to be removed if the foreign policy debate on the Middle East is ever to be fairly conducted is its 'oppression of human rights'. No one could seriously dispute that the current Tehran regime is heavily stained in blood and that huge numbers of ordinary and innocent Iranians have suffered very badly at the hands of its security forces. Yet whenever this record is highlighted in foreign policy debate, then the effect is just the same as with the terrorism label: it distorts and manipulates discussion because it is extremely difficult to take sides with any individual or regime that is characterized as having a dire record on human rights. Instead policymakers in Washington need to recognize that another government's domestic track record has no necessary bearing at all on the outside world, and that its behaviour within its own borders is ultimately a matter on which only the nationals of that country are in a position to pass judgement and pronounce sentence. By condemning Tehran in the language of 'human rights', the outside world instead deludes itself that it has an intrinsic superiority over an unquestionably evil regime whereas, in international affairs, there can never be such a thing as 'human rights' any more than there can ever be such a thing as 'terrorism': there are only particular interests on which particular people place particular value at particular moments. Instead other terms, such as the 'unpopularity' or 'unaccountability' of the regime before ordinary Iranians, should be deployed.

These are the terms that need to be dropped from use if the debate on Iran is ever to be conducted fairly. Without such open and fair discussion, proposals to withdraw or scale down the scope of existing primary and secondary sanctions are likely to fall only on deaf ears, and fail to prevent the United States from effectively writing part of its own obituary.

Notes

Introduction

1. Edward Gibbon, *The Decline and Fall of the Roman Empire* (London and New York: Penguin, 1978), chapter VIII, p 260.
2. Speech to Baltic and Black Sea leaders in Vilnius, the Lithuanian capital, 4 May 2006.
3. See generally Michael Klare, *Blood and Oil: How America's Thirst for Petrol is Killing Us* (London: Hamish Hamilton, 2005).
4. Such as Evo Morales' movement in Bolivia. Chavez has also blocked US-led political initiatives. In November 2005, for example, he was a leading light in the effort to block the US-led proposal to restart talks on the Free Trade Area of the Americas (FTAA).
5. 'IEA warns of 50% oil price rise by 2030', *Financial Times*, 2 November 2005.

Chapter 1. Why Iran's Natural Resources Matter

1. Persia was officially renamed Iran in 1935.
2. Michael B. Stoff, *Oil, War and American Security: The Search for a National Policy on Foreign Oil 1941–1947* (New Haven: Yale University Press, 1980) pp 48–51, 58–9.
3. India is formally a member of the Non-Aligned Movement. See Chapter 3.
4. 'Iran's zealot in chief does Bush a favour', *Sunday Times*, 30 October 2005. Ahmadinejad had made a speech a few days before calling for the annihilation of the Jewish state.
5. 'Proven reserves' include only those reserves that can be exploited with currently available technology at conservatively projected prices. 'Recoverable reserves', meanwhile, are not necessarily 'proven', but are expected to meet that standard in the foreseeable future. What is and is not 'recoverable' is always inherently uncertain but all the more so in Iran, which has suffered from the effects of international sanctions and where the extent of 'recoverability' is therefore even more unclear.
6. An analyst for Barclays Capital quoted in 'How much oil do we really have',

BBC News, 15 July 2005.

7. Such as the *Oil and Gas Journal*, which quotes this upward figure in its World-wide Report of 20 December 2004.

8. FACTS Inc., *'Iranian Oil Industry: A Status Report'*, November 2003.

9. See also Chapter 2, pp 59–61.

10. 'Iran's Gas Industry and Export Projects', 2005.

11. Author's correspondence with Professor Stern, November 2005.

12. These Executive Orders were pursuant to the International Security and Development Cooperation Act and the International Emergency Economic Powers Act.

13. On 17 March 2000 Secretary of State Madeleine Albright announced that sanctions against Iran would be eased to allow these products to be imported. The change was implemented through amendments to the Iranian Transactions Regulations.

14. *Middle Eastern Economic Survey*, 25 February 2002.

15. *Petroleum Economist*, vol. 67, no. 2 (February 2000), p 26.

16. Meeting of the National Security Council, 4 March 1953.

17. See Stephen Kinzer's account of the 1953 coup in *All the Shah's Men: An American Coup and the Roots of Middle East Terror* (New York: John Wiley, 2003).

18. William E. Griffith, 'Iran's foreign policy in the Pahlavi era', in George Lenczowski (ed), *Iran under the Pahlavis* (Stanford, California: Hoover Institution Press, 1978) p 375.

19. This was introduced into the House of Representatives as legislation number H.R. 282 and into the Senate as S.333.

20. *Middle Eastern Economic Survey*, 7 February 2005 and 22 December 2003.

21. See Chapter 2, pp 57–8.

22. 'Iran's nuclear threat', *Time*, 8 March 2003.

23. On 2 August 2005 the National Intelligence Estimate projected that Iran was about a decade away from manufacturing HEU. On 6 September 2005 Gary Samore of the IISS published a report, *Iran's Strategic Weapons Programme: A Net Assessment*, arguing that Iran was still 'at least several years' from reaching the nuclear threshold.

24. Quoted at the 'Investing in Iran' conference in London, 24–25 October 2001.

25. See Chapter 2, pp 57–8.

26. On 22 October 2005 IRNA quoted an analyst for the US-based Jamestown Foundation, Mahan Abedin, as saying that the UK was using its allegations of Iranian involvement in southern Iraq as a 'smokescreen' for its plight in Basra.

27. 'President Bush renews anti-Iranian sanctions', Iran Press Service, Washington DC, 14 March 2003.

28. See Michael Klare's book, *Blood and Oil*.

29. Cited in Doris Leblond, 'IEA: $16 trillion in energy investment needed by

2030', *Oil and Gas Journal*, 20 November 2003, p 37.

30. Klare, *Blood and Oil*, p 80.
31. 'IEA warns of 50% oil price rise by 2030', *Financial Times*, 2 November 2005.
32. US Department of Energy (USDOE), *International Energy Outlook 2003*.
33. USDOE, *International Energy Outlook 2001*.
34. USDOE, *International Energy Outlook 2003*.
35. *New York Times*, 17 May 2001.
36. 'Oil prices may slow EU growth', BBC News, 10 September 2005.
37. An ABC/*Washington Post* poll, 6–9 April 2006, showed that 74 per cent of Americans were unhappy on this score.
38. 'Tehran warns of $100 barrel', *The Age*, 2 November 2004.
39. FACTS Inc., 'Iran's Oil Industry: Year End Update', April 2005.
40. *Oil and Gas Journal*, 1 November 2004.
41. IRNA, 21 April 2006.
42. *Oil and Gas Journal*, 24 May 1999.
43. *Ibid.*, 12 July 2004.
44. *Ibid.*, 5 April 1999.
45. *Ibid.*, 14 February 2000.
46. *Ibid.*, 4 August 1997.
47. *Middle Eastern Economic Survey*, 24 January 2005. This was a survey of representatives of Western international oil companies and banks in Iran and was taken shortly after *The New Yorker* published Seymour Hersch's article claiming that US forces were already inside Iran, preparing for possible military strikes.
48. 'New man in Iran', *New York Review of Books*, 11 August 2005.
49. Joseph S. Nye, *The Paradox of American Power* (Oxford: Oxford University Press, 2002) p 4.
50. *Ibid.*, p 8.
51. 'Turkey upsets US military plans', BBC News, 1 March 2003.
52. Curt Tarnoff and Larry Nowels, 'Foreign Aid: An Introductory Overview of US Programs and Policy', Congressional Research Service Report, updated 6 April 2001, p 23.
53. *Oil and Gas Journal*, 24 April 2000.
54. See generally Chapter 3, pp 111–22.
55. 'Bush warns of China arms sales', *Washington Times*, 23 February 2005.
56. Associated Press, 'Policing the Net', CBS News, 22 November 2001.
57. Quoted in Fred Kaplan, *The Wizards of Armageddon* (New York: Simon and Schuster, 1983), p 176.
58. 'Iran's oil gambit and potential affront to the US', *Christian Science Monitor*, 30 August 2005.
59. *Oil and Gas Journal*, 6 October 1997.
60. *Ibid.*, 3 June 1996.

Chapter 2. Breaking US Alliances

1. Information to the author from Michael Thomas, 26 October 2005.
2. Quoted in Christopher Bollyn's article, 'The oil monarchs: George W. Bush and his royal kin', posted at http://www.thetruthseeker.co.uk/article. asp?ID=553.
3. On 15 September 2005, for example, French Prime Minister Dominique de Villepin 'strongly' urged Iran to keep its non-proliferation promises or face action before the UN Security Council.
4. See Chapter 1, p 21, and Chapter 4, p 143.
5. 'EU intensifies pressure on Iran to accept inspections', *Guardian*, 17 June 2003.
6. Just occasionally it seemed to have one: in September 2003, for example, a ten-page IAEA report, claiming that Iran could not have built its massive facility at Natanz without having tested its equipment with heavily enriched uranium, appeared to be just such an indictment because such operations should have been declared to the IAEA.
7. *The Washington Post*, 23 October 2003.
8. 'Blueprints prove Iran is pursuing nuclear weapons', *The Times*, 13 February 2004.
9. 'Iran "has secret atomic bomb project"', *Daily Telegraph*, 6 February 2004.
10. 'Iran gathers allies in nuclear row', CNN, 19 September 2005.
11. See Chapter 3.
12. 'Cracks appear in united front as oil price threatened', *Daily Telegraph*, 16 January 2006.
13. 'Split emerges in West's front against Iran', Reuters, 20 May 2006.
14. See Chapter 1, p 14.
15. See below, p 79.
16. *Middle Eastern Economic Survey*, 11 February 2002.
17. Reuters, 26 August 1997.
18. Reuters, 8 January 1998.
19. *Guardian*, 28 September 2005. Rumours of disagreements between Straw and a more hawkish Tony Blair were reported in Toby Harnden's report, 'Blair and Straw split by Iran nuclear crisis', *Daily Telegraph*, 20 September 2005.
20. Reuters, 1 July 1998.
21. These and other trade statistics are taken from the OECD report, *Monthly Statistics of Foreign Trade*, January 1996–May 1998.
22. Solana, 'The transatlantic rift', *Harvard International Review*, vol. 24, no. 4 (1 January 2003), p 62.
23. Quoted in the *Los Angeles Times*, 31 December 2000, pp 16–34.
24. 'The curse of Euro-nationalism', *National Review*, 6 August 2001, pp 33–6.
25. 'Iran still has nuclear deadline', *Washington Post*, 23 October 2003.
26. 'Preventing Iran from acquiring nuclear weapons', Speech to the Hudson Institute, 17 August 2004.

27. FACTS Inc., 'Further Developments in the Japanese Power Sector', September 2002.
28. FACTS Inc., 'Japan's NG Fundamentals and Forecasts'.
29. See the report of the International Energy Agency, *Analysis of the Impact of High Oil Prices on the Global Economy*, May 2004.
30. Quoted in *Oil and Gas Journal*, 22 May 2000.
31. On 10 July 2001 Iran's Deputy Oil Minister, Kazempour Ardebili, told reporters that ExxonMobil and Conoco had expressed an interest in wanting to join the Azadegan development, *Middle Eastern Economic Survey*, 16 July 2001.
32. *Financial Times*, 28 June 2003.
33. BBC News, 1 July 2003.
34. *Oil and Gas Journal*, 7 July 2003.
35. *Middle Eastern Economic Survey*, 7 July 2003 and 10 February 2003.
36. 'Bush's Iran policy falters amid futile sanctions, diplomacy', Bloomberg, 7 November 2005.
37. *Oil and Gas Journal*, 20 September 2004.
38. 'Support for Iran embargo losing ground', *Financial Times*, 12 March 2006.
39. 'Japan vows to keep developing giant Iran oil field', AFP, 23 March 2006.
40. Energy Information Administration, 2000.
41. These figures were quoted by Dr Naved Hamid of the Asian Development Bank at the Pakistan Oil and Gas Conference 2004, jointly organized by the Petroleum Institute of Pakistan (PIP) and the Mediators Conferences on 4 May 2004 at the Marriott Hotel, Islamabad.
42. *The Daily Times*, 18 April 2003.
43. *The Daily Times*, 17 November 2004.
44. *Times of India*, 11 September 2000.
45. BBC News, 13 July 2005.
46. 'India against referring Iran's nuclear dossier to Security Council, *Tehran Times*, 29 October 2005.

Chapter 3. US Rivals and Non-Aligned States

1. Speech to an Iranian trade delegation, Beijing, 8 April 2004.
2. Statement by the Chinese Ministry of Foreign Affairs: 'President Hu Jintao meets with Iranian vice president Mohammed Reza Aref', 7 July 2005.
3. 'Backlash to Chinese bid for Unocal: Bush urged to block takeover because of energy, security fears', *San Francisco Chronicle*, 24 June 2005.
4. 'Analysis: Tension in US–China talks', BBC News, 2 March 2001.
5. Coral Brown, 'TK', *The National Interest*, Fall 1999, p 56.
6. Arthur Waldron, 'How not to deal with China', *Commentary*, March 1997. These views have also been reiterated by, for example, Robert Kagan in *The Weekly Standard*, 20 January 1997.
7. Quoted in Simon Tisdall's article, 'US attack over Taiwan's defences', *Guardian*, 21 October 2005.

8.   *Washington Times*, 18 January 2005.

9.   USDOE, *Annual Energy Outlook 2004*.

10. Cambridge Energy Research Associates (CERA).

11. IEA, *World Energy Outlook*, 2000, p 67.

12. Quoted by *Alexander's Oil and Gas Connections*, vol. 10, issue 17, 15 September 2005.

13. 'China: Electricity cuts and manufacturing', by Stephen Frost, *Asian Labour News*, 4 June 2004.

14. 'China's thirst for oil undercuts US efforts to rein in Iran', Bloomberg, 20 December 2004.

15. Source: *Yearbook of China Customs Statistics*, Relevant Issues, Customs General Administration, People's Republic of China.

16. See also Chapter 2, pp 47-8.

17. See Chapter 3, pp 98-9.

18. Quoted in *China Reform Monitor*, no. 442, American Foreign Policy Council, 22 April 2002.

19. 'US dissuades Sinopec from bidding in Iran', *People's Daily Online*, 6 February 2004.

20. 'Russia, China warn against antagonising Iran', *China Daily*, 22 September 2005.

21. 'Iran, China eye military cooperation', *Persian Journal*, 18 August 2005.

22. 'US experts fear Russia-China axis', *UPI*, 4 October 2005.

23. 'Bush and Putin stand firm on Iran', BBC News, 17 September 2005.

24. 'Russia and West split on Iran nuclear issue', *New York Times*, 6 March 2006.

25. USDOE, *International Energy Outlook 2004*.

26. *Washington Post*, 27 September 2005.

27. Reuters, 28 February 2002.

28. *Jane's Defence Weekly*, 29 January 2003.

29. CSIS, 'Iran's Developing Military Capabilities', Washington DC, 2004.

30. 'US objects to gas pipeline', *Dawn*, 28 July 2005.

31. Quoted in Zlatica Hoke's report, 'US and India getting closer than ever', *VOA*, 24 July 2005.

32. See Chapter 2, pp 57-8.

33. 'India against referring Iran's nuclear dossier to Security Council', *Tehran Times*, 29 October 2005.

34. 'UN nuclear watchdog debates Iran deadline', *Financial Times*, 11 August 2005.

35. *Iran Daily*, 14 July 2005.

Chapter 4. Supporting the Iranian Regime

1.   Hamid Algar, *Religion and State in Iran 1785-1906: The Role of the Ulama in the Qajar Period* (Berkeley, CA: UCLA Press, 1969), p 57.

2.   Petroleum Industry Research Foundation, 'Gasoline 101: A Politically Explo-

sive Topic', June 2000.
3.   *New York Times*, 17 May 2001.
4.   'Iran pours oil fund billions into wooing disaffected youth', *Independent*, 1 September 2005.
5.   Bill Samii, 'Iran: Paramilitary force prepares for urban unrest', *Pakistan Today*, 7 October 2005.
6.   *Jane's All the World's Armies*, 2004.
7.   'Tehran lends Pyongyang a helping hand', *Der Spiegel*, 28 November 2005.
8.   All quotes in this paragraph are from *Jane's All the World's Armies*, 2004.
9.   See Chapter 2, p 51.
10. Quoted in Professor Vladimir Sazhin's article 'On Iran's nuclear programme', Centre for European Policy Studies, June 2005.
11. Israeli warplanes attacked targets in Syria on 5 October 2003 in retaliation for a suicide bombing that left 19 Israelis dead.
12. 'A strategy for a nuclear Iran', American Enterprise Institute, 30 September 2004.
13. In contrast to Saddam's Osirak reactor, struck by Israeli planes in 1981, Iranian nuclear installations are dispersed, buried underground and well defended.
14. See Chapter 1, pp 11-12.
15. Herodotus, *Histories*, Book One, Chapter 135, translated by George Rawlinson (Wordsworth Classics, 1996).
16. 'Iranians assert right to nuclear weapons', *Washington Post*, 11 March 2003.
17. 'Iranians unite over nuclear row', BBC News, 20 October 2004.
18. Quoted in George Perkovich's, *'India's Nuclear Bomb'* (Berkeley and Los Angeles: University of California Press, 1999), p 343.
19. See, for example, William Vaughan, *Romanticism and Art* (London: Thames & Hudson, 1994), chapter 5.

Conclusion

1.   See Chapter 1, p 23.
2.   See Richard Aldrich's report, 'America used Islamists to arm the Bosnian Muslims', *Guardian*, 22 April 2002. Aldrich summarized the findings of Dutch intelligence reports on the subject of US support to the Bosnian Muslims.
3.   Kenneth Kyle, *Suez* (London: I.B.Tauris, 1985), pp 144-5.
4.   Edward Gibbon, 'General Observations on the Fall of the Roman Empire in the West' in *The Decline and Fall of the Roman Empire* (London and New York: Penguin, 1978), p 621.
5.   George Ball, *The Past Has Another Pattern* (New York and London: W.W. Norton & Co., 1982), p 389.
6.   Kenneth Pollack, *The Persian Puzzle: The Conflict between Iran and America* (New York: Random House, 2004), p 384.
7.   *Ibid.*, p 207.

8.   *Ibid.*, p 361.

9.   *Ibid.*, p 380.

10. Typical examples are National Security Council documents such as NSC 64 (1950), 124/2 (1952) and 5504 (1954), quoted in *The Pentagon Papers*, vol. 1 (Boston: Beacon Press, 1971).

11. Pollack, p 355.

12. See Avi Shlaim, *The Iron Wall: Israel and the Arab World* (London: Penguin, 2000), p 396.

Index

Abadan, 1, 61, 84, 154
Abbott Group, 60
Abrams, Elliot, 25
Ackerman, Gary L., 120
Adeli, Mohammed Hossein, 114
Advanced Research Projects Agency
    (ARPA), 41
Afghanistan, 8, 82, 98, 113, 116, 117,
    119–20, 129, 139
Aghamohammadi, Ali, 122
Aghazadeh, Gholamreza, 143
Ahmadinejad, Mahmoud, xii, 3, 29,
    36, 37–8, 49, 57, 71, 101, 102, 123,
    131, 136, 137, 150, 151, 152, 158
Ahwaz, 126
Ahwaz-Bangestan field, 50, 59, 74, 75,
    105–6
Aiyar, Mani Shankar, 83, 113, 115, 117
Aker Kvaerner, 63
Al Qaeda, 2, 42, 101
Albright, Madeline, 13, 69
Alexander the Great, 148, 150
American–Israeli Public Affairs
    Committee (AIPAC), 18–19
American Enterprise Institute, 144
Aminuddin, Usman, 83
Amrollahi, Reza, 106
Anglo-Iranian (Persian) Oil Company,
    16, 47, 148, 152, 153
Anglo-Persian Agreement (1919), 16

Angola, 27
Ansari, Hamid, 117
Aref, Reza, 144
Asad, President, 145
Atomic Energy Agency of Iran, 143
Atomic Energy Organization, 141
Austria, 8
Aviation Week and Space Technology, 103
'Axis of Evil', 66, 124
Azadegan field, 5, 48, 60, 62, 74–6
Azerbaijan, 90, 154
Azeri Gas Company, 8
Aziz, Shaukat, 84

Baghdad, 85
Baharat Indaa, 114
Baker, Norman, 50
Bakrie field, 15
Balal field, 15, 33
Balkans, 162
Ball, George, 162
Bam Earthquake, 13, 149
Bandar Assaluyeh, 74
Bangestan field, 33
Bank Mellat, 64
Bank Tejarat, 63
Basiji Resistance Force, 137–8
Basra, 61, 84
Bay Oil Company, 11
Berlin, 65

Blair, Tony, 24, 85
Blank, Stephen, 104
Bolsheviks, 1, 16
Bolton John R., 54, 70, 77, 80
Booz Allen Hamilton, 92
Boroujerdi, Alaeddin, 62
Bosnian Civil War, 157
Boucher, Richard, 22, 76, 78, 85, 122
Bow Valley Energy, 14, 36
Brent Crude, 115
Brill, Kenneth, 45, 55
British Petroleum, 50, 59, 116
Britain, 26, 41
    allegations of Iranian involvement in
    Iraq, 24, 85
    ties with US, 41–2
    trade with Iran, 49
    see also E3; European Union
Brittan, Leon, 44
Broken Hill Petroleum, 113
Browne, Gordon, 29
BTC pipeline, 154
Burns, Nicholas, 20, 25, 117
Bush, George W., 13, 20, 23, 25, 30,
    44, 65, 66, 71, 76, 81, 83, 88, 98,
    110, 117, 118, 121, 124, 144, 147
Bushehr, 4, 36, 106–7, 142
buyback contracts, 33–6, 78

Cairn Energy, 36
Caltex Oil Company, 11
Caspian Sea, 108, 139
Center for Strategic and International
    Studies, 138
Central Bank of Iran, 134, 135
Cepsa, 60
Ceyhan, 154
Chavez, Hugo, x–xi
Cheney, Dick, x, 59, 110
China, xi, 3, 27, 36, 41, 43, 47, 58, 71,
    86, 119, 140, 152, 160
    demand for energy, 91–5
    relations with the US, 89–93, 98–
    101

ties with Iran, 95–104
China Business Weekly, 95
China North Industries, 103
China Petrochemical Corporation
    (Sinopec), 96, 98
China Precision Machinery Import/
    Export Corporation, 103
Chinese National Offshore Oil
    Company (CNOOC), 89
Chinese National Petroleum Company
    (CNPC), 96, 146
Chirac, Jacques, 42
Chittagong, 92
Christopher, Warren, 65
Churchill, Winston, 16
CIA, 17, 92
Clinton, Bill, 12, 18, 22
Coastal Oil Company, 11
Cohen, William, 69
Cold War, 17, 45, 104, 144
ConocoPhillips, 74, 146, 149
Cook, Robin, 52
critical dialogue, 64–9
Cuba, 13
Cuban Missile Crisis, 17
Curzon, Lord, 16

D'Amato, Senator Alfonse, 12, 14, 36
D'Arcy, William Knox, 16
Danesh-Jafari, Davoud, 30
Daneshyar, Kamal, 35
Daqing field, 94
Davies, Pat, 123
Denmark, 68
Deora, Murali, 121
Der Spiegel, 140
Devon Energy, 146
Donnelly, Thomas, 144
Dorood field, 14, 33
Dresdner Kleinwort Benson, 33
Dulles, John, 17

E3, 25, 45–69
Ebrahimi-Asl, Asghar, 146

Elf Acquitaine, 14
Eni, 14, 50, 60
Erler, Gernot, 58
Etemad, Akbar, 141
European Union, 13, 29, 44, 45–71;
    see also critical dialogue
Expediency Council, 32, 35
ExxonMobil, 11, 74, 146

FACTS, 7, 79
Fakuda, Yasuo, 77, 78
Ferrouz field, 62
First World War, 91, 160, 162
Fischer, Joschka, 56
Fleischer, Ari, 152
Foruzande, Mohammed, 105
French government, 67
Fukaya, Takashi, 73
Al Furat Petroleum Company, 146

Gail, 106, 114
Gan, Sun Bi, 99
Gazprom, x, 14, 18, 106, 108, 109
Genscher, Hans-Dietrich, 67
Germany, 29, 67-8, 97
Ghanimifard, Hojatollah, 136
Gibbon, Edward, ix, 161
Gilman, Rep. Ben, 14
Golovinky, Stanislav, 143
Greece, 8
Greeks, Ancient, 148
Greenspan, Alan, 73
Guangya, Wang, 100
Gulf Cooperation Council, 64
Gulfsands Petroleum, 146

Habibollah Seidan, 86
Haddad, Ibrahim, 147
Hadley, Stephen, 25
Haldor Topsoe, 63
Halliburton, 19, 37
Hamas, 157
Hansa Chemie, 61
Hansen, Peter Lysholt, 66

Hariri, Rafik, 147
Helms, Jesse, 69
Helms–Burton Bill, 13
Herodotus, 150
Hezbollah, 23, 145
Hill, Christopher, 93, 100
Hiranuma, Takeo, 75
Hiroshima, 72
Hitler, Adolf, 162
Hosseini, Haidar Mostakhdemin, 43
Hosseinian, Hadi Nejad, 115
House International Relations
    Committee, 117
HSBC, 63
Hunter, Rep. Duncan, 89
Hurricane Katrina, 27, 29, 104
Hyde, Henry, 99
Hyundai, 63, 86

India, 8, 40, 41, 86
    energy requirements, 27, 111–13, 127
Indian Oil and Natural Gas Company
    (ONGC) Videsh, 115
Indian Oil Corporation, 106, 114, 115
Indonesia Petroleum Ltd (Inpex), 75
Intecsa-Uhde, 60
International Atomic Energy Agency
    (IAEA), 19, 21, 45, 51-9, 77-9, 99,
    102, 109, 110–11, 118, 120, 122
International Court of Justice, 31
International Energy Agency, xi, 26
International Monetary Fund (IMF),
    40
Iran
    domestic economy, 130-7
    domestic politics, 135
    military forces, 138–41, 144–5
    nuclear programme, 4, 21–2, 29–30,
    51-9, 76–80, 99, 141–4, 159
    revolution of 1979, 9, 10–11, 18, 33,
    38, 88
    security services, 137–8
    sense of isolation, 148–50
    state bureaucracy, 131–4

status and prestige, 150-5
war with Iraq, 11, 31, 128, 142, 157,
    164
Iran Freedom and Support Bill, 19
Iran-Libya Sanctions Act (ILSA), 14-
    15, 18-19, 24, 44, 74, 83, 157, 161
Iran-Libya Sanctions Enhancement
    and Compliance Act, 20
Iran LNG, 50, 116
Iran Non-Proliferation Act, 103
Iranian oil and gas
    announcements of 'new reserves', 4,
        59-60
    export earnings, 127-31
    exports, 7-9, 11, 30
    foreign investment, 30-6, 60-1
    history of oil, 16-18
    output, 5-6, 31-2
    refined oil, 135
    refineries, 7, 135
    size of reserves, 5-9
Iranian Southern Petroleum Company,
    105
Iraq, ix, 11, 23, 38, 41, 61, 117, 124,
    160, 162, 163
Isfahan, 69, 110, 122
Islam, 151
Islamic Jihad, 157
Israel, 3, 39, 98, 101, 141, 144, 145,
    149, 153, 157, 160, 162-3
Itochu Corporation, 74

Jadoon, Amanullah Khan, 84, 113
Japan, 48, 65, 71-81
Japan Petroleum Exploration Company
    (Japex), 75, 79
Japanese Bank for International
    Cooperation, 64, 74, 75
Japanese National Oil Company
    (JNOC), 75, 78
Jerusalem, 148
Jianchao, Liu, 100
Jintao, Hu, 88, 99
Johnson, Lyndon B., 163

Jones, Frederick, 121

Kahuta, 153
Kalaye Electric Factory, 51-2, 102, 143
Kant, Immanuel, 160
Karine A (ship), 23, 157
Kashmir, 8
Kasuri, Kurshid Mehmood, 83
Kasyanov, Mikhail, 105
Kawaguvhi, Yoriko, 77
Keshavarzi Bank, 137
Khalilian, Sadeq, 137
Khamanei, Ali, 30
Khamushi, Ali Naqi, 97
Kharg Island, 14, 128, 154
Kharrazi, Kamal, 66, 84, 85, 97
Khatami, Mohammed, 21, 37, 65, 67,
    68, 73, 82, 96, 106, 114, 115, 130,
    131, 139
Khazai, Mohammed, 31, 119
Khomeini, Ruhollah, 128, 138, 164
Khristenko, Viktor Borisovich, 106
Kinkel, Klaus, 67
Kish Island, 7, 32, 33, 43
Kish Oriental, 37
Kissinger, Henry, 149
Koizumi, Junichiro, 76, 77
Korin, Anne, 93
Kosovo, 162
Kupal field, 105
Kuwait, 7, 26, 35, 73
Kyoto Agreement, 72

Larijani, Ali, 61, 62, 79, 89
Lantos, Tom, 117, 119
Larson, Alan, 65
Lavrov, Sergei, 107, 110
Lebanon, 145, 164
Leffler, Christian, 66
Lugar, Richard, 127
Lukoil, 108

McCarthy, John, 11
McCormack, Sean, 85

Machimura, Nobutaka, 78
Mahmoudzadeh, Ebrahim, 140
Majlis, 16, 33, 62, 136, 145, 149
Majnoon field, 74
Malaek, Mohammed Hossein, 96
Mao, Chairman, 90
Masjid-i-Suleiman, 1, 14, 96
Mbeki, Thabo, 122
Mehir field, 62
Mexico, 26
Middle East Association, 49
Mikhailov, Viktor, 106
Miller, Alexei, 106
Milošević, Slobodan, 39
Minnikhanov, Rustam, 105
Mirahmadi, General, 137
Mirdamadi, Mohsen, 145
Mitsubishi Tokyo Financial Group, 75
Mitsui Financial Group, 75
Mizuho Financial Group, 75
Mofaz, Shaul, 23
Mohammed, 148
Mohammadi-Far, Nasser, 103, 104
Mollet, Guy, 159
Mongols, 148
Moslehi, Heidar, 137
Mossadeq, Mohammed, x, 16–17, 28,
    148, 152, 153
Mostazafan and Janbazan Foundation,
    105
Mottaki, Manouchehr, 80, 99
Mulford, David, 121
Mumbai field, 111
Murshed, Iftikhar, 106
Musavi-Jazayeri, Ali, 137
Musharraf, Pervez, 82, 83
Muzzaffar al-Din, 16

Nabucco Pipeline, 8
Naftiran Intertrade Company (NICO),
    75
Nagasaki, 72
Nasser, Gamal Abdul, x, 159
Natanz, 21, 69, 102, 142–3

Nateq-Nuri, Ali Akbar, 30
National Council of Resistance of Iran
    (NCRI), 143
National Iran Gas Exporting Company
    (NIGEC), 8, 64, 114
National Iranian Drilling Corporation
    (NIDC), 105
National Iranian Oil Company
    (NIOC), 9, 31, 33, 34, 47, 60, 62, 63,
    75, 78, 96, 115, 116, 123, 136
National Iranian Oil Engineering and
    Construction Company (NIOECC),
    73
National Iranian Tanker Company
    (NITC), 86, 96
National Review, 69
National Security Council, 121
NATO, 69
Nekoen, Zoa, 104
New Delhi Declaration, 114, 116
Nigeria, 135
Nikolayev, Andrey, 139
Nixon administration, 155
Non-Aligned Movement, 3, 87, 120
Non-Proliferation Act, 118
North Korea, 39, 43, 46, 56, 66, 71,
    72, 80–1, 101, 110, 124, 140–1, 151,
    160
Nuclear Suppliers Group, 118
Nye, Joseph, 38

oil
    future of, xi
    growing global demand for, 26–30,
    129
    price, xii, 29–30, 102, 129
    see also Iranian oil and gas
Oil and Natural Gas Corporation, 117
Oil India, 115
Oil Stabilization Fund, 130–1
Okuda, Hiroshi, 79
Oman, 7, 154
Operation Ajax, 17
Operation Eagle Claw, 10

Orange Revolution, 108
Organization of Petroleum Exporting
   Countries (OPEC), xi, 5, 28, 40, 130
O'Sullivan, John, 69
Al-Otari, Naji, 144
Ottomans, 148

Pahlavi, Shah Mohammed Reza, 10, 17,
   142, 154
Pakistan, 8, 81-4, 106, 114, 253
Palestinians, 23, 98, 124, 133, 157, 163
Paris Accords, 54-7, 62
Pars LNG, 60, 64
People's Daily, 96
Persepolis, 148, 155
Persian LNG, 62, 64
Peterloo Massacre, 125
PetroCanada, 146
Petronas, 14, 18, 33, 50, 60, 105
Petronet, 115
Petropars, 50, 115
PetroSA, 123
Plesetsk, 153
Pollack, Kenneth, 162-4
Powell, Colin, 25, 55
Prodi, Romano, 68
Project for the New American Century,
   23
Proliferation Security Initiative, 118
Putin, Vladimir, x, 107, 110

Qatar, 6, 7, 9, 26, 82, 113, 123
Qinghong, Zeng, 99
Qods Day, 133

Rafsanjani, Hashemi, 11-12, 149
Raha, Subir, 117
Ramshir field, 105-6
Reeker, Philip T., 107
Reliance, 116
Repsol, 62, 63, 88
Resalat, 31
Reshadat, 31
Revolutionary Guard, 137, 164

Reynolds, George, 1
Reza Love Fund, 136
Rhodesia, 160
Rice, Condoleezza, 25, 56, 59, 68, 69,
   83, 100, 107, 110
Richardson, Bill, 40
Rome, ix, 161
Roosevelt, Kermit, 17
Ros-Lehtinen, Rep. Ileana, 20, 24
Rowhani, Hassan, 30, 76, 77
Rumsfeld, Donald, 59, 91
Rumyantsev, Alexander, 107
Rushdie, Salman, 11
Russia, 104-11, 127, 139-40, 142, 152,
   153

Sadat, Anwar, 148
Saddam Hussein, 55, 163
Salehi, Ali Akbar, 95
Santorum, Senator Rick, 19
Sasol, 123
Sasolburg, 123
The Satanic Verses, 11
Saudi Arabia, xii, 2, 4, 5, 9, 26, 28, 73,
   102, 113, 128, 164
Schroeder, Gerhard, 68
Second World War, 16, 125
Senate Foreign Relations Committee,
   93, 127
Sergeyev, Igor, 139
Shamkhani, Ali, 139
Shandong Peninsula, 104
Shanghai Cooperation Organization,
   84, 102-3
Sheer Energy, 14, 96
Sheibani, Ebrahim, 135
Shell consortium, 14, 49, 62, 63, 78,
   79, 99, 146
Siam Cement Public Company, 74
Silk Road, 97, 98
Simon-Carves, 63
Sina-1 satellite, 139-40
Singh, Madhvendra, 116
Singh, Manmohan, 111, 118, 119

Singh, Natwar, 120
Sinopec *see* China Petrochemical
   Corporation
Sirri fields, 33
Smith, Gordon, 79
Société Generale, 64
Sofregaz, 61
Solana, Javier, 69
Sondel, 60
Soroush-Nowruz fields, 31, 60, 73
Souri, Mohammed, 96
South Africa, 122–4, 160–1
South Azadegan *see* Azadegan
South China Sea, 94
South Korea, 86
South Pars fields, 4, 6, 7, 15, 18, 33,
   35, 44, 50, 60, 62, 63, 75, 86, 105,
   115, 116, 123, 146
Soviet Union, 21, 46, 154
Stanford University, 109
Statoil, 60
Steinitz, Yuval, 153
Straw, Jack, 58, 68
Sudan, xi, 100
Suez Canal, x
Suez Canal Company, 158–9
Suez Crisis, 40, 158–9, 162
Sugiyama, Hideji, 80
Syria, 23, 127, 144–7,
Syria Accountability and Lebanese
   Sovereignty Act, 145

Tabnak field, 6
Taiwan, 71, 90, 104
Talabani, Jalal, 85
Tan, Lio G., 97
Tanganyika Oil, 146
Tatneft, 50, 105–6
Technip-Coflexip, 61, 63
Tehran Nuclear Research Centre, 141
Tehran Stock Exchange, 4
Tehran Times, 97
Tel Aviv, 68
terrorism, 1, 15, 22–6, 157–65

Tokyo, 73
Torkan, Akbar, 31
Total, 14, 33–5, 44, 50, 59, 60, 62, 63,
   67, 88, 105
Toyo Engineering, 74
Toyota, 79
Trans-Afghan Pipeline, 117
Turkey, 8, 90, 108, 109
Turkmenistan, 82, 113, 117, 120

UFJ Holdings, 75
UK Exports Credits Guarantee
   Department (ECGD), 63
Ukraine, x, 108–9, 140
Al-Ulum, Ibrahim, 84
UN General Assembly, 3, 57–9, 101
UN Security Council, xii, 30, 40, 45,
   58–9, 61, 102, 109, 110–11, 118,
   120–1
United Arab Emirates, 154
United States
   definition of its 'political power',
   38–42
   oil companies, 11–12, 74, 146
   sanctions against Iran, 12–13, 22, 49,
   159–65
   secondary sanctions, 130, 159–65
   State Department, 14, 23, 76, 85,
   107
Unocal, 89
USA Engage, 22
US Congress, 12, 18–26, 41, 43–4,
   100, 117, 118–21, 157
US–Taiwan Relations Act, 90
Uthman, Caliph, 126

Vaziri-Hamaneh, Kazem, 30
Vedrine, Hubert, 66
Venezuela, x, 26, 95, 122, 127, 146
Verdinejad, Fereydoun, 99
Vietnam, ix, 10, 102, 154, 163
Volner, Ludger, 66
Voss, Martha, 79
Waite, Terry, 11

Waqar, Ahmed, 83
Wayne, Anthony, 117
Woolsey, R. James, 89
World Bank, 40
World Trade Center, 10, 23, 129
World Trade Organization, 25, 44, 56
Wyden, Senator Ron, 19

Xiamen Polo Metal Industrial
    Company, 94

Yadavaran field, 62, 99, 115
Yi, Wu, 97

Youness-Sinaki, Hassan, 134
Yushchenko, Viktor, 109

Zagdeh field, 105
Zahedi, Fazlollah, 17
Zamzama field, 81
Zanganeh, Bijan Namdar, 4, 7, 32, 35,
    83, 84, 95, 115, 128
Zemin, Jiang, 97, 98
Zhaoxing, Li, 99, 102
Zhejiang province, 94
Zoellick, Robert, 80
Zukang, Sha, 90
Zuma, Nkosazana Dlamini, 124